RALEGH'S LAST JOURNEY

Paul Hyland was born in Dorset in 1947. An award-winning poet and writer, his books on English places, *Purbeck* and *Wight*, are modern classics. His most recent books include *Indian Balm* and *Backwards Out of the Big World*.

'[Hyland] has delved deep into the archives to produce a work which is a fascinating window into the past. While providing a factual narrative, Hyland still manages to inject humanity into his writing so that you have a feeling for the people involved and an understanding of what drove them.'

STEVEN MOORE *News Letter* (Northern Ireland)

'This is a little-known slice of a well-known life . . . there are plenty of adventures, many verging on farce . . . It challenges many of the assumptions behind the writing of a life . . . demonstrates that the subject's path to death is as important as the path through life.'

DEA BIRKETT *Independent*

'. . . what should have been a quick trip wound up taking nearly three weeks and was, as Paul Hyland makes clear in his engaging account, more than a little fraught. High treason? More like low comedy . . . Mr Hyland narrates the whole ignominious episode with aplomb.'

The Economist

By the same author

Travel

PURBECK: *The Ingrained Island*
WIGHT: *Biography of an Island*
THE BLACK HEART: *A Voyage into Central Africa*
INDIAN BALM: *Travels in the Southern Subcontinent*
BACKWARDS OUT OF THE BIG WORLD: *A Voyage into Portugal*

Poetry

RIDDLES FOR JACK
DOMINGUS
POEMS OF Z
THE STUBBORN FOREST
KICKING SAWDUST

Other

GETTING INTO POETRY
BABEL GUIDE to the Fiction of Brazil, Portugal and Africa
(with Ray Keenoy and David Treece)

RALEGH'S
LAST JOURNEY

*A tale of madness,
vanity and treachery*

PAUL HYLAND

HarperCollins*Publishers*

HarperCollins*Publishers*
77–85 Fulham Palace Road
Hammersmith, London, W6 8JB

www.harpercollins.co.uk

This paperback edition 2004
1 3 5 7 9 8 6 4 2

First published in Great Britain by
HarperCollins*Publishers* 2003

A catalogue record for this book
is available from the British Library

ISBN: 978-0-00-729176-2
ISBN: 0-00-729176-0

Set in Postscript Linotype Galliard with Spectrum display by
Rowland Phototypesetting Ltd, Bury St Edmunds, Suffolk

Printed and bound in Great Britain by
Clays Ltd, St Ives plc

to Sue

CONTENTS

AUTHOR'S NOTE   ix

Prologue   1

1 Destiny   3

2 Bess's Eyes   16

3 An Inevitable Rock   38

4 Cousin Lewis   50

5 The Chymist and the Soul   62

6 Osmund's Curse   74

7 Impostures   84

8 Apology   99

9 Hail Powdered with Diamonds   115

10 House Arrest   123

11 Flight   131

12 Tower   139

13 Judas   152

14 Intrigues and Interrogations   162

15 Last Judgment   183

16 Scaffold   199

Epilogue   215

NOTES   221
SELECT BIBLIOGRAPHY   235
INDEX   238

AUTHOR'S NOTE

APPROACH

I encountered Lewis Stucley, the man who arrested Ralegh and led him to London and the scaffold, by accident. While researching in the Stucley family archives for other reasons I stumbled upon what remains of his story. Sir Hugh Stucley of Affeton Castle discussed him with me and loaned me *The Humble Petition and Information of Sir Lewis Stucley* from his library at Hartland Abbey. It started me down the road to this book.

Stucley's side of the narrative is omitted from the nineteenth- and twentieth-century volumes in which primary sources for Ralegh's story are printed. But his *Appollogie* and *Humble Petition*, as well as Samuel King's *Narrative of Sir Walter Ralegh's Motives* and other obscure or uncollected documents, are peep-holes into Ralegh's last months. Writers on Ralegh have largely ignored or underplayed them.

Together with other accounts – Ralegh's own writings, letters by other hands, reports by the gaoler/spy Sir Thomas Wilson, transcriptions of evidence given to the Privy Council and intelligence shared with the Spanish and French courts – they contain not only vivid insights but also records of conversations which allow us to eavesdrop on important episodes.

In James I's *Declaration of the Demeanour and Cariage of Sir Walter Raleigh*, for instance, much of the discourse is presented as dialogue; in most sources, it is reported speech. Naturally it is partial, and often deliberately biased, but where it seems apt I have re-created conversations or speeches in order to get as close as possible to the minds and passions of my subjects. I have edited the script but I have not invented anything.

Ralegh's name has often been spelled 'Raleigh' and people still joke about his going to sea on a bicycle, but nowadays it is usually printed without an 'i'. His first published verses of 1576 are by 'Walter Rawley of the Middle Temple'. The first edition of his *History of the World* is anonymous, for in 1614 he was legally dead, but the title page of the second edition, published the year before he was executed, has him as 'Sr. Walter Ralegh'.

His contemporaries spelled his name in many ways, but he used just three variants. The facsimile signature stamped on his wine licences is 'W. Raleigh'. It has been claimed that he never wrote his own name that way, but he did; a single extant letter (c. 1584/5) is signed 'W Raleigh' in his best italic hand. That apart, surviving documents show that he wrote 'W Rauley' until 1584; after that, his signature became 'W Ralegh' and remained so until his death, more often than not elided: 'WRalegh'.

The name was not pronounced 'Rally', like the bicycle with three gears, or 'rah-rah-Rahley' like three cheers, but 'Rawley'. James I's pun, 'I have heard rawly of thee', makes that clear, while Henry Noel's riddling epigram, 'The foe to the stomach and the word of disgrace/Shows the gentleman's name with the bold face', demands the solution, 'Raw lie'. But be sure not to enunciate 'Rawley' in clipped county tones; speak his name in broad Devon brogue, for bold-faced 'Water' Ralegh from Budleigh kept his accent all his life.

As I have indicated, this is a true story based on personal and state letters, private journals, notes of interrogations, intelligence reports, official records and printed works of the time. Both main protagonists wrote and rewrote 'apologies' to James I, a fashionable means of defending oneself and attacking one's enemies before the King and the court. King James felt compelled, or was persuaded, to justify his own actions in a 'declaration' drafted by Francis Bacon and published soon after Ralegh's execution.

AUTHOR'S NOTE

Most of what we know of both the Spanish and native South American views of Ralegh's Guiana expedition is contained in Fray Pedro Simon's narrative, *Noticias de las Conquistas de tierra firme en las Indias Occidentales* (1626), in documents stored in the Spanish national archive at the castle of Simancas, near Tordesillas in Castile, and in the Archivo General des Indias at Seville, some of which were only rediscovered two and a half centuries after the event.

The sources are rich and deep. Nevertheless, the evidence is, as always, fragmentary; many papers have been lost. Primary sources are identified in the Notes, but it is worth noting here that many, though not all, of the most important documents have been gathered together in three volumes by editors to whom I am greatly indebted: Sir Robert H. Schomburgk (ed.), *The Discovery of the Large, Rich, and Beautiful Empire of Guiana . . .* by Sir W. Ralegh, Knt. (London, 1848); V.T. Harlow, *Ralegh's Last Voyage* (London, 1932); and Agnes Latham and Joyce Youings (eds), *The Letters of Sir Walter Ralegh* (Exeter, 1999).

ACKNOWLEDGEMENTS

I am grateful to Sir Hugh Stucley for inspiration and hospitality. For their patient help I am indebted to librarians and archivists, particularly at the British Library, Plymouth City Library, Exeter University, North Devon Library, North Devon Record Office, Dorchester Museum, Dorset County Library and Salisbury City Library. For stimulating information about Drake properties in Musbury, Devon, I offer thanks to Mr Francis Greene. For access to Clifton Maybank house and Poyntington Manor in Dorset I am grateful to Mrs Patricia Jaffé and Mrs T.P.S. Woods respectively. For assistance with seventeenth-century anglicised French I thank Mrs Sue Cottam, and especially M. Jean-Christophe Sorin for particularly problematical French translation.

I hope that this book justifies the faith of my publisher, Michael Fishwick, and the work of my editors, Kate Johnson and Janet Law.

Sir W.R. was condemned for being a friend to the Spaniard; and lost his life for being their enemy.

Carew Ralegh

Rawleigh is a great name in our history, and fills a space in our imagination.

Isaac D'Israeli

PROLOGUE

When Sir Walter Ralegh laid his head on the executioner's block in Palace Yard in 1618 he knelt facing the wrong way. He looked west towards Devon, where he was born sixty-five years earlier, and in the direction of a New World which had seduced and undone him. The Dean of Westminster pointed out his error. A man about to cross the threshold of eternity must lie with his face towards the east, the promised land and the resurrected Christ.

It was a question of piety, the questionable piety of a man once investigated for atheism. Perhaps Ralegh would have preferred to die facing his source and lifelong muse rather than some supposed spiritual destination; nevertheless he stood up, stepped around and got to his knees on the other side of the block.

Despite the extreme pressure of the moment, a *bon mot* occurred to him that he could not resist. Onlookers recalled many choice sayings from Ralegh's last performance; in most of us they would have remained undelivered lines, *l'esprit de l'escalier*, brilliant responses that came to mind too late. Ralegh, though, had the wit and composure instantly to retort to the Dean's reproof.

'So the heart be right,' he declared, 'it is no matter which way the head lieth.'

Ralegh's last journey took him from Plymouth to London and the block. Spanning just two hundred and fifty miles and twenty weeks, it encapsulates an epic life and reveals a character, unlike 'the last Elizabethan' we think we know, who behaves in stark contrast to the dignified role he acted out on the scaffold.

DESTINY

alegh's last voyage ended at Plymouth in mid-summer 1618. On the final leg of a traumatic transatlantic voyage his ship the *Destiny* sailed out of Kinsale at the south of Ireland, rounded Land's End, left the Lizard and Rame Head to larboard and, passing between Penlee Point and the Great Mew Stone, entered Plymouth Sound where the waters of the St Germans, Tamar, Tavy and Plym rivers, the lifeblood of Ralegh's western terrain, meld and run into the sea.

Once he had resolved to steer the *Destiny* to a Plymouth berth, Ralegh could no longer escape his fate. It was the second week of June, a year since King James had allowed him to sail from this haven to Guiana in search of gold, and twenty-two years since he had led Queen Elizabeth's fleet to victory over the Spanish at Cadiz. He had fetched no gold from Guiana, only tobacco, regret and guilt. His glory days were long gone. The sun could only lower in the sky, the days shorten.

Ralegh need not have come back. He had prepared the ground for landfall in France; when the Guiana expedition went sour he often talked about a French destination. He could have finished up in Ireland; 150 of his crew abandoned ship there. Criminals and freebooters with no appetite for justice at home, they had mutinied and compelled him, on pain of death by drowning, to promise them landfall before they reached

England. They insisted he put them ashore in the north, at the pirate haunt of Killybegs on Donegal Bay, but he held out against that demand and made them grateful for Kinsale, the southern port of his old stamping ground.

There Sir Richard Boyle, who had bought Ralegh's Irish estates in 1602, told Sir Walter how badly the failure of his Guiana expedition had been received in London and Madrid. Ralegh's fleet now consisted of four ships, rather than the fourteen with which he started out. With the deserters gone, the *Destiny* had limped home manned by a skeleton crew. The short voyage from Kinsale to Plymouth proved the most hazardous of all.

Plymouth had been good to Ralegh. When the townsfolk knew his fleet was gathering there in the spring of 1617 before embarking for Guiana, they prepared a public send-off in his honour. He had an acknowledged part in the town's illustrious Elizabethan past along with his elder kinsmen, the circumnavigator Sir Francis Drake, with whom he had sailed in revenge against the Armada, and the slave trader Sir John Hawkins, whom he had irritated by making tobacco fashionable twenty years after Hawkins had first introduced it to England. A portrait of Drake and the arms of Hawkins were being hung in Plymouth Guildhall as Sir Walter readied his expedition. By popular consent, the mayor was allowed £9 to entertain him and his followers, and a drummer was paid a shilling to beat his men aboard the ships.

He was lucky to be in good odour with anyone. The Tower of London might have been his *oubliette*, his cell of oblivion. After thirteen years' incarceration most men would have been forgotten, but Plymouth remembered him. Ralegh had come a long way to eat that feast, drink those toasts and hear that rousing tattoo.

Soon after the turn of the century Ralegh's reputation had reached its lowest ebb. His part in the downfall of the popular Earl of Essex in 1601 had turned the people against him.

> Ralegh doth time bestride;
> He sits 'twixt wind and tide
> Yet uphill he cannot ride,
> For all his bloody pride.[1]

In 1603 he had been implicated in the Bye plot to oust James I in favour of Arabella Stuart. Because plague raged in London, his trial was shifted to Winchester. When Ralegh was escorted from the Tower by a guard of fifty horse, it was touch and go whether he would make it out of the city alive, for the mob was determined to see the disdainful courtier dashed to the ground.

At Winchester Ralegh's eloquence won him the sympathy of his peers and turned public opinion around. He was sentenced to death for treason. He would have been hung, drawn and dismembered had not King James granted a last-minute reprieve. Confined to the Tower indefinitely, Sir Walter remained dead in the eyes of the law. He had been stripped of his West Country titles – Lord Warden of the Stannaries and Vice Admiral of Cornwall and Devon among them – and he probably relinquished his Plymouth house in Notte Street at this time. His letters reveal the depths of his depression and hopelessness. Gradually, by absorbing himself in projects alchemical, historical and navigational, he began to revive. Of the extant letters that he wrote from the Tower in the decade before his release, 1607–16, half are about proposed voyages to the Americas; of those, all but one concern Guiana.

The truth is, not just the last ten but the last thirty years of Ralegh's life were dominated by the idea of Guiana. Since 1588, the year of the Armada, he had brooded over it. He had sent Captain Jacob Whiddon to Trinidad on a prospecting mission in 1594. The following year, with his right-hand man Laurence Keymis, he made his own first voyage there and on his return quickly published *The Discovery of the Large, Rich, and Beautiful Empire of Guiana with a relation of the great and Golden City of Manoa (which the Spaniards call El Dorado)*. It was potent propaganda.

Backed by heavyweights – Lord Treasurer Burghley, Sir Robert Cecil, Sir George Carey and Thomas Lord Howard – Ralegh sent Laurence Keymis back to Guiana almost at once, in January 1596, with the pinnace *Darling* and two smaller ships; Keymis's otherwise upbeat report included ominous news of a newly-built Spanish fortress at the junction of the Orinoco and Caroni rivers.[2] Ralegh aimed to oust the Spanish and establish an English colony there with access to the Andes and Panama, not to mention the lost empire of the Incas and the golden city, a heady cocktail of realpolitik and myth. Less than a year after Keymis sailed, in December 1596, Ralegh despatched Leonard Berry to Guiana in command of the *Wat*, a ship named after his infant son, Walter junior.

Ralegh himself would not return to the Caribbean for more than two decades, but every two years or so he sent another ship to nurture his relationship with the Amerindians, who were intrigued by the idea of an English queen quite as much as they resented Spanish dominance. Ships' masters of various nations found that people along the coast asked earnestly after the 'Anglee' Guattaral, the Englishman Sir Walter Ralegh.

Even if they had been told where he was, the Amerindians could hardly have visualised Guattaral's situation: confined in the Tower of London, doggedly petitioning the likes of Sir Robert Cecil, Queen Anne, King James himself, and the new anti-Spanish principal secretary to the Privy Council, Sir Ralph Winwood, to allow him to revisit Guiana.

Exploitation of Guiana's gold mines accorded well with England's political struggle against the Spanish for control of the Atlantic and Caribbean regions. A powerful faction at James's court clamoured for the kind of seaborne colonial crusade that had characterised the reign of Elizabeth. The King thought otherwise and was suspected of being a crypto-Catholic. Keen to secure a Spanish marriage for Prince Charles, and a Spanish dowry to offset his debts of £700,000, James had no intention of offending his 'dear brother the King of Spain'.

However, the pro-Spanish faction, led by Robert Carr, Earl of Somerset, was on the wane. Carr, who as the King's favourite had had the benefit of Ralegh's castle at Sherborne in Dorset for a time, was himself in decline. Through his wife, who masterminded the poisoning of Sir Thomas Overbury, he was implicated in murder; scandal shook court and kingdom; the King's love for Carr was overtaken by the royal infatuation with the beautiful George Villiers, who belonged to the anti-Spanish party.

Many men were enchanted by Villiers; Francis Bacon, in one postscript, thanked him 'for your inward letter; I have burned it as you commanded: but the flame it hath kindled in me will never be extinguished'; Archbishop Laud recorded a delightful dream in which Villiers came into his bed; King James nicknamed him Steenie and, seeming to forget his own family, addressed him as 'my only sweet and dear child', 'sweetheart' and 'wife'.

Queen Anne, who championed her husband's new lover out of jealousy of Carr, also supported Ralegh's scheme. 'If it go on and succeed well,' Ralegh wrote to Winwood in July 1615, 'his Majesty shall have reason to acknowledge it towards you ... and if it shall please God that I shall perish in it yet His Majesty shall lose but a man already lost,' and again, in early 1616, 'to die *for* the King and not *by* the King is all the ambition I have in the world'. Villiers was lobbied and, once his half-brother and one of his associates had each received persuas-ive gifts of £750 (worth something approaching £400,000 today), he joined Winwood in pressing the King to let Ralegh go to Guiana.

Ralegh wrote gratefully to Villiers on 17 March 1616: 'Sir, you have by your mediation put me again into the world.'[3] Two days later he was released from the Tower; Carr and his wife were imprisoned there the next week, she in the apartments Ralegh had just vacated.

Though out in the world again, Ralegh was not free; he was barred from the royal courts – King James's, Queen Anne's and Prince Charles's – and from public assemblies. Nor could he move freely, for he was in the custody of a keeper who shadowed the ageing adventurer as, one gentleman noted, he went 'up and down seeing sights and places built or bettered since his imprisonment'.

With Ben Jonson, who had been young Wat's tutor for a time, Ralegh dined at the Mermaid Tavern and was made much of by old friends. For the first time he saw the effigy of his old mistress, Queen Elizabeth, in Westminster Abbey, one with Mary Tudor in death, and read the inscription: 'sharers of king-dom and tomb sleep here, sisters, in hope of the Resurrection'. He passed by his old home, Durham House, with its turret study where he had supervised the Thames, held court and, under the influence of Dr John Dee, studied mathematics and hermetic science with Thomas Hariot and Laurence Keymis and plotted exotic expeditions. He had invested thousands in this private palace, a theatre and laboratory for imagining and investigating the New World, until King James handed it back to the bishop of Durham. Now he saw it re-faced with freestone and in its grounds, where he once dried tobacco harvested in Ireland, he grudgingly admired the New Exchange that his sometime friend and enemy Sir Robert Cecil had erected ten years earlier. So much in London was new and grand, though the fashions were strange: men's hats were taller, their clothes more drab.

Friends, aware of Ralegh's age and infirmity, and of the political sensitivity of his Guiana enterprise, cautioned him against leaving prison for something worse. Sylvanus Scory – friend to both Ralegh and Keymis and once a handsome, witty favourite at Elizabeth's court, but now melancholic and impotent 'through much lechery' – put his advice, paradoxical enough to fit both poetic conceit and the situation's implicit contradictions, like this:

> Ralegh in this thyself thy self transcends,
> When hourly tasting of a bitter chalice,
> Scorning the sad faces of thy friends,
> Thou smil'st at Fortune's menaces and malice.
> Hold thee firm *here*, cast anchor in this port,
> *Here* art thou safe till Death enfranchise thee.
> Here neither harm nor fears of harm resort,
> Here, though enchained, thou liv'st in liberty.[4]

As it turned out, Sylvanus Scory would be in his grave by the time Ralegh returned from Guiana.

Ralegh was fixed on the course that would lead him to death. His immediate concern was to raise money (£30,000 in all) and commission a new ship to be built in the dockyards at Woolwich. Within days of leaving the Tower he put down £500 on account with a trusted collaborator, the royal shipbuilder Phineas Pett. It would be a ship incorporating the latest advances, a beautiful creature, fit to redeem time lost and win back life and fortune. Of 440 tons' burden, it must carry two hundred men and thirty-six guns. It would have 5-inch-thick planking of solid English oak from Kent; ironwork from Lewis Tite the anchorsmith; the best hempen cables; the finest sailcloth sewn in the lofts; and strong linen shirts for the crew. Ralegh's new-found faith in himself overcame his doubts and, surely aware of tempting fate, he determined to name the vessel the *Destiny*.

In June it was rumoured that Ralegh, legally dead these thirteen years, was to be pardoned; a resurrection to encourage the others, the gentlemen-adventurers, to risk voyaging with him.[5] But the rumour was groundless, for it became clear that Sir Walter would not be forgiven until after his return. It is a measure of their faith in his good faith that so many gentlemen, most of them from his old West Country power base, hazarded their fortunes and lives with him, despite King James's laggardly mercy.

On 26 August Sir Ralph Winwood obtained a royal commission for the voyage to Guiana. It was issued under the privy seal but without the customary approbation; Sir Walter was not addressed as 'trusty and well-beloved'; those words were erased after the document had been written. He took legal advice on whether or not the commission was a *de facto* pardon. His sometime friend Sir Francis Bacon, Lord Keeper of the Great Seal and, in Ralegh's son Carew's words, 'no fool, nor no ill lawyer', strolled with Sir Walter in Gray's Inn Walks and told him not to waste his money buying a formal pardon. Carew later maintained that another £1,500 to Villiers's connections would have done the trick, but Bacon assured Sir Walter that he had 'a sufficient pardon for all that is past already, the King having under his Great Seal made you Admiral, and given you power of marshal law'.

Then Bacon asked shrewdly, what Ralegh would do if, for all his investment, he missed the gold mine. 'We'll look after the plate fleet,' Sir Walter replied, meaning the Spanish treasure ships. They would be his insurance policy; there would be no need to refine *their* gold. 'Then you'll be a pirate,' said Sir Francis. Ralegh didn't see himself as some small-time freebooter. 'Did you ever know of any that were pirates for millions?' he laughed. 'They that risk for small things are pirates. I could give

£10,000 to this one, £10,000 to that one, and £600,000 to the King and several more besides.'[6]

King James would not have seen the joke, and did not share Bacon's interpretation of the commission. When the Spanish ambassador, Don Diego Sarmiento de Acuña,[7] protested loudly at the aggressive posture implied by the gathering fleet, King James promised that Ralegh, not the Crown, would be liable for injuries to Spanish subjects, and that, if this responsibility were shirked, Ralegh would forfeit his life. Either way, Ralegh would be the loser.

The autumn turned exceptionally cold. Shortly before Christmas 1616, Sir Walter and Lady Elizabeth Ralegh with their sons Wat and Carew were at the forefront of the crowd that gathered at Phineas Pett's Woolwich shipyard to watch the *Destiny* launched. Downriver, at Deptford, lay the hallowed relics of Drake's *Golden Hind* in her shallow dock, ribs picked clean by trophy hunters. On her circumnavigation of the globe Drake had won more than £300,000 in gold bullion and jewels, of which the largest single haul came from the galleon *Nuestra Señora de la Concepcion* whose formidable cannons gave her the nickname *Cacafuego or* 'Fire-shitter'. The Spanish King had wanted Drake's head. Queen Elizabeth announced that she had a golden sword to strike it off. But at Deptford, on the *Golden Hind*'s quarterdeck, she handed the sword to her French suitor, the Duke of Anjou, who knighted Drake on her behalf. Now, as Ralegh's family warmed their hands at a glowing brazier, France and Spain, gold and death were elements in the dread equation repeatedly recalculated in Sir Walter's head. The handsome *Destiny* stumbled off her stilts and glided into the freezing flood tide.

She became one of the 'sights', visited by many grandees to the consternation of the Spanish ambassador. Following her launch George Lord Carew wrote of Ralegh to a friend: 'In February next he purposes to set sail towards his golden mine, whereof he is extremely confident. The alarm of his journey is flown into Spain . . . but he is nothing appalled with the report, for he will be a good fleet and well manned.'[8] Ralegh's keeper was relieved of his duties and Sir Walter was free at last to make his arrangements without being overseen and overheard.

A contemporary noted in his diary, 'Sir Walter Ralegh purposeth to be gone the first of March', but this new deadline came and went.[9] Ralegh had hoped secretly to enlist French help. He sent a messenger, Captain Faige of La Rochelle, to Henri, Duc de Montmorency, the Admiral of France begging him to obtain Louis XIII's permission to enter a French port on his return from Guiana. Faige was ordered to pursue earlier covert negotiations for fitting out French ships and recruiting men to join the expedition. The best way to avoid conflict between his men and the Spaniards in Guiana, so complying with the terms of his commission, Ralegh decided, was to let the French do the fighting while the English mined for gold.[10]

The French ambassador, Count Des Maretz, recorded that he several times visited the *Destiny* on the Thames. On one occasion he claimed to have had a conversation with Ralegh on board, though he did not report it in his dispatches until some weeks after she had sailed. Ralegh, he wrote, complained of tyrannical treatment in England, of being stripped of his property and imprisoned unjustly; he had resolved to leave the country and offer himself to the French king.

The Spanish ambassador, Don Diego Sarmiento de Acuña, had had not gone aboard, but had had himself rowed round the *Destiny* several times in order to study her well. He knew Ralegh's pedigree. When Don Diego was eighteen, the Governor of Galicia had taken him to parley with Drake and Frobisher's fleet off Bayonne, and the infamous English pirate

'Francisco Draques' had grasped the young man by the hand and helped him into his boat.

Seven of Ralegh's ships gathered in the Thames: the *Destiny*, burden 440 tons; the *Starre* alias the *Jason*, 240 tons; the *Encounter*, 160 tons; the *John and Francis* alias the *Thunder*, 150 tons; the *Flying Joane*, 120 tons; the *Husband* alias the *Southampton*, 80 tons, and a pinnace, the *Page*, 25 tons.[11]

Ralegh was obliged to let the Privy Council have details of both his manpower and firepower, along with a map of the Orinoco region on which his destination was pinpointed. This he did reluctantly on 15 March, the day King James departed London for Scotland, leaving Francis Bacon as regent, much to Queen Anne's chagrin.

All this time Ralegh feared being countermanded. On the 19th, aboard the *Destiny* at Lee on the Thames, he described himself as 'ready to set sail'.[12] A week later most of his fleet sailed out of the river, while he went overland to Dover. 'God grant', wrote one of his friends, 'he may return deep laden with Guianian gold ore!'[13] Before their admiral rejoined them, scoundrels among his force took on the townsmen of Gravesend in a drunken contest. It was a bad omen, though probably all they deserved, that 'in the end the townsmen prevailed and drove many of Sir Walter's men into the mud of the river'.[14]

There were yet more delays. Ralegh was beset by his captains' problems with men, money, tackle and supplies for the long voyage. Off the Isle of Wight Captain Faige rejoined Ralegh with promising news of French reinforcements. Ralegh sent him back to France to continue the good work. Meanwhile the *Thunder* was still berthed at Lee on the Thames. The *Starre* also procrastinated, arriving at the Isle of Wight after the *Destiny* had already left; her captain, finding himself unable to pay for bread, travelled from the Solent back to London to beg money from Lady Elizabeth Ralegh. To redeem wasted time, the captain of the appropriately-named *Husband* got married on the island. A month passed before the fleet assembled at Plymouth.

Three more vessels awaited the fleet at Plymouth: an un-named caravel and two flyboats, the *Pink* and the *Supply*, the latter commanded by one Captain Samuel King. Four larger ships soon joined the expedition: the *Chudley*, the *Flying Hart*, the *Confidence* and the *Convertine*, the last commanded by Laurence Keymis.

On 3 May Ralegh published his orders to the fleet, for both his naval and military commanders. He stipulated that divine service be read aboard each ship, morning and evening, 'or at the least (if there be interruption by foul weather) once the day, praising God every night with singing of a psalm at the setting of the watch'. He forbade blasphemy and demanded total obedi-ence. These were the first three of twenty-four short and long paragraphs, the words not of a 'dead man' but of a proud admiral with the power of life and death over his men, clarifying the chain of command, detailing policy and procedure, the code of signals and severe penalties for misdemeanours such as piracy.

Captain Faige came back again from France with a hopeful letter from the Admiral of France. Ralegh also heard the news that Louis XIII had turned against his pro-Spanish faction. The signs were favourable. On 14 May Ralegh wrote to an old acquaintance, a former French ambassador in London, urging him to help Faige obtain the commission Ralegh wanted from the French king.[15] For the third time, Faige sailed to France with letters, Ralegh worked in Plymouth, trying to pull his fleet into shape and raising money – for instance, for Captain Whitney by selling off his personal plate – but his mind must have been half on France and half on Guiana, at the Orinoco's mouth where French ships would rendezvous with his. He was not to know that Faige would abscond, that his letters would never be delivered, that the French vessels would never arrive. He was not to know how swiftly King James would betray him. He was not to know that bad weather would force him into Falmouth where his men would fight violently among themselves, nor that storms would quickly claim one ship and confine the fleet at Cork until 19 August.

After all his troubles, the omens seemed deceptively good. Plymouth gave him a rousing send-off. He was feasted in the mayor's house. His men were drummed aboard their ships. On 12 June 1617 the fleet finally sailed for Guiana.

A year later, almost to the day, the *Destiny* made fast at Plymouth once again. A public notary by the name of Thomas Harding boarded and arrested the ship. He was acting on the orders of his master the Vice Admiral of Devon, Sir Lewis Stucley, a relative of Ralegh.[16] Then, by a letter from the Lord High Admiral of England dated 12 June 1618, Stucley received the command to apprehend his 'cousin' Sir Walter Ralegh personally.

2

BESS'S EYES

ady Elizabeth Ralegh was not in Plymouth to meet her husband off the *Destiny*, but long before she set out from her house in Broad Street in the City of London she knew something of what would confront her there. In fact, she knew too much. She had a heap of papers that had been delivered to her intermittently and by various hands in the months since her husband had left.

Ralegh had written to Bess when he could. He entrusted a packet to Captain Peter Alley, a soldier so disabled by an 'infirmity of his head' that he was deemed unfit and sent back from Cayenne. 'He', Sir Walter wrote, 'can deliver you all that is passed.' So, on his return to England in January 1618, Captain Alley handed over the letters, filled in gaps, coloured in details and answered Lady Elizabeth's questions. He did not spare her the scares and escapades of the outward voyage.

First among the folded papers was a letter Sir Walter had written to her seven months before, on 14 November 1617, just two days after reaching the coast of Guiana.[1]

'Dear heart,' it began,
I can yet write unto you but with a weak hand for I have suffered the most violent calenture [delirious fever] for fifteen days that ever man did and lived. But God, that

gave me a strong heart in all my adversities, hath also now strengthened it in the hell fire of heat.

In his journal of the voyage[2] Ralegh put his sickness down to rising from bed on the last night of October in a great sweat because a sudden gust caused 'much clamour in the ship' before his men could haul down sails. 'I took a violent cold which cast me into a burning fever' and 'for the first twenty days I never received any sustenance but now and then a stewed prune, but drank every hour day and night, and sweat so strongly as I changed my shirts thrice every day and thrice every night.'

Contrary weather had held them back. The passage from the Cape Verde Islands to Guiana, one that should have taken fourteen days, took forty. Ralegh was still confined to bed in his cabin when the *Destiny* entered the great bay where the river Oyapock flows into the Atlantic between two capes.

In 1596 Laurence Keymis had christened the southern cape Cape Cecyl. Eight years later it was occupied in King James's name by Captain Charles Leigh, but after his sudden death the colonists abandoned the settlement and sailed for England. When Robert Harcourt put into the Oyapock river in 1609, local people came aboard dressed in the European clothes that Ralegh had sent them; they were disappointed not to find the legendary Sir Walter Ralegh, whom they called Guattaral, on Harcourt's ship. Now he was back in person, anchored in six fathoms five leagues offshore, too ill to see anyone. Still, he wrote to Bess, he sent his skiff in to enquire for his old servant 'Leonard the Indian' who had stayed with them in England for three or four years. The skiff returned with information that Leonard Regapo had moved thirty miles inland. Ralegh dared not wait for him to be sent for, and consoled himself with fruits of the country.

The *Destiny* sailed up the Guianese coast and anchored at the mouth of the Cayenne river. There Ralegh sent his barge ashore to look for 'Harry the Indian' who, like Leonard, was once his servant and had lived with him for two years in the Tower. Harry did not come to Ralegh's ship at once, but sent his brother on board for the night with two other Indians and the promise of provisions.

'We have had most grievous sicknesses in our ship,' Ralegh confided from afar. Forty-two men had died and many were sick. All Sir Walter's servants had suffered, but only Crab and Francis his cook had died. There were still two hundred men on the *Destiny* and almost a thousand in his fleet. His letter was quick to reassure Bess about the fate of one man, their elder boy Wat: 'Your son had never so good health, having no distemper in all the heat under the line,' meaning south of the Equator.

As a measure of his suffering he listed the 'men of sort' who had been lost. They included John Pigot, the fleet's sergeant major; Edward Hastings, the Earl of Huntington's younger brother, the rear admiral of the fleet, 'who would have died at home, for both his liver, spleen and brains were rotten'; Richard Moore, ex-governor of the Bermudas; William Steed, the provost marshal; Newball, the *Destiny*'s master surgeon; John Fowler of London, master refiner, a grave loss to an expedition in search of gold; and 'to my inestimable grief' Christopher Hammond and John Talbot. The last had been an honest friend and scholar who had lived in the Tower with Ralegh for eleven years.

'By the next I trust you shall hear better of us. In God's hands we are, in him we trust.' The rest of the fleet were reasonably fit, and strong enough to accomplish their aim, he added, 'if the diligent care at London to make our strength known to the Spanish King by his ambassador have not taught the Spaniards to fortify all the entrances against us'.

Bess well understood her husband's fury and the reference to James's 'diligent care'. In March 1617 the King had passed Ralegh's inventory of ships, burden, ordnance and men to Don

Diego Sarmiento de Acuña, the Spanish ambassador, who forwarded it post haste to Madrid. Philip of Spain sent a dispatch to the Americas warning his governors there of Gualtero Reali's hostile intentions and ordering them to prepare for an attack. It was received at Puerto Rico, New Granada, Trinidad and at San Thomé on the Orinoco river by Don Diego Palomeque de Acuña, a relative of the ambassador in London. The Spanish King's order was dated Madrid, 19 March 1617, a full week before Ralegh's ships had even left the Thames. King James, unsubtle spymaster, could hardly have leaked intelligence more swiftly about an expedition he himself had authorised.

'Howsoever we must make the adventure,' Ralegh's letter continued, 'and if we perish it shall be no honour for England nor gain for His Majesty to lose among many other an hundred gent[lemen] as valiant as England hath in it.'

It was not only his King who had betrayed him. Ralegh wrote of Captain Baily's 'base running from me at the Canaries'. For the story of that and the rest of their desperate voyage he referred Bess to another letter in the same packet. This second letter was from Laurence Keymis, Ralegh's old collaborator and commander of the *Convertine*, to their friend Sylvanus Scory (whose poem had urged Ralegh to stay put in the Tower rather than risk everything).[3] Keymis recounted how Baily had deceived Ralegh and deserted at Lanzarote, possibly to sail home to the wife he had just married in the Isle of Wight, but more probably because his ship, the *Husband*, was insufficiently victualled.

Bess was already aware that Baily had returned to the Isle of Wight from the Canaries. His noisy blackening of her husband's name had scandalised her. He claimed to have left the fleet because he suspected that Ralegh was about to turn pirate. Examined by the Privy Council in January 1618, Baily was committed prisoner to the Gatehouse in Westminster and only released to return to his new wife when he retracted his allegations.[4]

Of Lanzarote, Keymis's letter protested, 'we could get no water there, but by force'. Ralegh told the edgy story at length in his journal but his letter to Bess only recalled how he 'took water in peace' at La Gomera, another of the Canary Islands, and how the Spanish governor's half-English wife regaled him with 'a present of oranges, lemons, limes and pomegranates, without which I should not have lived. Those I preserved in fresh sands and I have of them yet to my great refreshing.'

Captain Alley informed Bess how a Captain Janson of Flushing, a trader at Cayenne for a dozen years,[5] had gone aboard the *Destiny* and offered help, for Sir Walter was still very weak and trapped aboard an unsavoury ship, 'pestered with many sick men which being unable to move, poisoned us with a most filthy stench'. In his desire to be carried ashore Ralegh risked taking his ship over the bar at the Cayenne river's mouth, which no great vessel had ever done. At 440 tons with a draft of seventeen feet, the *Destiny* was by far the biggest ship of the fleet. Janson's advice enabled Sir Walter's crew to get her over the bar in less than three fathoms.

Captain Alley told Lady Elizabeth that Harry the Indian had visited Ralegh soon afterwards. Harry had almost forgotten his English, but brought a generous supply of food for his old master's company: a quantity of good cassava bread, roasted mullet, ground-nuts or cashews, plantains, pineapples and a variety of other fruits. Much as he longed for it, Ralegh dared not touch pineapple to start with in case it upset his stomach, but after a day or two, having been lifted ashore to sit under a tent, he ate some and was greatly refreshed. Later, Alley said, he fed well on 'the pork of the country', the hoglike peccary, and on roasted armadillo. He began to regain strength.

All the sick men were set ashore there. Ralegh was carried about in a chair. From his seat he oversaw the interment of Lieutenant General Pigot and Captain Hastings to a peal of

cannon fire from the fleet and three volleys of musket shot from
the land force. He had the *Destiny* made clean and trim. Its
great cask was scoured and refilled with fresh water. Alley
described how the smiths set up a forge, blew up a fire and
hammered out whatever ironwork the fleet required. Five small
boats – barges and shallops brought from England in quarters
– were unpacked, assembled and tested on the Cayenne river
in readiness for their ascent of the Orinoco. With the noise of
industry, and the songs that accompanied it, the expedition's
sense of purpose, dissipated by so long and enervating a voyage,
began to reassert itself.

Bess was reassured by Alley's words. They also confirmed
the gentle boast with which Ralegh concluded his letter: 'To
tell you that I might be here king of the Indians now were a
vanity, but my name hath still lived among them. Here they
feed me with fresh water and all that the country yields, and all
offer to obey me.'[6]

There was a third document in the packet. It was headed:

Newes
of S[r] *Walter Rauleigh*
with
The true *Description of Guiana.*
Also a *Relation* of the excellent *Gouerment*, and much
hope of the prosperity of the *Voyage.*
from a *Gentleman of his Fleet*, to a most especiall *Friend*
of his in *London.*
from the *River of Caliana*, on the *Coast of Guiana*,
November 17. 1617.[7]

'In these queasy and most dangerous times,' it began,
'wherein truth is manacled by opinion and imagination, every
man making his own thoughts a comment upon other men's
labours, and by screws and wrests winding every design to that
which best suits with their fancies . . .' The gentleman author,
identified only as 'RM', had written a nervous broadside. Bess

[21]

could not tell whether its voice was RM's alone, or whether he was Sir Walter's ventriloquist. Even at the other side of the world Ralegh was obsessed with what London would make of his exploits. The language was tortured, full to the brim with self-justification; unendingly anxious about the ways in which the Guiana expedition would be misinterpreted.

'I know the malice of many envious and evil disposed people who build the ground work of their own honour upon other men's disgraces, and with the venom of their aspersions seek (as much as in their malice lies) to poison the worthy labours of the most noble attempters: To which our voyage . . . is infinitely subject.' RM praised his general, Ralegh, for his government of the fleet and gives high-flown precedents for his motives and objectives; he transcribes Ralegh's written orders to his commanders in their entirety, and quotes inspirational passages from Ralegh's account of the search for El Dorado in the *Discoverie of Guiana*.[8]

RM puts it in his own words too: 'And what prince soever shall possess it, shall be lord of more gold, of more beautiful empire, and of more cities and people than either the King of Spain or the great Turk . . . To mine eye the country hath appeared a very earthly paradise, and therefore doubtless is full of strong promises, that our attemptings cannot return without much honour and reward.'

The *Newes* was printed and sold at a shop called the Sign of the Bible outside Newgate, allowing the public to share in a faraway fantasy conjured up by RM's all-consuming fears and aspirations.

Did Lady Elizabeth see gold and nobility in this document, or dark foreboding? 'By the next I trust you shall hear better of us,' Ralegh had written. She longed to receive the best news, but trusted in little.

For thirteen years Bess had wished her husband to be free, but not to escape his apartments in the Tower for the liberty of the grave. Or Guiana, which amounted to much the same thing. What had been a healthy obsession in his imprisonment, when mental adventuring took him out of himself and that stone fortress on the Thames's north bank, had now become a dangerous gamble. She had argued with him, but he talked of honour. She had fought to keep Wat at home, but Sir Walter saw the expedition as an ideal opportunity to harness his son's hot blood. She would soon get the news she wished least to hear.

In May 1618 Bess's cousin, William Herbert, landed at Plymouth with a party of sick men sent home from the Caribbean in the fleet's nimble flyboat. Ralegh thought Herbert 'a very valiant and honest gentleman', in contrast with the 'scum of men' he accompanied. He commissioned him to deliver a second packet of papers to Broad Street, three months after the first, this time written from the island of St Christophers in the Lesser Antilles.

Twenty-three miles by five and fringed by black volcanic sands, the island was christened by Christopher Columbus in 1493. In 1623 settlers would give it the pet name St Kitts and plant on its west coast the first profitable English colony in the West Indies. Anchored off it on 22 March 1618, Ralegh sat down aboard the *Destiny* in a miasma of failure and dishonour to compel himself to write two letters: the first to Sir Ralph Winwood, Ralegh's only remaining ally on the Privy Council;[9] the second to Bess.

'I was loath to write,' his note to her began,

because I know not how to comfort you. And God knows I never knew what sorrow meant till now. All that I can say to you is that you must obey the will and providence of God and remember that the Queen's Majesty bore the loss of Prince Henry with a magnanimous heart, and the Lady Harington of her only son. Comfort your heart (dear

Bess): I shall sorrow for us both and I shall sorrow the
less because I have not long to sorrow, because not long
to live.[10]

Wat was dead, aged twenty-four. And Sir Walter had led him
to his death.

'I refer you to Master Secretary Winwood's letter,' he continued, 'who will give you a copy of it if you send for it. Therein
you shall know what hath passed, which I have written by that
letter, for my brains are broken and 'tis a torment to me to
write, especially of misery.'

Bess did not send to Sir Ralph Winwood for a copy of his
letter for he too was in his grave. Ralegh's only voice in the
King's ear, the man who had helped secure his release from the
Tower and who had urged him to venture to Guiana, had fallen
silent. On 27 October 1617, when Ralegh's fleet was becalmed
between Cape Verde and Cayenne, Winwood died very
suddenly.

Sir Walter continued with mundane details:

> I have cleansed my ship of sick men and sent them home
> and hope that God will send us somewhat ere we return
> . . . You shall hear from me, if I live, from Newfoundland
> where I mean to clean my ship and to re-victual, for I have
> tobacco enough to pay for it. The Lord bless you and
> comfort you, that you may bear patiently the death of your
> most valiant son.
> Your W Ralegh.

As if to underscore that Wat had died in vain, Bess now
knew that there was no gold, only tobacco. There followed a
postscript four times as long which contains hardly a word about
Wat. In it Ralegh protested before God that, just as Sir Francis
Drake and Sir John Hawkins had died heartbroken when their
enterprises failed, he could willingly do the same if he did not
struggle against his own sorrow in order to comfort her. 'If I

live to return, resolve yourself that it is the care for you that hath strengthened my heart.'

While Ralegh had been languishing at anchor off Trinidad, too sick to head his expedition, his nephew George Ralegh had taken overall command of the five land companies, one led by Wat, which Sir Walter had dispatched in five boats up the Orinoco on 10 December. Laurence Keymis was responsible for leading the party to the mine. Their brief was to outflank the Spanish based in the outpost town of San Thomé, to locate the mine and to bring back gold ore.

Ralegh complained to Bess about Mr Keymis, their old friend, habitué of their homes and accessory to the dream of El Dorado. Keymis, Ralegh wrote, could have gone directly to the mine but, after Wat was killed, he pretended that he did not know the way. Lack of water in the river was the second excuse he offered and, 'counterfeiting many impediments', he left the mine unfound. 'When he came back I told him that he had undone me and that my credit was lost for ever.'

The two men had sat in Ralegh's cabin, their friendship and mutual trust shattered by anger, recrimination and guilt. Keymis protested that with Wat dead and Ralegh so weak when they parted that he did not expect to find him alive on his return, there seemed no reason for a venture that would only enrich a company of men who accorded him no respect, or be a gift to the Spaniards. In any case, he said, he had too few men to defend the settlement of San Thomé, which he had been forced to take from the Spanish, while at the same time traversing the forest to the mine and keeping the mining party in the mountain supplied with victuals.

It was true, Ralegh wrote, that after the governor of San Thomé and four Spanish captains were slain at the town's entrance, the rest of the Spaniards went off in a body and took more care to defend the routes to the mines – 'of which they had three within a league of the town, besides mine, which was about five leagues off' – than they did to hold the town. Keymis, he admitted, had resolved to go to the mine, but an ambush on the riverbank killed two of his men and wounded six. Captain Thornhurst, commander of one of the land companies, was shot in the head, 'of which wound and the accidents thereof he hath pined away these twelve weeks'.

Ralegh, though, rejected all his old comrade's arguments and told him that he must answer for his actions, or lack of them, to the King. Keymis then 'shut himself into his cabin and shot himself with a pocket pistol which brake one of his ribs. And, finding that it had not prevailed, he thrust a long knife under his short ribs up to the handle and died.'

He had written all this to Sir Ralph Winwood too, but more graphically:

> I heard a pistol go off over my head and, sending up to know who shot it, word was brought that Keymis had shot it out of the cabin window to cleanse it. His boy, going into his cabin, found him lying upon his bed with much blood by him and, looking on his face, saw he was dead. The pistol being but little did but crack his rib but he, turning him over, found a long knife in his body, all but the handle.

There was nothing more about Wat, but much more about Sir Walter's predicament. 'For the rest, there was never poor man so exposed to the slaughter as I was,' he wrote, reminding her how King James had commanded him to detail his Orinoco plans, with his vessels, ordnance and manpower. 'For', he confided to Winwood's ghost, 'it pleased His Majesty to value us at so little.' His soldiers had found a copy of this intelligence among the governor of San Thomé's papers, dispatched by Philip of Spain on 19 March 1617. This paper he enclosed in his letter to Winwood, little knowing it would end up in the hands of less sympathetic privy councillors.

Ralegh kept four other documents in reserve 'not knowing

whether this may be intercepted or not'. One, so he tells Bess, was King Philip's commission for the speedy levying of three hundred men and ten brass cannon from his Caribbean garrisons 'to entertain us', and an armada by sea to set upon the fleet. 'It were too long to tell you how we were preserved. My brains are broken and I cannot write much. I live yet and I have told you why.'

Ralegh had been further betrayed by two more of his own captains: as they ran past the island of Grenada on 6 March, Woolaston in the *Confidence* and Whitney in the *Encounter* deserted and turned pirate. Ralegh reminded his wife how, at Plymouth, a world away now, he sold all his plate to fund Whitney for whom he had previously had the highest regard. To Sir Ralph Winwood he vowed that if his captains had not left him he would have sailed back to San Thomé himself to finish what Keymis had hardly begun. 'I would have left my body at St Thomas by my son's', or else brought out of the mines enough gold ore to satisfy the King that his plans were not fanciful.

Of his remaining five ships, he told Bess, the flyboat was coming home with 'cousin' Herbert, the letters, and 'a rabble of idle rascals which I know will not spare to wound me, but I care not'. There was not a base slave in the fleet who had taken the pains and care he had, or slept so little and worked so much. 'My friends will not believe them and for the rest I care not. God in Heaven bless you and strengthen your heart.' And with that he signed off, 'Your W Ralegh.'

About her he cared, conventionally at least, she knew. About most else it seemed he was past caring.

The day that Sir Walter wrote to his wife from St Kitts, Charles Parker, fresh from commanding the first land company in Guiana, wrote to his friend Peter Alley,[11] the soldier Ralegh had invalided home from Cayenne, with information for Lady Elizabeth. She needed more news of Wat than his father had allowed her, but would have preferred to hear rather less of the truth than her son's comrade-in-arms passed on.

Alley had been lucky to retire from the expedition when he did, Parker told him, because by leaving he had missed unspeakable miseries. They were a month going up the Orinoco, at last landing within three miles of San Thomé. About one in the morning they made an assault on the town in which they lost Captains Ralegh and Cosmor, though 'Captain Ralegh lost himself with his unadvised daringness'. He explained: Cosmor had led with his fifty men; Parker followed with a division of musketeers; then came a division of pikes led by Wat, who no sooner heard the attack on Parker's men than he recklessly rushed from his command across to them, 'where he was unfortunately welcomed with a bullet', giving him no chance 'to call for mercy to our heavenly father for his sinful life he had led'.

They took San Thomé with the loss of only two more men while the Spaniards fled, unsure of the English strength, leaving their governor, Don Diego Palomeque de Acuña, and two of his captains dead. Once in possession of the settlement, Keymis took some gentlemen with him to locate the mine and 'trifled up and down some twenty days' keeping everyone in hope of finding it. 'But at last', said Parker, 'we found his delays mere illusions and himself a mere machiavell, for he was false to all men and most odious to himself, for most ungodly he butchered himself, loathing to live since he could do no more villainy.'

Parker briskly informed Alley that the fleet had already split up; that Captains Whitney and Woolaston had combined 'to look for homeward-bound men' (a euphemism for piracy); and that Ralegh and his vice admiral would re-victual at Newfoundland before making to the Azores for the same purpose. 'For my part by the permission of God I will make a voyage or bury myself in the sea,' Parker confided. 'About the latter end of August I hope we shall have feathered our nest.'

The patchwork of accounts Bess found herself obliged to stitch together was both enlightening and bewildering. In Sir Walter's absence she clung to that heap of words, stories, statements and expostulations; a fragmented history of the past year.

The fullest document sent from the Antilles was penned by the Reverend Samuel Jones, the chaplain or, as he designated himself, 'preacher' on Captain Chudleigh's *Flying Joane*. His report, dated 22 March, was addressed to the Right Honourable the Lords of His Majesty's most Honourable Privy Council.[12] A certain Captain Edward Giles obtained a copy and forwarded it to Lady Ralegh from Plymouth on 24 May. So, a fortnight before her husband berthed at Plymouth, Bess was in possession of almost all the information she would get before she met him face to face.

The preacher made a show of being fair to all parties. Delays when the voyage had barely begun, being forced by foul weather into Falmouth, and driven to shelter from storms at Cork for almost eight weeks, he said, had compelled many gentlemen and others to sell their personal supplies of clothes and food, 'to the untimely death of many of them'. These frustrations had made them unreasonably suspicious of Ralegh's motives.

There was no piracy at first. Four ships which Ralegh took, Frenchmen and Basques who claimed, falsely as it happened, to be fishermen not men of war, were simply escorted southwards for two days, a hundred leagues out of their way, because they were bound for Seville; nothing was taken from them by force but a pinnace and a supply of fish oil which were paid for.

At Lanzarote Ralegh requested only water and provisions which he offered to pay for, but the islanders murdered three of his men. While at La Gomera, once fear of pillage was allayed, his ships were given leave to replenish their fresh water.

Sir Walter's restraint in these confrontations, Jones wrote, reassured many gentlemen that he was sure of his project, something the earlier delays had made them doubt. Still, a deserted Spanish caravel was captured at Gran Canaria and, nearby, a small boat was taken, manned by fourteen Spaniards who were set free, except for one who begged to join the expedition.

From there the fleet made for the Cape Verde Islands, unwisely in the seamen's judgment, and in the preacher's too, 'for by steering such uncertain and unnecessary courses we were so becalmed, that above a hundred persons, gentlemen most of them, died between those islands and the continent of Guiana'.

During this 'great mortality' the preacher, in the course of his solemn duties, heard many of the sick and dying gentlemen complain of Sir Walter's stern treatment, denying even those who had invested heavily in the voyage water and other essentials, even though there was no shortage of stores at that time. On his deathbed John Pigot, Ralegh's Lieutenant General, protested. So did others who survived. Jones pointed out that Mathew Rogers, surgeon's mate aboard the *Flying Joane*, could testify to this.

Then, he wrote, Ralegh fell down in his ship, bruised himself badly, brewed up a dangerous fever and called for the chaplain to pray for him. Sir Walter spoke religiously and told Jones that he grieved more for the gentlemen whose estates his death would put at risk than for himself. To cover them he vowed to leave promissory notes, 'which notes neither I, nor for aught I know any man else in the fleet, yet saw'.

Bess too had invested heavily in the voyage. She had sold her own estate at Mitcham for £2,500. She had induced relatives to give sureties against which she raised £15,000. She and Sir Walter had called in £8,000, paid to them in compensation for the loss of Sherborne Castle, which they had lent to the Countess of Bedford. She had even pledged a portion of her £400 annuity, granted in lieu of jointure, to supply the enterprise. As the fleet laboured in mid-Atlantic she was reduced to complaining to Sir Julius Caesar, judge of the High Court of the Admiralty, about a functionary who daily delayed her payment: she should have received £200 at Michaelmas, most of it owed to poor men for supplies her husband had had, 'and the rest to maintain me till our Lady day; but I have not received one penny from the Exchequer since Sir Walter went'.

Elizabeth Ralegh's fortune, with those of others, was locked up in Ralegh's hopes of Guiana gold. However, what struck her most in Jones's report was the passage about Sir Walter's fall. His letters had not mentioned it; his own journal was silent about the humiliating tumble. He hated to admit disability or clumsiness, although, ever since a cannonball hit the deck of his ship at Cadiz in 1596 and lamed him, he had limped and walked with a stick. Splinters from that impact had skewered and deformed his right calf. Until she read the preacher's tale she had had no clue that her husband had toppled unheroically in stormy darkness and aggravated an old but glorious injury.

She devoured Jones's disturbing narrative: how, after the expedition disappeared up the Orinoco in search of the mine, he waited with Ralegh at Punto Gallo, Trinidad, near the main mouth of the river. They heard nothing from the exploring party for two months. During this time Ralegh talked less, and less confidently than before, about the mine, and more about new projects. His head was in turmoil. One of the successes of his 1595 expedition had been the sacking of San Joseph, Trinidad's main Spanish settlement, later Port of Spain. Now he toyed with taking it again for its treasure and tobacco, saying that it did not matter whether or not his men emerged from the Orinoco. They were good for nothing but eating victuals, he said, having been sent to sea by friends who wished to be rid of them. Despite his promise that Keymis would find him at

Punto Gallo, dead or alive, Ralegh now considered abandoning them. His captains would not countenance the notion.

The attack on San Thomé had been provoked by a late-night Spanish ambush from the skirt of a wood as the expedition settled down for the night. When the town had been taken, Keymis was reported to be more concerned with tobacco, apparel, household stuff and other pillage than with finding the mine. One night, though, he went out with his own men and brought back ore. Cheerfully he showed this to Captain Thornhurst, but when a refiner assayed it, it proved worthless. The party believed him deluded, or deceived by Ralegh, about both the ore and the mine's location. There were desperate searches, an ambush by Spaniards and Spanish Indians, a planned four-day upriver expedition that did not return for three weeks, but pressed inland for 180 miles (or 300 according to Spanish accounts). Even if they had found a vein of ore they would have had to send back for spades, pickaxes and refiners, for they took none with them. All this for a mine that was supposed to be three miles downriver from San Thomé.

On 13 February, Peter Andrews, one of Keymis's men, with an Indian guide, emerged from the Orinoco delta carrying a parcel of documents from San Thomé, a roll of tobacco, a tortoise, oranges, lemons, and a letter which he delivered to the *Destiny*. The letter was in Keymis's hand, dated 8 January.[13] It put Ralegh's worst fears into words. The Spanish town had been attacked. His son, Wat, was dead. As yet there was no gold. His own death warrant was surely signed. From this day on his journal is a blank; he no longer had the heart to write in it.

Sir Walter protested his integrity to his captains and vowed to call Keymis to account publicly. He never did. When Keymis and the expedition rejoined the fleet on 2 March, Ralegh made as though to go back himself and lead them to the mine, but it was 'altogether improbable, if not impossible. Our men weary, our boats split, our ships foul, and our victuals well-nigh spent.'

After abandoning a botched attempt at plundering San Joseph, the fleet sailed from Trinidad to Nevis where Ralegh promised a new project and spoke of a French commission of which no one saw any evidence. Sir Warham St Leger, in overall charge of the land forces, asked him privately whether he intended to return to England. Never, he swore, for once they got him there they would hang him. He told Sir Warham he would first sail for Newfoundland to victual and trim his remaining ships, then make for the Azores to waylay homeward-bound Spanish ships and win treasure that would buy him a welcome in France or elsewhere.

At Nevis, the preacher continued, the desperate nature of these plans and the facts of Keymis's suicide turned men's minds to mutiny. All felt abused by Keymis or Ralegh, or both. The captains feared to lose their ships if they followed Sir Walter any longer. Most left him. Near Newfoundland banks, the *Destiny*'s own men mutinied. It was touch and go. Some wanted to sail for English terra firma and more profitable employment. Others, pirates and criminals who feared justice at home, planned to stay at sea as freebooters and make fortunes. Ralegh emerged from his cabin, outfaced the ringleaders on the quarterdeck and read out His Majesty's commission for the voyage in a loud voice. Then he put it to a vote. He himself voted firmly for England. Indeed, the preacher added, to his knowledge Ralegh never slighted the King's majesty, nor tolerated such a fault in any one.

The Guiana voyage should have transported Ralegh from impotence to mastery; it should have set right the wrongs he had suffered and given life back to the dead man. His whole career had been one of opportunity and triumph blocked or curtailed by betrayal and obstruction. On the *Destiny* this pattern had been repeated. Bess knew how he thrashed about when thwarted. She understood his panic and the expedients he must have contemplated to lift himself from the mire.

On 23 May, the day before Captain Giles sent Lady Elizabeth preacher Jones's report to the Privy Council, Captain Roger North was granted an audience with the King. It is impossible to say how quickly this news came to Bess's ears, but some account of it, wreathed with rumour, oppressed her soon enough. Captain North, Lord North's brother, fresh from commanding one of the five companies in the Orinoco fiasco and soured by the experience, had left Ralegh at Nevis to sail home. He furnished King James with a full recital of events and the benefit of his strong opinions:[14] Sir Walter had invented the notion of a gold mine; his anger with George Ralegh and Laurence Keymis was unreal, acted out to preserve the semblance of integrity; he had always planned to seek sanctuary in France.

On 9 June the King issued a proclamation from Greenwich Palace: while he had given licence to Sir Walter Ralegh and others for a voyage to Guiana 'where they pretended great hopes and probablities to make discovery of certain gold mines for the lawful enriching of themselves, and these our kingdoms', he had forbidden any act of of hostility against the territories, states or subjects of any friendly princes, 'and more particularly those of our dear brother the King of Spain'.[15] Since the peace had been infringed by killing, sacking and burning, he was obliged to make a public declaration of 'our own utter mislike and detestation of the same insolences, and excesses' if such had been committed, and to require anyone with information to reveal it, 'that we may thereupon proceed in our princely justice to the exemplary punishment and coercion of all such as shall be convicted and found guilty of so scandalous and enormous outrages'.

King James reissued the proclamation from Westminster two days later, just as Ralegh's skeleton crew eased the *Destiny* into the welcoming arms of Plymouth Sound.

As soon as the *Destiny* was sighted rounding Rame Head a message was sent to London. Lady Elizabeth boarded a coach, with her surviving son, Carew, her servants, food and drink and sweetmeats, fresh clothes and shoes to put on her husband and a terrible bundle of papers to put before him. As if in sympathy, the weather was unseasonal: summer hail one day, foul rain the next. By stages, with changes of horses at successive inns, the coach rolled towards Sir Walter with jarring thuds, jolts and sickening swerves through landscapes performing their usually so enticing metamorphoses: heathy Surrey to forested Hampshire, chalky Wiltshire, voluptuous Dorset and at last into ruddy Devon, the county of his birth. That he had come back alive was joy. That he must fall into the snare set for him was agony.

Sir Walter had appeared and disappeared many times into and out of her life. At his first appearance he was 'Water', the Queen's dear minion, dressed in dazzling clothes, ornamented with gold and jewels, a wheel-ruff edged with lace framing his head and setting off his thick dark hair, his neatly trimmed pointed beard and curled moustache. Queen Elizabeth had nicknamed him 'Water' in gentle mockery of his Devon brogue and in reluctant recognition of his attachment to the sea, the sea she always tried to keep him from. Water he was. He glittered. He ran through your fingers.

In poems Ralegh called the Queen Cynthia, the chaste goddess of the moon, and named himself Ocean, far greater than Water but none the less ruled in all his tides, in his every ebb and flow, by the moon, his Virgin Queen. In *The One-and-Twentieth and Last Book of the Ocean to Cynthia* he later wrote:

> To seek new worlds for gold, for praise, for glory,
> To try desire, to try love severed far,
> When I was gone she sent her memory,
> More strong than were ten thousand ships of war,

To call me back, to leave great honour's thought,
To leave my friends, my fortune, my attempt;
To leave the purpose I so long had sought,
And hold both cares and comfort in contempt.

Towards the end of 1584, when Bess's brother Arthur
Throckmorton had negotiated a place for her in the royal
household as a maid of the Privy Chamber, there he was. Walter
Ralegh, not yet Sir Walter. That year he had sent a reconnoitring
expedition to the New World; he gave the territory his scouts
discovered the name Virginia, in honour of the Queen who
would not permit him to cross the ocean to see it for himself.

Elizabeth Throckmorton was enchanted and flattered by
Ralegh. Walter, at thirty-four, was captivated by this Maid of
Honour, twelve years his junior. That she shared the Virgin
Queen's name was tantalising. Ralegh's fantasies had been
invaded by a fresh Elizabeth, a tall, unusual beauty with her
long face, luminous eyes, strong nose and provocatively modest
lips.

> Her eyes he would should be of light,
> A violet breath and lips of jelly,
> Her hair not black nor over-bright,
> And of the softest down her belly;
> As for her inside he'd have it
> Only of wantonness and wit . . .
>
> The light, the belly, lips and breath,
> He dims, discolours and destroys;
> With those he feeds but fills not Death,
> Which sometime were the food of joys.
> Yea, Time doth dull each lively wit
> And dries all wantonness with it.
>
> O cruel Time, which takes in trust
> Our youth, our joys and all we have,
> And pays us but with age and dust,

Who in the dark and silent grave
When we have wandered all our ways
Shuts up the story of our days.[16]

The two Elizabeths overlapped in his courtly, carnal imagination. He had had to curb lechery in order to retain his standing in the Queen's pleasure, his footing in the wild discipline of her dancing, his place at the Privy Chamber's door and, at her whim, his passage through it. He married Bess Throckmorton secretly, probably in the spring of 1588. Four years later she fled to her brother's house at Mile End to be delivered of a boy, Damerei, their first-born. He died early, and was the involuntary cause of her, and her no-longer-secret husband's fall from grace.

Now Wat, their second son, was dead. And Lady Elizabeth, with Carew, their third and last, was approaching Plymouth in a stage coach to meet old Sir Walter, limping, grey-haired, weakened and desperate but still damnably proud. Water. Her Walter, the man legally dead but risen again from the waves.

3

AN INEVITABLE ROCK

ristóbal Guayacunda walked the deck of the *Destiny*. He watched the crew furl, lower and fold the sails, lash them into bundles and carry them ashore. Guayacunda was a Moxan Indian from the town of Sogamoso, to the northeast of Bogotá, in the new kingdom of Granada. From the moored vessel he watched the dense, apparently erratic movement of women, men, horses, carts and carriages on the quays and wharves of Plymouth's Sutton Pool. He gazed at vessels on the water and at buildings climbing the low hills. This Old World was his New World. He had not been prepared for a port like this, not by the towns he had recently seen in the Spanish Indies, nor even by Kinsale. Plymouth was the twentieth town in England by population, and the fifth or sixth port by trade, after London, Hull, Exeter and Bristol, and in 1617 its customs returns had outstripped even Newcastle. Compared with the village-sized town of San Thomé on the Orinoco, where Guayacunda had served the Spanish governor, Plymouth was bafflingly vast.

Guayacunda had stood fast in a private room within the governor's house when the English came. Pedro the Creole, servant to a Spanish captain, was in the house too. Pedro was in chains, for on the day that sails appeared on the Orinoco river he had said how glad he was; he was going to join the

English. Guattaral's men relished releasing him from his fetters. They dressed him in finery looted from abandoned houses, and fêted him, calling him Don Pedro. Accordingly, Guayacunda pretended to be of mixed race too; but without the benefit of Spanish chains, Spanish blood was a handicap he soon disclaimed. The English took his clothes away and made him grind their corn. San Thomé was part-razed and simplified by fire. The English employed the negro slaves who deserted to them, 'enjoyed' three captured Spanish-speaking Indian women for twelve days until they ran away to rejoin the Spaniards in hiding, but confined Guayacunda on one of their boats.

After an uncertain interval Guayacunda found himself carried away, with another Indian named Josef by the Spaniards, to the ship of the legendary Guattaral. There, aboard the *Destiny* off Trinidad, they saw how old and sick the legend was; they witnessed Sir Walter weeping over the death of his son. After grief and anger had subsided, Ralegh interrogated and threatened the prisoners at intervals, then cajoled and conversed, especially with Guayacunda because of his status as the governor's servant; then with Guayacunda alone, for on the voyage to Guattaral's country Josef died.

Guayacunda is not mentioned in any of the extant letters or reports sent from Guiana and the Spanish Indies by Ralegh or members of his expedition. Ralegh refers to him, not by name but as 'the governor's servant who is now with me', in a letter he wrote on his arrival in Plymouth. Guayacunda's name occurs in documents relating to the hearings that led up to Ralegh's execution. After witnessing Guattaral's beheading, Guayacunda travelled to Madrid and back to South America where, at Cartagena, he was interviewed by the Spanish friar Pedro Simon, who used the story in his account of the conquest of the West Indies.[1]

Once at Plymouth Guayacunda found himself a member of Guattaral's entourage along with Captain Samuel King and Sir Walter's page Robin. Captain King had commanded one of

the fleet's flyboats, survived near-shipwreck and the fruitless
Orinoco adventure, but remained loyal to his friend and admiral.
The Indian was more than a prisoner or a servant or a hanger-on,
he was corroborative evidence.

As soon as he berthed at Plymouth, Ralegh sat down to write,
or to finish writing, a letter. There is no copy of it in English
but it exists in a Spanish translation sent to Madrid from London
on 24 June.

Until very recently the date of Ralegh's landfall at Plymouth
was believed to have been 21 June 1618. We now know that
he arrived a few days before 14 June.[2] The translator or copyist
dated his letter 'Plymouth 1 June 1618'. This too is wrong,
and probably a slip of the pen for 11 June. The ten-day difference between the Old Style calendar then in use in England
and the New Style employed in Catholic Europe does not solve
the problem because it works the wrong way, though it is con-
ceivable that the copyist meant to translate the date into Spanish
time, but subtracted ten days instead of adding them.

The mystery is that Ralegh was not arrested until the second
week of July, a month after he landed. In London the Spanish
ambassador had sought an audience with King James as soon
as he got news of the assault on San Thomé. The King had
been reluctant to see him, being preoccupied as usual with sport,
but Don Diego Sarmiento had insisted he wanted to say only
one word. He burst into the royal presence, so the story goes,
and shouted it three times: '*Piratas! Piratas! Piratas!*'[3] Then
he stormed out. Obediently James issued a proclamation against
Ralegh from Greenwich on 9 June, and from Westminster on
the 11th.[4] Next day the Lord High Admiral ordered Ralegh's
cousin Sir Lewis Stucley, the Vice Admiral of Devon, to apprehend Sir Walter at Plymouth. But nothing happened for a while.

Ralegh was already back, urgently writing a letter to George
Lord Carew, Privy Councillor and Master of the Ordnance. 'Sir:

I am sure your lordship has received a copy of my letter sent with Captain North to Secretary Winwood, of whose death I heard with great sorrow in Ireland,' he began.[5] He doubtless hoped that Lord Carew could be persuaded to be as faithful a friend and ally to him as Sir Ralph Winwood had been. Of Laurence Keymis's excuses for not discovering the gold mine, he wrote that a chief of the country, an old aquaintance, would have shown Keymis the way if he had stayed upriver just two more days.

Moreover the governor's servant [Guayacunda], who is now with me, could have led them to two gold mines not two leagues from the town as well as to a silver mine not three arquebus shots distant, and I will demonstrate the truth of this when my health allows me to go to London.

He acquainted Lord Carew with the mutiny on the *Destiny*: how, approaching Newfoundland, he learned that a hundred of his men had determined to join the English settlers there or turn pirate. He assembled the ship's company and told them he would not clean his ship in Newfoundland, nor take in fresh water and provisions, but would order the master to sail for England. They voted by moving to larboard or starboard. The conspirators were a clear majority, he says, including some of the best men he had and some gentlemen. They resisted and shouted that they would die rather than go home. They occupied the magazine full of arquebuses, swords and armour, and refused Ralegh entry. 'Finding myself in this peril I gave way to the mutiny for a time.'

Delicately he negotiated with two or three of the leaders and urged them to abandon their side. It was touch and go, but they relented, on condition that Ralegh promised on oath not to return to England until they had obtained pardon for past piracies. Hence the return to Ireland. 'If I had not agreed they would have killed me and those who stood by me, or else

I should have killed them, in which case, as the mutineers were my ablest men, I would have been unable to bring the ship into port.'

It had alarmed him, he wrote, on arrival in Kinsale to hear that he had fallen into His Majesty's grave displeasure for having taken a town from the Spaniards. His men were so afraid of being hanged that they were on the point of forcing him to sail away again from Ireland. He protested that he had given no authority for San Thomé to be taken, but that in any case the Spanish ambush forced his men to subdue it. They were obliged too to burn the houses overlooking the Plaza because the Spaniards 'had made loop-holes in the walls and kept up so hot a fire that in a quarter of an hour they would have killed them all'.

Then, referring back to his expedition of 1595, he added his key point: 'And, my lord, that Guiana be Spanish territory can never be acknowledged for I myself took possession of it for the Queen of England by virtue of a cession by all the native chiefs.' King James knew this very well, he argued; the commission to explore Guiana that His Majesty granted Robert Harcourt in 1609 was proof of it.

He countered the accusations of those who deserted him: he had not turned pirate and fled, but risked his life instead to get himself and his ship to England. 'I have suffered as many miseries as it was possible for me to suffer ... If His Majesty wishes that I should suffer even more let God's will and His Majesty's be done, for even death itself will not make me turn thief or vagabond.' Nor, he added, would he abuse the courtesy of those gentlemen who put up money for the expedition. With this he signed off, 'Your poor kinsman, W. Ralegh'.

A postscript begged Lord Carew to excuse him to the Privy Council for not writing earlier: 'Want of sleep for fear of being surprised in my cabin at night has almost deprived me of my sight and some return of the palsy which I had in the Tower has so weakened my hand that I cannot hold the pen.'

A second, longer, postscript informed Lord Carew that since his arrival in Plymouth he had been handed a copy of the statement against him delivered to the Privy Council by the preacher Samuel Jones. He briefly responded to its slurs, but added, 'I hope to live to answer them to their faces and prove them all cowards, liars and, in spirit, thieves', and concluded, 'I wrote this after having sealed the other letters and I pray you give a copy of them to my poor wife who, with the loss of her son and these rumours, I fear will go mad.'

Dear Bess was on his mind. To her he had written, 'My brains are broken.' We do not know how soon she got to Plymouth or where they lodged at first. They might have stayed just north of Plymouth Hoe, in Notte Street where they once had a house. Members of the Drake family may have offered them accommodation in Looe Street, that climbs steeply from Sutton Pool, where the late Sir Francis Drake had one of his many Plymouth properties. They could have found a temporary home with Ralegh's old friend and agent Sir Christopher Harris at Radford House, across Cattewater; we know they stayed there later. They may have spent time aboard the *Destiny*, in the cabin where Sir Walter had studied his maps and hopes, and which, during the mutiny, had become his prison for a time.

The company all waited for an agent of the King to knock on the door. No one came. Lady Elizabeth consulted Samuel King about getting a passage across the Channel. While others could hear the axe on the stone, Sir Walter remained deaf to its grinding. He believed too much in honour and in his capacity to sway the King by reasoned argument. After all, his reasons were justifiable in his own eyes. While his entourage worried about partial, irrational justice, Ralegh set about rebutting the complaints of the Spanish ambassador.

He wrote to King James on 16 June.[6] It was a short, beautifully-wrought letter designed to pull the rug, with a rhetorical flourish or two, from under the feet of the Spanish. For all its conventional deference, it ruthlessly attempted to throw the King off balance too, partly by reason and partly by an appeal to His Majesty's better nature. Despite his own cunning and duplicity, Ralegh, like many men with large but vulnerable egos, was endearingly naive when it came to others. At bottom, he had faith in reason and goodness.

In fewer than five hundred words he demonstrated his restraint at the Canary Islands, his honour in returning Spanish ships without taking spoil, and his forbearance in the Spanish Indies where he might have sacked twenty coastal towns but spared them, 'and did only follow my enterprise ... upon Guiana, where (without any directions from me) a Spanish village was burnt which was newly set up within three miles of the mine'. If it was lawful, he wrote, for the Spanish to kill thirty-seven English traders by tying them back to back and cutting their throats – a reference to a notorious recent atrocity – and it was not lawful for His Majesty's subjects, being attacked first, to repel force by force, 'we may then justly say: O miserable English'.

If English privateers like William Parker could burn towns and kill Spaniards in the heart of the Spanish Indies without reproof on their return, while Ralegh himself forbore because he had no wish to offend,

> I may justly say: O miserable Sir Walter Ralegh. If I have spent my poor estate, lost my son, suffered by sickness and otherwise a world of miseries; if I have resisted with manifest hazard of my life the robberies and spoils which my companies would have made; if, when I was poor, I could have made myself rich; if when I had gotten my liberty ... I voluntarily lost it; if when I was master of my life I have rendered it again; if when I might elsewhere have sold my ship and goods, and have put five or six thousand pounds in my purse, I have brought her into England.

All this, he wrote, so that it should not be said that His Majesty had given liberty and trust to a man whose only aim was his own freedom and the betrayal of that trust. 'My mutineers told me that if I returned for England I should be undone, but I believed more in your Majesty's goodness than in their arguments.'

It was a plausible and passionate defence, but at its core lay a doubtful notion: that San Thomé was not where he or Keymis expected it to be. He refers to it as 'a Spanish village . . . which was newly set up within three miles of the mine'. Was he really surprised by its location, or did he wilfully reposition it in order to convince the King and his enemies on the Privy Council that he had honestly thought he could exploit the mine without coming into conflict with Spain?

This letter was the second shot in what even Ralegh must have known would be a difficult campaign. He must have thought he could win it, unless he had deliberately set his course for death.

❦

Why did the knock on the door never come? Sir Lewis Stucley was in London when he received his orders on 12 June. Perhaps he dawdled because he had scruples about arresting his kinsman, or simply out of decency allowed Sir Walter and Lady Elizabeth a space to reacquaint themselves and share their grief. He must soon have learned that Ralegh had put his sails ashore, that the *Destiny* would not carry him off unexpectedly. His delay may have been a matter of policy. His deputy in Plymouth, the public notary Thomas Harding, arrested the ship. Maybe Stucley set spies to watch the Raleghs, but did not intervene in the hope that, given enough rope, Sir Walter would hang himself. Perhaps he hoped that Ralegh would make good his escape. There is reason to believe that this is what the King and the Council wanted; it would save them the ticklish task of dealing with so problematic a man; it would save His Majesty the embarrassment of fulfilling undertakings he had agreed privately with Madrid. The Spanish ambassador was due to finish his term shortly. Perhaps once he had left London the last act in Ralegh's drama, whatever it might be, could be quietly played out.

Wearing fresh clothes, a crisp ruff, clean hose and unsalted shoes, Ralegh had time to recuperate a little. However rhetorical they were, his protestations of misery and sickness were without doubt genuine enough. In the last image we have of him – a miniature believed to have been commissioned by Lady Ralegh after his death – his beard is almost white, his hair thinning, his face drawn, his eyes unsettlingly astray.[7] The old man's likeness is set above a tiny inset scene of one of his greatest exploits: the capture of Fayal in the Azores, twenty years before. The face may have been a copy, appropriately aged, of an earlier portrait or it may have been drawn from his death's head. It is the closest we can come to seeing him in his last months.

In Plymouth, the ghost they could hardly speak of was Wat's. His spectre stood between them in the street and sat down with them at table. Sir Walter told Bess and Carew many hair-raising and picturesque stories of the voyage that he had not recounted in his letters, but it was hard for him to place Wat in them. When he did talk about him, he told Bess how her son was buried. He did not want her to believe him abandoned in the jungle or thrown into some ditch in the town of San Thomé. Samuel King had witnessed the funeral. The bodies of Wat, Captain Cosmor and three others had lain in state in the town's guard house. On the morning of Sunday 5 January 1618 the English force paraded, armed, with drums muffled, pikes at the trail and five banners dipped. The bodies were borne from the guard house on planks shoulder-high in solemn procession and marched slowly round the plaza three times. Then they were carried into the larger of San Thomé's two churches where a pair of pits had been dug. Captain Ralegh and Captain Cosmor were lowered into one by the high altar, the other three into one in the nave. Before the ceremony was over two ships dropped anchor in the town harbour: Captain Woolaston's *Confidence* and Captain Whitney's *Encounter*, delayed for days after running aground on a shoal in the Orinoco delta. Because of the *Encounter*'s size, the ensign that it flew and the salute of more than thirty guns with which the other English ships greeted it, the Spanish assumed that it was the fleet's flagship with Admiral Ralegh aboard. But Sir Walter, off Trinidad, missed his son's funeral by more than a few minutes.

Ralegh reassured his wife that her elder boy had died bravely. Towards midnight on 2 January the three companies of English soldiers, led by Indian guides, had come within half a mile of San Thomé. They were three companies, not five, because the rest were aboard the grounded ships. The Spanish governor had sent Captain Geronimo de Grados with ten men to man a high point about three musket shots from the town. The English fell into the ambush. Grados had match-cord cut in pieces, lighted and set at intervals so that his force would seem larger than it was. Captains Cosmor, Parker and Ralegh's companies bettered them, so that they fell back upon the town. The Spanish charged again and Wat, crying 'Victory!' and 'Come on, my hearts!', ran ahead of his company to the front of Parker's men where he was hit by a bullet. Still he thrust at a Spanish captain with his sword, but this Captain Errinetta grasped the small end of his musket and swung it, felling Captain Ralegh with a blow to the head. 'Lord have mercy upon me, and prosper your enterprise,' were Wat's dying words. This, or something like this, was the version of events Sir Walter and Samuel King, who had been part of the skirmish, told Bess.

The second ghost that haunted them was that of Laurence Keymis, the man Ralegh had harangued for the failure of his hopes. A tall, slender figure with a scholarly gaze and a cast in one eye, Keymis had lived in their London home, Durham

House, and at Sherborne Castle in Dorset as a member of the household. Ralegh told his wife how Indians of a tribe ruled by chief Carapana, uncowed by the Spanish, had met the expedition between San Thomé and the Orinoco delta with the gift of a big canoe full of fruits and provisions, and repeatedly offered to take them to a mine or bring them samples of ore. Samuel King confirmed this. Two men, Mr Leake and Mr Mollineux, had volunteered to go but the rest refused and Keymis, by not asserting his authority, lost his last chance of gold. He ended his life, at fifty-six, in a cabin on the *Destiny*, in a welter of blood with a wound from a pistol ball in his chest and a long knife thrust up to the handle into his heart.

It rekindled a yet more intimate and uncomfortable vision: of a knife in the Bloody Tower, a duller knife Sir Walter had used. In 1603, his fiftieth year, Ralegh, awaiting trial for treason, had asked his keeper Sir John Peyton to buy him a long thin knife 'with which to stir his wine'. Sir John understood the metaphor and refused, or simply forgot the request. He 'never saw so strange a dejected mind', he said. 'Five or six times in a day he sendeth for me in such passions as I see his fortitude is not competent to support his grief.' Sir Walter resorted to a broader, blunter instrument. On Wednesday 27 July, when the Lords of His Majesty's Council had convened in the Tower to examine the prisoners, he stabbed himself between the ribs, under the heart.

'The stab was ungentle,' wrote a pamphleteer, 'savouring of barbarism, and too much tasting of desperation, together it had a spice of atheism; for he that denies himself, denies him that made him, and he that kills himself kills him in himself that redeemed him.'[8] Surgeons who dressed the wound reported that he had come within less than half an inch of his life. Perhaps he feared the Lords' questions or the rack that might extort the answers they wished to hear. While protesting and arguing his innocence, he acted guiltily. Bess had been close by, powerless to restrain him. At almost the same hour his faithful secretary Edward Hancock poisoned himself. King James urged the Lords to take a good preacher to Ralegh, 'that he may make him know that it is his soul that he must wound and not his body'. In the last stanza of an angry poem he wrote much earlier, *The Lie*, addressed to the soul, Ralegh seems to allude prophetically to this terrible moment and transform it:

> So when thou hast, as I
> Commanded thee, done blabbing,
> Although to give the lie
> Deserves no less than stabbing,
> Stab at thee he that will,
> No stab the soul can kill.

Bess once more feared that her husband would fall into a pit of despair, but time spent in the company of family and Plymouth friends had done him good. He gathered himself for the battle ahead. Letters had been written, sad words spoken, tears shared and fleet business concluded. It was time to face whatever future he had. Contemporaries, who did not believe he would survive, simply could not understand why he had risked coming home to Plymouth. As one wrote: 'The world wonders extremely that so great a wise man as Sir Walter Ralegh should have returned to cast himself upon so inevitable a Rock.'[9]

In the second week of July Sir Walter and Lady Elizabeth's party, with Carew, Robin (Walter's body servant), Samuel King and Cristóbal Guayacunda among them, boarded coach and mounted horse and started out on the road east. Since the knock on the door had never come, they would take themselves to London.

They did not imagine they would be back in Plymouth so soon.

4

COUSIN LEWIS

Ralegh did not know it, but in London his most implacable enemy was in trouble. The Spanish ambassador – Don Diego Sarmiento de Acuña, the Count de Gondomar, cousin of the late governor of San Thomé – had trampled a small boy while out riding and the incident aroused popular anti-Spanish sentiment. It did not take much to stir up Hispanophobia, or hatred of any foreigner, in England. Ralegh was no xenophobe, but he was an implacable enemy of Spain and therefore of James's *rapprochement* with Madrid. Like the country at large, he retained an Elizabethan habit of mind, formed during long wars, fanned by anti-Catholicism and refined by fear and triumphalism over the Armada. King James was now committed to a Spanish marriage (and a Spanish dowry) for Prince Charles, but there were many, including some in and near to the Privy Council, who still abhorred the very notion. Both crude prejudice and sophisticated policy focused on this riding accident: the Spanish grandee who had so carelessly mauled a little English boy. Crowds rioted, stoning Gondomar's house and pelting his carriage. Sir Walter had no more love for the rabble than the Spanish count, but, when he heard about these scenes, the picture of an unruly mob flinging brickbats at the licentious Don who had such unwarranted and inexplicable power over the King of England very much pleased him.

Ralegh's progress was uneventful. His party crossed the bridge over the river Plym and skirted the southern edge of Dartmoor. To the left slabs of cloud overhung hills topped with granite tors; to the right they floated in watery light, though the sea was long out of sight. Ralegh had once been lord of all this territory. Now he was an outlaw.

His company had been barely twenty miles on the road and was approaching Ashburton when a posse of horsemen came up at the rear. Several horse overtook them and wheeled about. Everyone halted. One of the gentlemen doffed his hat and Ralegh at once found himself face to face with his kinsman, Lewis Stucley.

Stucley came of old, distinguished stock. He was related to the Paulets, Courtenays, Grenvilles, Carews and all the great West Country families. His great-great-grandfather had been Knight of the King's Body in Henry VIII's time. His grandfather Lewis Stucley had been standard-bearer to Queen Elizabeth. His great-uncle Thomas 'Lusty' Stucley had had ambitions to be king of Ireland and raised forces for the purpose in Catholic Europe. Sailing out of the Mediterranean in leaky boats he put into Lisbon and tried to recruit the Portuguese King Dom Sebastião's support against Queen Elizabeth in Ireland. Sebastião agreed, on condition that Stucley first accompany his army to North Africa and finally defeat the Moors. In 1578 they set out accoutred like medieval knights on an anachronistic crusade and were soundly defeated at the battle of Alcaçer Kebir. Dom Sebastião died in the desert, or maybe he never died, for he is Portugal's King Arthur, asleep under a dune.

Another uncle was Sir Richard Grenville, the daring commander of the *Revenge* who had died of his wounds in 1591 following a famous battle with the Spanish fleet off Flores in the Azores. Through these connections he was related to Sir Walter, though his family had far greater hereditary weight than Ralegh's. He had come to arrest a lightweight in terms of blood, but one whose vanity, ambition and achievement he could never match.

Stucley had reason both to look down on Ralegh and to be envious of him. He had a grievance, too, dating from 1585 when he was ten and Ralegh was thirty: that Sir Walter had cheated his father John Stucley of at least £10,000 due to him for his part in Ralegh's Virginia voyage abroad the Queen's ship *Tiger* with Thomas Hariot and other gentlemen under Sir Richard Grenville's command. Ralegh had not sailed himself; he had sent his relatives and friends along with the ill-fated settlers, but had taken the voyage's bounty for his Queen and himself and been elevated to the status of governor of Virginia. Despite his unscrupulousness, Elizabeth 'had raised him from such meanness to such greatness'.

Lewis had been one of the many gentlemen, courtiers and would-be courtiers who had been knighted by King James in May 1603 when, in Camden's words, he 'created eighty knights in a bunch'. Then, before his coronation in July, the King sent Ralegh to the Tower. Laurence Keymis was imprisoned too and endlessly interrogated concerning Ralegh. Thomas Hariot went into hiding. James's accession exalted Stucley and toppled Ralegh.

Sir Lewis was the new Vice Admiral of Devon; a big man in his mid-forties,[1] he probably took some pleasure in overtaking his senior cousin. There was nothing exciting or unconventional about Grenville's nephew, 'Lusty' Stucley's great-nephew; Sir Lewis was an unexceptional courtier, a useful tool of the Crown, a small fish in the big pond. Not entirely scrupulous, he would make or take money where he found it, so long as not too much risk was involved. Last year he had been made guardian of Thomas, the son of Virginia tobacco baron John Rolfe and the 'Indian princess' Pocahontas, who had died of smallpox at Gravesend. John Rolfe trusted Stucley enough, or was sufficiently desperate when Pocahontas died, to leave their infant son in his charge. King James trusted him, or his duplicity, enough to command him to fetch his kinsman from Plymouth to London.

Sir Walter Ralegh was a subtle, multi-faceted creature who, like many such men, viewed other people in two dimensions. It was as if they were not worth his better judgment. They were simpler than he was: simpletons or wise men, wholesome or wicked. He believed in them as such, though at key moments of his life faulty estimates of individuals and misplaced faith in them had cost him dearly. It is hard to tell whether or not he liked Stucley, but Stucley was family, and Ralegh's own deviousness and sense of superiority inclined him, paradoxically, to trust him.

Sir Lewis probably offered his commiserations on the outcome of Ralegh's late enterprise. Sooner or later he got around to telling him that he was acting on the instructions of the King. As yet he had no formal warrant, but he had letters: that of 12 June from the Lord High Admiral ordering him to apprehend Sir Walter, and another from Sir Robert Naunton, the King's principal secretary, in which His Majesty commanded him to bring Ralegh to appear before the lords.[2] The night-time knock on the door had been translated into a civil, even affectionate, encounter on the open road. Stucley's duty, which he had sought, he insisted, only for Ralegh's comfort, was to escort him to London. 'By easy stages,' he said, 'as your health will allow.'

Sir Walter replied that he could save him the labour, for London was his destination; but Stucley turned everyone around and escorted them back towards Plymouth. Perhaps London was not ready for Ralegh. Don Diego Sarmiento de Acuña had not yet left for Spain. Perhaps Sir Lewis needed Ralegh's authority, or simply more time, to dispose of the *Destiny*'s cargo of tobacco to his own advantage. Maybe he was implicitly offering his cousin a real chance of escape, or another length of rope.

Sir Walter and Lady Elizabeth were conducted not to Plymouth itself where the *Destiny* lay in Sutton Pool, but to Radford near Plymstock. They did not re-cross the Plym that day but kept east of it, arriving at Radford House at the head of Hooe Lake, an inlet that opens into Cattewater opposite Cattedown. It was a place Ralegh knew well, the home of Sir Christopher Harris and his third wife Lady Frances. Harris had been a friend of Sir Richard Grenville and had bought Buckland Abbey from him on behalf of Sir Francis Drake to whom Grenville would never have knowingly sold his property. Harris had assisted Drake with the extraordinary feat of civil engineering which brought fresh water in a leat from Dartmoor to Plymouth. He was also Drake's executor. Long before he was knighted he had served Ralegh well on Admiralty business and in connection with Sir Walter's roles as Lord Lieutenant and Lord Warden of the Stannaries. Then their concerns were tin mines, customs dues and prizes taken at sea.

In August 1592, when the Queen had clapped Sir Walter and Lady Elizabeth in the Tower as a punishment for their liaison and marriage, ships of Ralegh's West Indian fleet helped capture the East Indiaman *Madre de Dios* off the Azores. A Spanish carrack of 1,600 tons, she was brought to Dartmouth loaded with pepper, spices, drugs, jewels, perfumes, silks, cottons, carpets, ivory and other opulent cargo. Ralegh promised Queen Elizabeth a minimum of £80,000 as her portion if given his freedom to police the matter. After just a month's imprisonment he was conditionally released, on Sir John Hawkins's recommendation, to ride west and join his nephew Sir John Gilbert, Sir Francis Drake, Sir Robert Cecil and Master Christopher Harris to safeguard and administer this, the greatest prize ever taken by the English.

At the turn of the century Ralegh feasted with Harris at Radford off a magnificent set of silver dishes with gilt rims which became known as the Armada service, although all but two of its pieces were hallmarked after 1588.[3] In November 1600, when Harris was his deputy warden, Ralegh wrote from Radford to the Lord High Treasurer and Sir Robert Cecil concerning negotiations with the tinners over a favourable minimum price at which the Queen might exercise her pre-emptive right to purchase tin.

Radford was a house accustomed to power. On one occasion the Corporation of Plymouth had hired 'a great boat' to convey its members across Cattewater and up the Hooe to pay court to Ralegh. Its cellars were repositories of piratical prizes and of goods seized by customs. Its upper rooms spawned initiatives which benefited the people of Devon and Cornwall and certainly bolstered Harris and Ralegh's wealth. Now, shorn of power, with the Guiana albatross hung about his neck, Ralegh was delivered to Radford and held under benign house arrest, leaving his keeper, Sir Lewis Stucley, free to do business in Plymouth itself.

❧

Sir Walter may have given Stucley the benefit of the doubt, but Sir Christopher Harris, Lady Ralegh and Samuel King were not so inclined. King negotiated with a Huguenot captain and engaged a barque for his master's passage to France. For four nights he detained the French vessel at anchor in Plymouth Sound, 'beyond command of the fort'. Sir Walter was persuaded to go. He was later accused of attempting an escape in this way before Stucley arrested him. On that occasion he is supposed to have offered twelve crowns to the barque's owner for the passage of 'a friend'.

It may be that he did. But now he said his farewells and grieved to leave his wife and son again so soon. At one o'clock in the morning when the tide was full Captain King conducted him from the house to the waterside where, at Radford's private quay overhung by trees, a boat awaited them. Men rowed them down the broadening Hooe and out into Cattewater. Some accounts describe the night as moonless or misty and claim they thrashed about unable to locate the French ship. Samuel King makes no mention of mist in his account of the affair, but states that 'before they reached the barque ... Ralegh changed his mind and returned to Radford unsuspected by anyone'.[4]

Whether mist really hung in the night air, shrouding the means of escape, or in Ralegh's mind hardly matters. Samuel King wrote: 'I, who was with him, will take my oath, that if he had been only willing to have rowed a quarter of a mile further, he might have seen her. Besides, if that night would not have served, one of the other three would, the wind being fair, and the tide falling out conveniently.'

Bathetically, Sir Walter was reunited with family and friends and limped upstairs to his bed. Next day he sent money to the barque's master, to retain him one more night, but did not venture near the ship again.

Soon the dream of escape faded. Ralegh passed a few more summer days in Radford's idyll, talking now to Bess and Carew, now to Sir Christopher and Lady Frances, and now in Spanish to Cristóbal Guayacunda. The stay rested his body but could not soothe his agitated brain.

On 16 July Don Diego Sarmiento de Acuña left London. Four days later, with a company of priests released from prison at his request, the Spanish ambassador departed English shores for home. It is possible that the news of his going prompted Stucley to make a move. In any event, having sold the *Destiny*'s cargo of tobacco, he returned to Radford and stirred the party into action. With him he brought armed men, his personal page, Cuthbert, and a French physician and chymist, Dr Guillaume Manoury. Since the late eighteenth century, 'chymist' has been spelled 'chemist', but the archaic form is appropriate here because it retains an alchemical aura the modern word lacks.

Manoury's ostensible purpose was to keep Sir Walter in good health.

The official report of these events, written for the King by Sir Francis Bacon, states that 'upon Saturday 25th July, Sir Walter Ralegh, Sir Lewis Stucley and Manoury went to lie at Mr Drake's'.[5] Those few histories and biographies that have anything to say about it assume that Mr Drake's house was in Plymouth. It was not Buckland Abbey, due north of Plymouth on a tributary of the river Tavy, which Sir Francis had bequeathed to his younger brother Thomas. That would have been quite out of their way. Thomas Drake had also inherited a number of his brother's tenements in the city, but there would have been no reason to return from Radford to Plymouth itself. In any case, the dates and places that we can fix during this shadowy time strongly suggest that, to make the journey feasible, Mr Drake's house must have been east of Plymouth by quite a long way; Mr Drake's house was a staging post on the road to London.

For the second time the Raleghs and their entourage set out for the capital, this time under guard. They passed through Ashburton and crossed the river Exe at Exeter. Soon Sir Walter found himself disturbingly close to his birthplace, East Budleigh, both a comforting and discomfiting experience, for a man approaching the end may be supposed to have mixed feelings about his beginnings.

In his will, and in other official documents, he described himself as 'Walter Raleghe of Colliton Raleghe'.[6] Colaton Raleigh lay just south of their road, and just south again was the village of East Budleigh with its church where his father, in an excess of reforming zeal, had torn down the crucifix in 1546 and, as churchwarden, had the family coat of arms, with its pair of prancing roebucks, carved on his pew end.

In All Saints' churchyard, as if to prove that East Budleigh men were no strangers to ambition, there stood a stone inscribed, *Orate pro anima Radulphi Node*. Node is said to have broken his neck when he attempted to fly from the church tower wearing artificial wings. Walter Ralegh senior was less flamboyant, a squire with a few ships, a farm called Hayes Barton and two sons, George and John, to help him run his sheep on the ewe-lease and administer his cargoes. Though an influential man and heir to his own ancient manor in Colaton Raleigh, he chose to lease the cob-and-thatch farmhouse from a Mr Duke. His third wife Katherine, a widow, brought her sons John, Adrian and Humphrey Gilbert into the household and bore two more, Carew and, around 1553/4, Walter junior. When he grew up Walter would have his mother and his famous step-brothers, with all their connections, to thank for thrusting him into the ambitious, expanding Elizabethan world.

The family moved to Exeter when he was in his teens, but he never forgot his childhood home. From the house he could run down through Hayes Wood to the red cliffs at Salterton, the river Otter's mouth, a sprinkling of boats beached at the brink of the seductive salt sea that reached away to the flat threshold of the horizon and the puzzling notion of infinity, of infinite possibility. Walter. Water. Ocean. Ireland. Cadiz. Fayal. Univisited Virginia. Guiana. The boy had run a long way; the road now brought him within a short walk of his origin.

There is a glimpse, allowed us by the antiquary Thomas Fuller, of Ralegh and Queen Elizabeth standing by a window looking out.[7] For now, they are both on the same side of the glass. The world lies beyond, full not just of promise and reward but of infinite danger. Ralegh had scratched a line on the pane with a diamond. The Queen added a second to complete the couplet:

> Fain would I climb, yet I fear to fall.
> If thy heart fails thee, climb not at all.

Perhaps it was because he wanted a secure place on which to fall back, a spot in which his heart could be still, that he tried to buy Hayes Barton in July 1584, in the early days of his ambition. (We have an inkling of his wealth and style at the time, for that May a Welsh gentleman had robbed him of some articles. A note of them survives: five yards of white silk damask, a hatband of pearls valued at £30 and an £80 jewel.) Ralegh was willing to pay well for his birthplace. With naive candour he wrote from Court to Mr Richard Duke to say as much. 'I will most willingly give you what so ever in your conscience you shall deem it worth . . . I am resolved, if I cannot entreat you, to build at Colliton, but for the natural disposition I have to that place, being born in that house, I had rather seat myself there than anywhere else.'[8] For all Ralegh's wealth and strong desire, Mr Duke was unforthcoming.

On 25 July the company crossed the river Axe and joined the Fosse Way, the Roman road that links Axmouth with Bath, Cirencester, Leicester and Lincoln. Almost at once they entered the village of Musbury, between Axmouth and Axminster, where 'Mr Drake' had at least three properties: the venerable seat Mount Drake, half a mile north of the village, Ashe House, a quarter of a mile further along the Fosse Way, and Great Trill, almost a mile to the west of Ashe.

Barnard Drake of Ashe had been Ralegh's stepcousin. About 1580 he incurred Queen Elizabeth's displeasure when, 'within the verge of the court', he boxed the ears of the *parvenu* Sir Francis Drake. Barnard was outraged that the upstart circumnavigator had appropriated the ancient Drake arms – a *wyvern gules* or red dragon – without being able to establish his lineage. If he was a member of the family at all, his was a humble branch. The Queen responded by presenting Sir Francis with his own coat-of-arms in 1581. This too annoyed Barnard: its shield was emblazoned with a *fessy wave*, representing ocean, between two polar stars Arctic and Antarctic; its crest was a ship on a globe, drawn by a cable in the hand of God, with a *wyvern gules* hung by the heels in its rigging. The motto was appropriate: *Sic Parvis Magna*, 'great things from small'. Of Sir Francis's new arms Barnard observed that 'though Her Majesty could give him a nobler, yet she could not give him an ancienter coat than mine'. Brilliant naval actions reinstated him and won him a knighthood in January 1585. That June he and Ralegh's brother Carew led a fleet, to which Ralegh lent his ship the *Job*, to Newfoundland where they protected English fishing vessels and captured rich Spanish prizes. It was one of the first overt acts of war with Spain.

It was Sir Barnard's son, fifty-two-year-old John Drake and his wife Dorothye of Mount Drake and Ashe, who most probably welcomed Ralegh's party and escort to their house for the night. There Lewis Stucley received a warrant from London. It had been entrusted to James Taylor, messenger, at 10 a.m. on 23 July, and carried post-haste to the west. (On the vital road to Plymouth, as well as to Dover and Southampton, fresh horses were kept in readiness every ten miles in order to speed royal dispatches.) On the 25th, at Mr Drake's house, Stucley digested the following stern words:

> You have under your charge the person of Sir Walter Ralegh, knight, touching whom and his safe bringing hither before us of his Majesty's Privy Council you have received sundry directions signifying his Majesty's pleasure and commandment.
>
> Notwithstanding we find no execution thereof, as had become you, but vain excuses unworthy to be offered unto his Majesty or to those of his Council from whom you received his pleasure. We have therefore now dispatched this letter unto you, and hereby do and will command you in his Majesty's name and upon your allegiance, that all delays and excuses set apart (of which we will hear no

more) you do safely and speedily convey hither the person of the said Sir Walter Ralegh, to answer before us such matters as shall be objected against him on His Majesty's behalf. And of this you are to be careful as you will answer the contrary at your peril.

From ... Lord Archbishop of Canterbury, Lord Chancellor, Lord Privy Seal, Lord Chamberlain, Earl of Arundel, Lord Carew, Mr Treasurer, Mr Vice Chamberlain, Mr Secretary Naunton.[9]

Sir Lewis was bruised by the reproof. No more delays, no more excuses. He knew he must prove his loyalty and aptness for the task.

He showed the warrant to Sir Walter, who felt its impact too. It was irrefutable proof of his cousin's commission. He must be escorted to London to answer official charges. Excusing himself from the company Ralegh climbed the stairs to the room the Drakes had allotted him. There, thinking himself alone and unobserved, he stamped his feet and pulled his hair and swore.

5

THE CHYMIST AND
THE SOUL

Ralegh was not unobserved. Dr Guillaume Manoury, the French chymist employed to keep Sir Walter in good health, was watching him. He noted how profoundly Sir Walter's aspect changed on reading Stucley's commission.

A doctor, or quack, of the period understood that a man's temperament was governed by four cardinal humours: blood, phlegm, yellow bile (or choler) and black bile (or melancholer), each ruled by the planets. A predominance of one or another rendered an individual sanguine or phlegmatic, choleric or melancholic. Suddenly put out of humour, Ralegh hovered between anger and despair. The Frenchman could not at once tell which would be predominant.

Manoury later passed on his observations to the Privy Council and Sir Francis Bacon incorporated them into the propaganda issued in the King's name, the *Declaration*.[1] Much of the material on which this part of the story is based comes from Manoury's own account in his interrogation by the King's Privy Councillors and as recorded by Francis Bacon. It is therefore open to question. However, the salient episodes are corroborated by Ralegh's subsequent admissions and by information from both Captain Samuel King and Sir Lewis Stucley, so we can take the Frenchman's version of events as being broadly accurate.

When Ralegh left the dining table in Mr Drake's hall and retreated to his room, Manoury followed softly after and scrutinised him from the head of the stairs. The door of Ralegh's chamber stood ajar. Through its squint Manoury observed how, like a child, Sir Walter 'stamped with his feet, and pulled himself by the hair, swearing in these words, "God's wounds, is it possible my fortune should return upon me thus again?"'

At the sight of that warrant Ralegh could not help revisiting the darkest moments of his life. Stucley's unaccustomed sense of urgency added to Sir Walter's sense of foreboding. Unease exacerbated disease, the constellation of symptoms that accrued from old wounds, the palsy he suffered in the Tower, the fever that gripped him on the Guiana voyage and the lowering of spirits that haunted him whenever the world turned on him.

Early the next morning, Sunday, they made 'a sudden departure, with much more haste than was expected before', according to the story Francis Bacon gleaned from Manoury, and 'from Mr Drake's they went on their journey to the house of Mr Horsey, distant from thence four miles or thereabouts'. In fact, Horsey's house at Clifton Maybank is about twenty-four miles from Mount Drake in Musbury. It seems that Manoury's 'four miles' was a slip of his pen, or of Francis Bacon's secretary's, for 'twenty-four'.[2]

Holding to the Fosse Way for a dozen miles or so the company passed from Devon into Somerset before turning off the Roman road and making for Clifton Maybank just over the Dorset border on the river Yeo. At Ralegh's instigation, Captain King made it his business to chat to Dr Manoury and win his trust as the journey progressed. His instructions were to sound out what was in the doctor's heart. King enlarged upon Sir Walter's misfortunes and gauged the Frenchman's reactions.

There is a fragmentary, albeit biased, record of this intimate conversation, as reported by Manoury to the Privy Council.[3]

'I would we were all at Paris,' sighed Samuel King.

'Oh, I would we were all at London,' Guillaume Manoury responded, tired of the ruts in the road. 'Alas, what shall we do at Paris?'

'I would we were there,' King explained, 'because as soon as we come to London they will commit Sir Walter Ralegh to the Tower and cut off his head.'

'I hope better than that,' said Manoury.

There was a pause during which King waited to see if he might hear something still more positive.

'I am sorry for his ill fortune,' the doctor added, 'and I am ready, according to my small ability, to do him all the honest service I can, so long as it may be done without offence.'

This was a very promising start. Manoury had to hedge his bets for he was in Stucley's employ, after all, and must be loyal to his interests. But it seemed to King that the Frenchman's heart was in the right place. His sympathy sounded genuine enough, and his willingness to be of service was encouraging. Captain King would tell his master what he had gleaned as soon as they had an opportunity to confer privately at Mr Horsey's. There was a chance they might turn Manoury and make good use of him.

In the seventeenth century Clifton Maybank was a parish in its own right. The church, now nothing more than a lumpy crop-mark in a field, stood between the road and the manor house. Clifton Maybank House was grand, rebuilt by Sir John Horsey in about 1540 on a site noted in both the Domesday Book and the Saxon Annals of 1001. Moulded panels below the oriel window in the west wing displayed Tudor roses and horses' heads from the Horsey coat of arms. The river Yeo, well stocked with pike and carp, encircled the house at a good distance, except on the east side where it ran by the garden. To the west lay an expansive bowling green with four raised paths around it, surrounded by an embattlemented wall and set with fruit trees. Broad walks shaded by mature elms fanned out from the bowling green and, behind the house, an easy ascent led to a rabbit warren and an ash plantation, while another path descended to coppiced walks by the river.

Ralegh had known Clifton Maybank in its heyday. The last Sir John Horsey died with no heir in 1589 and his cousin Ralph, whom Bess described as her 'very good friend', inherited the house. Sir Ralph had died in 1612, when Sir Walter was in the Tower, but the dowager Lady Edith Horsey still lived there, with her eldest son George and Elizabeth his wife.

At about noon, on Sunday 26 July, the company's horses and carriages entered the drive, passing first the church, set in a square fenced green, and then the distinctive gatehouse in front of the house, before halting beneath the magnificent south front, whose half-octagonal buttresses of local, warm Ham stone soared to a pierced stone parapet set with quatrefoils. The mounts and equipages were accommodated in a large outer court flanked by a coach house and three stables, a big barn and good housing for cattle.

The Raleghs received a warm welcome and as good a repast as the house could afford. Sir Walter and Bess had spent time with the Horseys in 1593 after their imprisonment in the Tower by Queen Elizabeth in punishment for their liaison. When Ralegh was not busy in Parliament, they retreated to nearby Sherborne, away from the Queen's displeasure, to manage their affairs from Dorset. Bess was pregnant with Wat. Work on their new house, on the site of a hunting lodge beside Sherborne Castle, was in progress under the supervision of Sir Walter's half-brother, Adrian Gilbert. In any case it was a good time to be out of London. Plague was raging there in 1593 and there was ferment in the underworld of Catholic agents and government spies which threatened to discredit Ralegh's circle.

With his Dorset gentleman friends Ralegh had engaged in other sorts of business at a slower pace than London's. He also brought members of his London circle to Sherborne where they could pursue arcane interests away from the capital's scuffle and gossip and spying eyes. One day in the summer of 1593 Ralegh's bucolic and secretive worlds collided at a supper party he attended, together with his brother Carew, governor of Portland Castle, and Sir Ralph Horsey, at Wolfeton House near Dorchester, the home of Sir George Trenchard.

Towards the end of the meal, having eaten and drunk well, Carew Ralegh indulged in loose talk, sure to upset some of the local gentlemen present, not to mention two men of the cloth, the Calvinist Reverend Ironside of Winterborne Abbas and Parson Whittle of Fordington. Sensitive to the situation, Sir Ralph Horsey swiftly interrupted, no doubt with an apologetic smile, and said, '*Colloquia prava corrumpunt bonos mores*,' which the company well understood: evil words corrupt good morals.

Carew was not to be muzzled. 'What danger', he asked Roger Ironside, 'might talk such as mine incur?'

'The wages of sin', Ironside responded ponderously, in St Paul's words, 'is death.'

'Ah, but death is common to all men, both the sinner and the righteous,' said Carew.

'But just as that life which is the gift of God through Jesus Christ is life eternal,' the reverend gentleman countered, 'so that death which is properly the wages of sin is death eternal, both of the body and of the soul also.'

'Soul?' said Carew. 'What is that?'

Sir Walter knew what treacherous ground his brother trod. Such things could be debated with trusted friends. Among his circle they were tame considerations but here, in the presence of potentially hostile witnesses, it was foolish to question received doctrine.

Only the previous year the Jesuit Robert Persons had published his *Responsio*[4] to Queen Elizabeth's *Declaration* against the treasonable activities of seminary priests and Jesuits who infiltrated her realm. Published first in Latin, its slurs were disseminated throughout Europe, and in two years it went through eight editions in four languages. 'There is a flourishing and well known School of Atheism which Sir Walter Ralegh runs in his house, with a certain necromancer-astronomer as teacher . . .' the relevant paragraph began. If Ralegh was elevated to the Privy Council, it predicted that some day an edict might appear in the Queen's name in which belief in God would be denied, while those who publicly opposed it would be accused of *lèse-majesté*.

A condensed English version exploited popular prejudice about the black arts and talked 'of Sir Walter Ralegh's School of Atheism . . . and of the conjuror that is Master thereof and of the diligence used to get young gentlemen to this school, where both Moses and our Saviour, the Old and New Testaments are jested at, and the scholars are taught among other things to spell God backward'.[5]

There had indeed been a collection of thinkers, tightly knit or loosely grouped, whose passion was to explore the world and the mind. They gathered, some regularly and others occasionally, under the patronage of 'the Wizard Earl' of Northumberland, Henry Percy, at Syon House, and of Sir Walter Ralegh at Durham House and Sherborne. The 'school' included Thomas Hariot, the mathematician and astronomer; his friend Christopher Marlowe, the popular poet, playwright and notorious atheist; Walter Warner, the one-handed mathematician and alchemist who anticipated William Harvey's ideas concerning the circulation of the blood; Robert Hues, the geographer; the poets George Chapman and Matthew Roydon; and Emery

Molyneaux, a globemaker who studied longitude at the feet of the conjuror Simon Forman.

Thomas Hariot believed himself to be the teacher of the school, the necromancer-astrologer, to whom Persons referred, while Dr John Dee, Queen Elizabeth's conjuror, considered that he was the 'master' of the School of Night,[6] as he later made clear in a petition to James I.[7]

On 20 May 1593 Christopher Marlowe was arrested and charged with blasphemy and treason; heretical papers of his were discovered when his fellow dramatist Thomas Kyd's lodgings were ransacked. Kyd was tortured and interrogated, and he, along with other witnesses and informers, avowed that Marlowe and Hariot attended meetings where forbidden matters were discussed, that Marlowe joked how all those who loved not tobacco and boys were fools, and that he talked of Jesus Christ and St John as bedfellows enjoying 'an extraordinary love'.

The agent Richard Baines, unmasked after training under cover as a seminary priest, compiled a note on Marlowe's opinions, including the view 'that Moses was but a juggler and that one Hariot, being Sir Walter Ralegh's man, could do more than he'. Richard Cholmeley, one of Sir Robert Cecil's spies who also belonged to the Earl of Essex's circle, claimed that Marlowe 'is able to show more sound reasons for atheism than any divine in England is able to give to prove divinity, and that Marlowe told him, he hath read the atheist lecture to Sir Walter Ralegh and others'.

Marlowe too had been employed as an agent by Cecil. He was allowed bail, on condition that he report daily to the Star Chamber. Ten days later at Deptford he was killed, stabbed above the right eyeball, brawling over who should pay the bill in a tavern owned by Eleanor Bull. Or so the story went. Eleanor Bull had a house, not a tavern, in Deptford. She was one of Cecil's relatives. Marlowe and his three companions that day were all spies, Cecil's or Essex's. Essex was Ralegh's deadly enemy. Cecil had just clashed with Ralegh in Parliament. Shortly he would announce an inquisition to enquire into Ralegh and the 'School of Atheism'. Marlowe had had a choice that fatal day at Deptford: to betray Ralegh or be gagged for good. Several gentleman slept more easily once he was dead.

So soon after such events, and in such a gathering as the dinner party at Wolfeton House, it was hardly wise for Carew Ralegh to ask, 'Soul? What is it?'

Sir Walter should have known better than to engage in a dangerous dispute, but his fellow guests' equivocation riled him.

'I think you should answer my brother's question for our instruction,' Sir Walter said. He had been a scholar at Oxford – an Oriel man like Ironside – and had talked with many, he continued, and yet until now 'in this point, to wit, what the reasonable soul of man is, I have not by any been resolved'.

In the cut and thrust that followed, Ralegh became frustrated with the obscure and intricate Scholastic points that the patronising Ironside made, and with the circularity of his arguments. Finally Ralegh had had enough. He wished the conversation over and grace said, 'for that is better than this disputation'.

The Reverend Ironside duly said the grace. Then he quickly departed from Wolfeton House for Dorchester, in the company of Parson Whittle, and noted down an account of the dinner-table conversation before he forgot it.

Ironside's eyewitness account was brought to Sir Robert Cecil's Court of High Commission which convened to enquire into heresy on 21 March 1594, at the small town of Cerne Abbas, between Sherborne and Dorchester.[8] Its purpose was to investigate unorthodox beliefs in the context, always unstated, of black magic, alchemy and arcane sexuality. With a beautiful irony it went to work immediately under the hill on which a mighty figure is cut in the chalk: a giant; whom local people called Beelzebub, notable for the club he brandishes and the size of his erect penis.[9]

Ralegh's enemy Thomas Lord Howard of Bindon presided. Ralegh was fortunate that his friend, Sir Ralph Horsey of Clifton Maybank, sat on the commission. The Reverend Ironside had been instructed not to quote hearsay evidence but simply to give his first-hand account of the supper-table conversation, but a succession of local clerics had a lot to say about Ralegh's circle, much of which was little more than gossip.

'Whom do you know or have heard to be suspected of atheism or apostasy?' was the first question each witness faced. They were asked whether anyone had said that Scripture was not to be defended by Her Majesty out of faith, but simply out of policy. More simply, could they name those who had blasphemed and cursed God, or any persons who had 'spoken against the being or mortality of the soul of man, or that a man's soul should die and become like the soul of a beast'?

Despite the claims of various witnesses, nothing of consequence came to light and the inquisition fizzled out. Horsey had worked hard, if circumspectly, to protect his friend Ralegh's reputation, and the Privy Council had gained more ammunition to discredit Jesuitical propaganda.

As if to prove his credentials to the Queen and her councillors Ralegh wrote to Sir Robert Cecil less than a month later: 'Sir, This night the 13th of April we have taken a notable Jesuit in the Lady Stourton's house, wife to old Sir John Arundell, with his copes and bulls.'[10] Sir George Trenchard and his men had ridden from Wolfeton to Chideock, between Bridport and Charmouth, where the Arundell household harboured priests who regularly celebrated mass. 'There hath been kept in this house,' wrote Ralegh, 'as I have formerly informed you, above thirty recusants.'

That night Trenchard's men climbed the walls. They scoured the castle for six hours and piled books, vestments and sacred vessels on to a cart. Sir George had been content with that, his duty as deputy lieutenant done; but a zealous servant jeered at his haul, provoking him to carry off more than books. Trenchard ordered a disenchanted servant to lead them to the priest's hiding-place. Inside, they found John Cornelius on his knees. 'He calls himself John Moone,' Ralegh wrote, 'but he is an Irishman and a notable stout villain and I think can say much.'

John Cornelius was a mystic, famous for visions and exorcisms, and said to be 'terrible to the devils'. He agreed to eat with the Trenchards but not to say grace at their table. Ralegh, Trenchard and Horsey examined him. Ralegh's tormentor, the Reverend Ironside, and three other clerics came to Wolfeton to hold disputations with the priest. Sir Walter 'passed the whole night with him alone that he might have certain doubts resolved'. Cornelius 'gently reproved him for his mode of life and conversation', and Ralegh promised to intercede with the Privy Council on his behalf.

In London, at the Marshalsea prison, the priest was subjected to persuasive torture on the rack but did not disclose his converts' names. He was brought back to Dorset where many venerated him and sought his blessing, but in Dorchester's Assize Hall he was indicted for high treason, rebellion and a list of offences including possession of pamphlets, such as Person's *Responsio*, that denounced Queen Elizabeth's *Declaration* against seminary priests.

Ralegh took charge of the execution. Hundreds gathered to watch. No man could be hired, for any money, to quarter the priest alive. John Cornelius kissed the ground at the gallows' foot, then kissed the feet of his fellows, hanged minutes earlier for the same faith. He addressed the crowd from the ladder. Ralegh tried to silence him. When, with the noose around his neck, he began to pray for the Queen's conversion, Ralegh commanded the ladder to be pulled away. The prayer did not reach its Amen. Cornelius was cut down and disembowelled, his private parts severed and his body dismembered. Ralegh ordered his head to be stuck on the pinnacle of St Peter's church, but the crowd's passions prevented it. It was nailed to the gallows instead.

❋

On this Sunday in July 1618 Ralegh may have thought back to the wet summer months that followed John Cornelius's execution. 'In the months of June and July,' the chronicler John Stow observed, 'it commonly rained every day or night till St James' Day.' The people murmured about the judgment of God, and by September, as we know from another of Ralegh's letters to Cecil, Dorset suffered again. 'I had a post this morning from Sherborne. The plague is in the town very hot. My Bess is one way sent, her son another way' – presumably the infant Wat was with his wetnurse – 'and I am in great trouble therewith.'[11]

Now Sir Walter was in trouble of a deeper sort and Wat was dead. Whatever talk of past escapades or present dangers he had had with the Horseys over dinner, it was cut short. Stucley was eager to move on. The grooms and pages had feasted in the kitchen. The horses were fed and rested.

After Samuel King's promising conversation with Manoury on the road to Clifton Maybank, Sir Walter decided that he himself must have words with the French physician on the next stage of their journey. The two men had interests in common, for Ralegh was no mean chymist. He was famous for the cordials he had concocted in the Tower and, in particular, for his legendary balsam of Guiana.

> O reputation! dearer far than life,
> Thou precious balsam, lovely, sweet of smell,
> Whose cordial drops once spilt by some rash hand,
> Not all the owner's care, nor the repenting toil
> Of the rude spiller, ever can collect
> To its first purity and native sweetness.

Now, the last dregs of his reputation spilt, Ralegh needed whatever sympathy and help he could elicit. On the road to London he must evaluate the French doctor's humour and reckon whether or not he could be persuaded to sell his services, if not his soul.

6

OSMUND'S CURSE

fter almost five miles on the road from the Horseys'
house, as they came within sight of the town of Sherborne, Sir Walter turned to Dr Manoury. He pointed
out the abbey rising above the yellow-ochre huddle of houses
like a cathedral dominating a small city; and, beyond the river
Yeo on a rocky hill to the east of the town, the old castle that
he had tried to rehabilitate for his own use before building his
new Sherborne Lodge on the site of an ancient hunting
lodge.

'This was all mine,' Ralegh confided to the Frenchman, 'but
the King unjustly took it from me.'[1]

The story goes that as a young man he first saw and coveted
Sherborne Castle on the ride from Plymouth to London with
his Gilbert half-brothers: 'He cast such an eye upon it as Ahab
did upon Naboth's vineyard.'[2] Then he had flung out an arm
to point at the glorious scene. The suddenness and exuberance
of the gesture spooked his horse, which stumbled and threw
him so that 'his very face, which was thought a very good
face, ploughed up the earth where he fell'.[3] It might have been
considered a bad omen; it was certainly an affront to his dignity,
but Adrian Gilbert, an astrologer, offered him a face-saving
conceit: the fall was a clear portent that he would possess the
ground he had so unceremoniously kissed.

Ralegh told Queen Elizabeth he wanted Sherborne and she approved her favourite's desire. It belonged to the see of Salisbury, but the diocese had been vacant for three years. Her Majesty could milk her church. As Ralegh wrote, 'I gave the Queen a jewel worth £250 to make a bishop', and she appointed his candidate, Dr Coldwell, who willingly leased Sherborne to the Crown for ninety-nine years, subject to an annual rent of £200 16s. 1d. After a few days, in January 1592, the Queen reassigned the lease to Ralegh.

William the Conqueror had granted the Sherborne lands to his knight and chancellor Osmund, who had a hand in the Domesday survey, was appointed bishop of Salisbury in 1078 and built the cathedral at Old Sarum before his death. He was eventually canonised, though the process begun in 1228 was not completed until 1457. On retreating to the religious life, the prelate had laid a curse upon his see's Sherborne property: 'Whosoever shall take these lands from the bishopric or diminish them in great or in small, shall be accursed, not only in this world but also in the world to come; unless in his lifetime he make restitution thereof.'[4] The poet William Crowe later recounted how the saint's curse fell most heavily upon Ralegh:

> War-glutted Osmund, superstitious lord!
> Who with heaven's justice for a bloody life
> Madest thy presumptuous bargain, giving more
> Than thy just having to redeem thy guilt,
> And darest bid th' Almighty to become
> The minister of thy Curse: but sure it fell,
> So bigots fondly judged, full sure it fell
> With sacred vengeance pointed at the head
> Of many a bold usurper, chief on thine,
> (Favourite of fortune once, but last her thrall,)
> Accomplish'd Raleigh! in that lawless day,
> When, like a goodly hart, thou wert beset
> With crafty blood-hounds, lurching for thy life,

While as they feign'd to chase thee fairly down;
And that vile Scot, the minion-kissing King,
Pursued with havoc in the tyrannous hunt.[5]

When Sir Walter showed Manoury what had once been his, he was already surrounded by King James's 'crafty bloodhounds'; indeed, the French doctor was one of them. On Ralegh's attainder for treason in 1603 King James had taken Sherborne from him and granted it to his favourite minion Robert Carr, Earl of Somerset. Laurence Keymis later negotiated the formal transfer and £8,000 in compensation which Ralegh invested in his last expedition.

The King bought the property back from Carr for £20,000 and gave it to Prince Henry who, if he had not died in 1612, would almost certainly have returned it to Sir Walter or his heirs. James re-granted it to Carr, for £25,000, until the earl was implicated in the poisoning of Sir Thomas Overbury and, with his wife, took Sir Walter's place in the Tower. Now the estate was in the possession of Sir John Digby, the King's ambassador in Madrid. Ralegh's memories of the castle his Queen gave him, the house he built, the grounds he nurtured and the society he cultivated there were touched with the taint of Spain.

During their Sherborne years Sir Walter and Lady Elizabeth had seats in the Abbey. In the east window of the choir, above the altarpiece, was a panel of brilliant stained and enamelled glass bearing the arms of Ralegh's friend Laurence Keymis, mathematician, alchemist and fellow of Balliol, above the date 1606.[6] Keymis had at that time been immersed in the life and work of the Sherborne estate, living in one of its farms and acting as his imprisoned master's castellan. Some time later, after it became public knowledge that he had disgraced himself at San Thomé and committed suicide, somebody scratched out his name and motto with a diamond.[7]

Sir Lewis led the party down into the town. Dr Manoury

[76]

and most of the entourage were lodged at the George Inn and the New Inn. Stucley conducted Sir Walter, Lady Elizabeth and young Carew through the town, and out on the Shaftesbury road where for a little while they rode alongside the wall of their old estate. Just beyond the church of St Cuthbert at Oborne,[8] they turned north off the London highway on a narrow road which ran beside the bed of a winterbourne up an increasingly intimate valley between infolded downs towards one of the Yeo's headwaters.

They were making for the village of Poyntington, just over the county boundary in Somerset and in the see, not of Salisbury, but of Bath and Wells.[9] It was as if Ralegh could not sup well or sleep soundly within the bounds of his old cursed territory. After a mile and a half, where the sinuous valley opens into a broad bowl of hills whose chalk springs fed an ancient mill-head, and where monks once cultivated vineyards on tier after tier of a Saxon earthwork called Poyntington Skait, they came to the village and passed through a gatehouse into the courtyard of the manor house.

Poyntington Manor was the home of old John Parham, his son Sir Edward and Sir Edward's wife Elizabeth, Ralegh's first cousin once removed. Under Stucley's eye, the Raleghs entered the main door beneath an ogee-headed arch. Their chamber for the night was set above the high arched gateway in the west wing.[10]

As at Clifton Maybank, the welcome they received must have been replete with nostalgia, for Sir Edward, though a staunch and active Catholic, was Sir Walter's close friend, and his cook had once been Ralegh's. The Parhams would have wished to offer hospitality, not custody. The two families had much shared history. Sir Edward was one of the attesting witnesses to the deed by which Ralegh set out to convey his Sherborne property to his family in perpetuity. Queen Elizabeth, by letters patent, had eventually granted it to Sir Walter 'and his heirs for ever all and singular' in 1599. He had lawyers draft a trust deed in favour of Wat in January 1603, which was signed and sealed on 13 April, in the month between the Queen's death and burial. But the clerk who had transcribed the deed left out a crucial phrase, by which Wat 'shall and will from henceforth stand thereof seised'. This omission rendered it void. The property remained Sir Walter's, and was soon forfeit to the Crown. When Ralegh wrote from the Tower to Sir Robert Carr, the Scottish favourite on whom King James was determined to bestow Sherborne, he referred to his children's inheritance as 'lost in law for want of a word' and begged him 'not to begin your first buildings upon the ruins of the innocent'.[11] He had written to Sir Robert Cecil from the Tower about Bess's fury: 'She hath already brought her eldest son in one hand and her sucking child in another, crying out of her and their destruction; charging me with unnatural negligence, and that having provided for mine own life I am without sense and compassion of theirs.'[12]

But it had been Sir Robert Cecil himself who had suggested that the King might creep through the legal loophole the deed left open. James was grateful to him. Bess was refused an audience. Fighting for her family, she ambushed the King at Hampton Court, threw herself down before his scrawny shanks as he shambled by and begged a house for herself and her child. All James could splutter was, 'I mun have the land, I mun have it for Carr'. In January 1609 the deed was judged invalid. Sherborne was forfeited for good, though a final settlement was made in the Court of Chancery in February 1610 whereby a one-off sum of £8,000, and an annuity of £400 while Bess or Wat lived, was to be paid to the trustees, Thomas Hariot, John Shelbury and Laurence Keymis. The deal might have been worse, but could never compensate the Raleghs for their loss. Unwittingly, Sir Edward Parham had set his hand to a paper which signed away their beloved estate.

A second unfortunate connection between the families

involved Lady Parham's father, George Tilley, and John Meere, the lawyer who was Ralegh's first bailiff at Sherborne. The Meeres were a substantial family in the town. Back in 1582, John Meere had been accused of 'a suspicion of a felony' by Justice George Tilley, who sent the case to the Bridport quarter sessions. In revenge Meere seduced Tilley's daughter and tried to elope with her two days before the trial. The girl's mother prevented the escape and Meere came to court charged with beating up a man and raping another woman. Tilley and Meere so insulted one another that the trial itself became a riot. Meere was clapped in the stocks by the dunghill in Poyntington. Tilley let his pigs loose so that 'they should come grunting at night'. When he was released the next morning Meere could not stand up.

Meere's father had been the bishop of Salisbury's steward with responsibility for Sherborne Castle and, although the son had been twice imprisoned in London for clipping coinage, Ralegh secured his release from Newgate and appointed him bailiff in 1592. It was another example of Sir Walter's lack of judgment. In the face of the obvious he made decisions which prejudiced his own interests. Ralegh wanted a hard man who knew his business. He got one who guaranteed local enmity and turned against his master.

Meere was a rapist, a litigious forger and a fomenter of feuds. By the time Ralegh dismissed him in 1601, Meere had got his wife's unmarried sister pregnant in his own house; Sir Walter noted that she was 'now by him thus undone, cozened and cast off'.[13] Writing to the Western Assize judges the following March, Ralegh wheeled out all the accusations, of gold clipping, of mischievous suits against himself and others in the Star Chamber, the Exchequer and the Assizes: 'I think that God hath worthily plagued me for entertaining such a wretch, whom I took eaten with lice out of prison because it was told me he had all the ancient records of Sherborne.' Further, 'I protest before the everliving God that I found him myself (coming on him on the sudden) counterfeiting my hand above a hundred times upon an oiled paper.' Ralegh begged their lordships to take action, for Meere 'sueth or terrifieth all those poor inhabitants who will not join with him in his devilish practises, counterfeitings and perjuries'.[14]

The saga continued after Ralegh's imprisonment for treason, and after Laurence Keymis, who was put into the Tower with him, had been released and made warden of Sherborne Castle. There is an extant letter of 1609, purporting to be in Ralegh's hand, requesting a trusted gentleman to draw up a good and perfect lease of Bishop's Down, Sherborne, for the benefit of John Meere.[15] It is almost certainly a forgery, for Sir Walter, in the Tower, would hardly have felt kindly disposed towards his ex-bailiff, or under any obligation to him for, as he had explained to the Exchequer in 1604, 'I do not pay the Bailiff because he is mine enemy and hath abused me'.[16] Both the Parhams and the Raleghs had cause to recall the torments they suffered at the hands of John Meere.

On this July Sunday evening, those torments were distant ones. Sherborne Castle's latest owner came to call at Poyntington Manor, wishing to speak with Sir Walter. Sir John Digby was King James's ambassador to Spain. He had come back to London from Madrid just as Ralegh was released from the Tower. He had joined the Privy Council as Ralegh began preparations for his last voyage. He had been granted Sherborne by King James – for a mere £10,000 in recognition of his services in Spain – while Ralegh was investing everything in the *Destiny*. He had resumed his duties in Spain when Sir Walter's fleet set sail. He had returned to King James's court just a month before Raleigh made fast at Plymouth. He was intimately aware of the political consequences of the Guiana expedition, and was renowned in the world of espionage for his boast 'that every single paper of the Spanish King's private cabinet came into his possession and, not only so, but that he was able to set his own private mark on each of them'.[17]

While Ralegh was still on his outward voyage the Spanish ambassador in London, Don Diego Sarmiento de Acuña, wrote to Philip of Spain saying that 'whatever measures Your Majesty may adopt to punish him will be fully justified, and many honourable Englishmen will be very glad of it. Amongst these is Sir John Digby, for he protested here frequently and vigorously against the evils which would arise to England if Walter Ralegh were allowed to go on this voyage.'[18] The King had sent Digby and Villiers to the Spanish ambassador with the assurance that 'Ralegh's friends and all England shall not save him from the gallows'. Moreover, Digby had witnessed James give Don Diego a written undertaking to King Philip that Ralegh and his leading captains would be sent to Spain aboard the *Destiny* so that their execution might take place in the Plaza Royal, Madrid.

It must have been with a peculiar sense of sympathy and self-justification, if not pleasure, that Digby rode to counsel the old adventurer riding to his death. When Sir John entered Poyntington Manor that night Sir Walter must have seen him as a usurper. He now possessed the old castle where the Raleghs had once lived and which they had intended to restore and convert. A flight of steps to the west of the keep may be evidence of Ralegh's endeavour to make it habitable, half a century before it was demolished during the Civil War. Digby owned the new house, Sherborne Lodge, which Ralegh had built on the foundations of a hunting lodge. It was a four-storey rectangular building, finished in 1594, rendered with stucco and lit by large square-headed windows of diamond-pane glass. In 1600 Raleigh had added hexagonal towers topped with heraldic beasts to the four corners of the house. Sir John had four wings with corresponding towers built on to Ralegh's house, and by 1618 Sir Walter's rooms were full of the Digbys' lives. In Sir Walter's Great Chamber, the Ralegh coat of arms with its prancing roebucks remained at the centre of the plaster ceiling but a new imposing fireplace was dominated by the Digby device, a fleur-de-lys argent on an azure ground.

Face to face with Sir John, Sir Walter was more than ever exiled from his Eden: the views from that Great Chamber over the lake to the old castle, over the walled garden on the east to the deer park and Jerusalem Hill, and south across the courtyard to Gainsborough Hill. It was a landscape he had shaped with Adrian Gilbert's skill, beautified with orchards, groves and gardens full of exotic plants brought from the Americas and set with trees from Virginia. In one grove was the stone seat on which he had smoked his pipes. The Black Marsh had been transformed into a water garden. To his nephew Sir John Gilbert, governor of Plymouth Fort, Ralegh wrote asking if he had cannon from Spanish prizes – 'a couple of fine little pieces of brass between minion and falcon' – that he could buy as decorative ordnance for his castle. His Wiltshire neighbour, the witty poet Sir John Harington, Queen Elizabeth's 'Boy Jack', was shocked by Sir Walter's extravagance and maintained that for what he had spent 'drawing the river through rocks into his garden he might very justly and without offence of the church or state have compassed a much better purpose'.[19] Harington entirely missed the point. Ralegh was enchanted and obsessed with Sherborne. Now Sir John Digby, the thirty-eight-year-old Spanish pensioner, had it.

Digby had come to offer Sir Walter advice, perhaps out of obligation and certainly with a sense of irony. What he had to say was to the point: the King would exercise strict justice upon him. He agreed with Ralegh that his actions did not justify an indictment under common law, but insisted that he was not beyond the reach of civil and Admiralty law.[20] Sir John did not stay long that night at Poyntington, but rode back to Sherborne Castle, his salutary mission accomplished.

The full weight of St Osmund's curse now bore down upon Ralegh's head. He may have hoped that Digby would inherit it in his turn, but he undoubtedly retired to his chamber with more matter in his head to fuel his fears. If he stamped his feet or tore his hair, Dr Manoury was not there to see him.

7

IMPOSTURES

arly on Monday 27 July, when Stucley and the Raleghs broke their fast, Sir Edward Parham offered Sir Walter a cup of ale. A drink which should simply have refreshed him would have bizarre consequences, real or imaginary. Meanwhile, Manoury, Captain King, Guayacunda and the rest of the escort left their Sherborne inns and rode to Poyntington to join their masters and continue towards London.

Sir John Digby's sober advice lay heavily on Ralegh's heart as the party clattered back down the valley towards the main road. At the point where they approached Oborne, the track unwound and offered Sir Walter and Lady Elizabeth a sudden vision across the meadows of Sherborne Castle standing proud on its hill, illuminated and thrown into relief by early light; it was the last glimpse he would have of the property so longed for, so cherished and so long denied him.

There is no clue as to how many horses the party had, or how many carriages. Private coaches were a badge of wealth, but at this period most gentlemen still regarded them as an effete means of transport, suitable for delicate ladies and children, the old and the sick. An attempt had been made in 1601 to prohibit men from using them altogether. But Ralegh was both old and sick and it is likely that he travelled with Bess and Carew in the relative comfort of a coach. However, we know from contemporary travellers that being driven by a too-keen coachman, even in a vehicle well upholstered with cushions, was a battering experience. Post routes were maintained better than most, but when they were not a mire they were ridged with ruts and pitted with potholes. Coaches were also vulnerable to highway robbers, though the entourage provided by Stucley and Ralegh's men would have intimidated any but the most desperate.

We do have a clear idea of travelling times: a letter that Ralegh dispatched to Sir Robert Cecil, marked 'Hast post hast', on 26 November 1595, half his lifetime ago, shows how quick they could be. The letter was despatched from Sherborne that morning and is endorsed by successive postmasters: Shaftesbury (17 miles) 1 p.m.; Salisbury (21 miles) 5 p.m.; Andover (18 miles) 8 p.m.; Basingstoke (22 miles) 11 p.m.; Hartford Bridge (10 miles) 1 a.m. the next day; Staines (25 miles) 8 a.m.[1] From Staines to central London is another 18 miles, so Ralegh's letter would have reached Cecil's secretary's hands well before midday on the 27th.

In May of that same year Lady Elizabeth's brother, Arthur Throckmorton, stayed at Sherborne in company with Christopher Harris of Radford while Sir Walter was away on his first voyage to Guiana. Throckmorton's journey back to London over the same 130-mile route took him three days and two nights. He dined at Shaftesbury and slept in Salisbury on the first day, then dined at Andover and slept at Hartley Row, between Basingstoke and Bagshot, on the second, and on the third dined at Staines before taking a boat down the Thames from Brentford to Ratcliffe Cross and so to his own bed at Mile End.[2]

Stucley's instructions were to convey Ralegh to London 'by easy stages as his health will allow' but, however easy the stages might be, the journey promised to be too fast for the prisoner. Ralegh needed time, as Digby's visit the previous night had confirmed, to prepare himself to confront his accusers. He needed time to write to King James who, he had heard, was on a progress which would take him to Salisbury at the end of the week. He might have audience with him there. He had to slow Stucley's intended pace. Sir Lewis planned to sleep at Salisbury that night and be on the road again the next day. Sir Walter would make sure that his health did not allow it.

The company dined in the town of Shaftesbury. That afternoon they proceeded over the Wiltshire hills and, when they came to the steep descent to the bridges over the Nadder and Avon and the city of Salisbury, Manoury tells us that Ralegh went on foot and took the opportunity of speaking privately with him.

'Have you any of your vomits or other medicines?' he asked in French.

'Sir, I have,' said the physician.

'Then I pray you make one ready against tomorrow morning,' said Ralegh, 'and tell nobody thereof.'

They walked down towards the town and St Mary's dizzying spire; beneath it was the Episcopal throne, seat of an earlier bishop whom Ralegh had 'made' by giving a jewel to the Queen; there too were the remains, translated from Old Sarum to the new cathedral in 1226, of Bishop Osmund, the saint who had cursed Sherborne.

Sir Walter enlarged on his predicament and his plan to escape it, which required Dr Manoury's good will.

'I know that it is good for me to evacuate many bad humours,' Ralegh pursued the matter, in French, 'and by this means I shall gain time to work my friends, give order to my affairs, and, it may be, pacify His Majesty before my coming to London.'

If Manoury is to be believed, Ralegh spoke frankly.[3] Medical treatment was not much more than a pretext for his plans.

'For I know well that as soon as I come there,' he continued, 'I shall to the Tower, and that they will cut off my head if I use no means to escape it, which I cannot do without counterfeiting to be sick, which your vomits will effect without suspicion.'[4]

Salisbury, or New Sarum, grew up with the cathedral at the confluence of rivers. Within early-fourteenth-century earthen ramparts pierced by gates, it grew fat and prosperous upon the wool and cloth trade. The gridiron pattern of streets survives, and narrow canals – John Leland's 'streamelettes' and Celia Fiennes's 'rivulets' – flowed through them in Ralegh's day.

The party entered the town up Exeter Street which, soon after passing the cathedral on the left-hand side, becomes St John's Street and leads north into the medieval centre. They stayed just outside the ancient town, at a house close to the White Hart Inn on St John's Street. It may have been the Greyhound and the Hare, where Lady Elizabeth's brother stayed in 1595, or the fifteenth-century King's Arms whose top-heavy, black-and-white timber-framed gable stands four floors high above the street, the second jutting over the first, and the first overhanging the ground floor. The King's Arms is in the right place: across the street from the gate to the cathedral precincts and a few doors down from the White Hart.

Ralegh retired to his room at once and 'laid him down upon a bed, complaining much of his head, and blaming his great day's journey'. Still, he supped very well. Soon after supper he seemed to be surprised by shaky vision, 'with a dimness of sight, by a swimming or giddiness in his head'. As he rose from his bed he held his hand in front of his face. Sir Lewis led him by the arm, but Sir Walter staggered and 'struck his head with some violence against a post of the gallery before his chamber'. Stucley was alarmed, thinking that Ralegh must indeed be sick.

For the moment Manoury said nothing to dispel that belief. Just as Sir Walter was trying to gain time 'to work his friends', the Frenchman could afford to wait, working both Ralegh and Stucley to his profit. That night Sir Walter conferred with Bess and Samuel King and persuaded them of his plan, for the next morning he sent them ahead to London, together with Carew and most of his servants, to prepare for his arrival and to make arrangements for his escape.

Ralegh's ill health would not allow him to travel. Stucley had decisions to make. He was in his chamber with his servant Cuthbert and Dr Manoury when Ralegh's body servant, Robin, came to tell them that his master was behaving strangely. Sir Walter had waited until Lady Elizabeth and Carew were gone. If they had been worried by the previous night's performance they would have been shocked by that morning's.

'My master is out of his wits,' reported Robin. 'He is naked in his shirt, crawling on all fours, scratching and biting the rushes upon the planks.'

Stucley pitied his cousin and, hurriedly getting up, sent Manoury ahead to Ralegh's chamber. The doctor found Sir Walter in bed.

'Sir, what ails you?' he asked.

'I ail nothing, monsieur,' said Sir Walter. 'I did it on purpose.'

Manoury understood that he was being drawn further into the plot. Ralegh asked him for the 'vomit' he had promised. Manoury proffered it at once and Ralegh 'made no bones, but swallowed it down incontinently'.

Sir Lewis, now dressed, entered the room. It was the cue for his prisoner to begin to cry and rave once more. When Manoury went out Sir Walter began to draw up his legs and arms, 'all on a heap', as if he was suffering a fit 'and contractions of his sinews'. These convulsions were so violent that Stucley tried his best to calm him. First he straightened one of Ralegh's arms, then a leg. As soon as he forced one limb down on to the bed another one flexed. He summoned help but, despite his servants' strength, between them they could not still Sir Walter's tormented body. When at last he seemed to exhaust himself, Sir Lewis felt great compassion for his kinsman and had him 'well rubbed and chafed'.

After the fit passed and the massage had taken effect, Sir Walter called for Manoury. When the doctor returned to his bedside Ralegh begged him to stay by him, and said he would rest for a while. As soon as the others had gone Manoury shut the door.

'I have exercised Sir Lewis well,' Ralegh told him, describing the scene with much laughter, 'and taught him to be a physician.'

Sir Walter was concerned that the vomit he swallowed had not yet taken effect and asked for another stronger dose, but Manoury assured him that it would work in a short time.

'Can you devise anything', asked Ralegh, 'that will make me look horrible and loathsome outwardly, without offending my principal parts or making me sick inwardly?'

Manoury considered this proposition. 'I will make a composition presently of certain things which will make you like a leper from head to foot, without doing you any harm.'

'Then, I beg you, effect it speedily.'

So Manoury set to work to create a mixture, one of whose chief ingredients was aqua fortis, or nitric acid.

'The reason for it', said Sir Walter, 'is that if I am in such a condition it will make the Lords of the Council afraid to come near me, and move them with more pity to favour me.'

Manoury applied his potion to Ralegh's brow, arms and chest. It quickly produced the desired result. Not long afterwards, when Stucley entered the chamber, Manoury left them alone together.

Sir Lewis was taken aback to see Sir Walter covered with pimples, his face full of lurid blisters, each with a yellowish heart surrounded by a purple tinge, and the rest of his exposed skin apparently inflamed with heat. All at once he grew anxious about the possible danger of the disease, that it might be contagious. Astonished, and frightened, by the sudden onset of the attack, he hurried out to consult Manoury. The doctor prevaricated, saying it might be this or it might be that, but confessed himself puzzled and unable to make a sure diagnosis.

Seeing that his Frenchman had insufficient skill to deal with the crisis, Stucley decided to go to the Bishop's Palace, on the other side of the cathedral precincts. The bishop of Ely, who had just been installed as bishop of Winchester after the previous incumbent died of dropsy at Greenwich,[5] was in residence there. He listened to Sir Lewis's account of Ralegh's critical condition and without delay sent two physicians back with him to the patient's bedside. The deception was not uncovered, for the bishop's doctors 'could tell nothing of what humour the said sickness was composed'.

Then a third medical man, a Bachelor in Physick, attended too. As if on cue, Manoury's vomit 'began to work both upwards and downwards' in their presence. Faced with such a spectacular array of symptoms not one of them, for all his science, could diagnose the disease. They gave their opinion and advice all the same: that the patient could not be exposed to the air without manifest peril of his life. They put their report in writing and, after all three had signed it, Manoury set his hand to it also.

Ralegh was very happy. The ruse had worked. Before the physicians revisited him he thought some more symptoms should be prepared to perplex them. He suspected that they might ask to see his urine.

'I pray you, do something to make it seem troubled and bad.'

Manoury took the urinal and rubbed the inside of the glass with 'a certain drug' before replacing it in the bed.

Ralegh was enjoying himself now. Anticipating what else the physicians might decide to examine, he unwound a black silk ribbon from the hilt of his poniard and made Manoury tie it tightly around his arm, 'to try if it would distemper the pulse'. But the ploy did not work as he had imagined it would. The artery in his wrist would not be coerced to lie about the state of his heart.

Still, he pissed in the physicians' presence, and when the vessel was lifted from his bed and put into their hands, they observed his urine turn to an earthy humour, a blackish colour, an ill-favoured water which compelled them to deduce that his disease was mortal and without remedy, unless heaven came to his aid.

Stucley was concerned for his kinsman's life, but was also committed to bringing him alive to the Tower of London to face the lords, his masters. Manoury and Ralegh rejoiced together when the medical men left. It had been a good day's work.

The next morning Sir Walter summoned Manoury and asked him to anoint him again, this time on his nose, his head, his thighs and his calves. The treatment again worked perfectly. Covered with a fresh rash of pustules, Ralegh became very jovial.

'But,' he said, 'the evacuation your physic caused has so opened my stomach that I am exceedingly hungry, monsieur. Pray go out and buy me some meat secretly, for if I eat publicly it will be seen that I am not sick.'

Manoury dutifully went to buy food. He must make his new master sick unto death and at the same time give him the strength to fight for his life. He walked to the White Hart, not many yards up St John Street. The landlord, George Staples, gladly supplied him with a leg of mutton and three loaves which he hid under his cloak and carried back to Ralegh's chamber.

Sir Walter concealed the victuals in his room and ate them covertly. He continued in this way until Friday, the last day of July, so that everyone but Manoury believed that he lived for three days without food.

In company Ralegh kept up the appearance of sickness, but left to himself he wrote. His quill scraped over the paper for hours, only ceasing when Stucley or Cuthbert or a doctor came to his bedside. Sometimes the ink flowed with the style he had brought to his great *History of the World*, written in the Tower for Prince Henry. Sometimes it was sucked from his pen by the necessity to express an anguished cry for justice, or mercy. When he had finished, he asked Manoury to transcribe it for him in a fair hand, ready for presentation to His Majesty.[6]

A loyal address, a political tract and an apology, it was urgently composed in extraordinary circumstances so that King James, due in Salisbury shortly, should read it and be moved.

Ralegh did not know that on Thursday, 30 July, the Privy Council sent a letter to the Lieutenant of the Tower:

> Whereas his Majesty has given special direction and commandment ... to pray and require you to receive the person of the said Sir Walter Ralegh into your charge and keeping within his Majesty's Tower, there to remain in that place under your charge with that liberty as he enjoyed when he was last discharged thence. For which this shall be your warrant.[7]

That Friday night Stucley, Manoury and other members of the party discussed the sickness with Ralegh and speculated about its cause. Was it a contagion brought back from the Indies? Could it be a consequence of the extreme fever Sir Walter had suffered aboard the *Destiny*? Or was its origin more recent? Could it have been the ale he had drunk at breakfast in the Parhams' house?

'As God save me,' said Ralegh, 'I think I have taken poison where I lay the night before I came to this town.'

This is what Stucley and Manoury later testified that he said about his stay at Poyntington, though he denied it vehemently. According to them he enlarged on the theme: 'I know that Master Parham is a great lover of the King of Spain, and a papist, and that he keeps always a priest in his house.' Ralegh paused, before adding, 'But I will not have any of you speak of it.' He shot a meaningful glance at Manoury, 'Nor you, monsieur.'[8]

If this is what Ralegh truly said, then it may have been a ploy to explain the seemingly inexplicable, a tactic his large mind happily employed to gull small-minded Sir Lewis and pander to his prejudice. By his command to his hearers not to speak of it he may have convinced himself that it was as good as unspoken. Or, in the search for a rational explanation of extraordinary symptoms, did Stucley himself suggest that Sir Edward Parham had poisoned Sir Walter, and agree with Manoury to pass it off as Ralegh's accusation? Or did he simply blacken Ralegh's name by inventing this slander of his friends?

When Sir Walter was again behind closed doors, with only Manoury for company, he rose from his sick bed, clad only in his shirt, and paced up and down the chamber. Then he picked up a looking-glass, studied his spotty face in it with inordinate pleasure and broke into guffaws.

'We shall laugh well one day, monsieur, for having thus cozened and beguiled the King, his council, and the Spaniards and all.'

The following day His Majesty King James I and his train arrived at Salisbury. His custom was to stay either in the Bishop's Palace or at Sherborne Place, in Cathedral Close, the home of local worthies Thomas Sadler and his elderly second wife Elihonor.

The King refused see Ralegh, who appeared far too distempered for an audience, but he heard about Sir Walter's condition, for it was the talk of the bishop's household and of the Sadlers' too. Ralegh's feigned sickness had both won him the time to write an apology to the King and rendered him unpresentable; Manoury had made a fair copy of Sir Walter's crabbed hand;

His Majesty and Ralegh were now within a stone's throw of each other but could not come face to face.

It was a tragi-comical stalemate, and Manoury observed that Sir Walter seemed suddenly to be overtaken by great apprehension. The proximity of power – the King and his accompanying courtiers – sharpened Ralegh's sense of impotence and of his status as a man dead in law whose only hope had been to please the King, whose only achievement was to earn his displeasure.

Sir Walter was painfully aware that his successful imposture as a diseased patient, a ruse only made possible by the excellent Manoury, was utterly dependent upon the Frenchman's discretion, and vulnerable to any change of heart he might have. He made Manoury shut the doors and asked him to fetch a coffer from his baggage, and from within it another red leather coffer which Ralegh took and opened. He gazed into it for some while before calling Manoury to his side. Then he put nine pieces of Spanish gold money into the physician's hand.

'There is twenty crowns in pistolets,' he said, 'which I give you for your physical receipts, and for the victuals you bought me.' It was a generous payment indeed for a potion of nitric acid and for mutton and bread. 'And I will give you fifty pound a year if you will do what I shall tell you.'

That was a good offer for almost any service.

'If it happen that Sir Lewis Stucley asks you what conference you had with me, tell him that you comfort me in mine adversity, and that I make you no other answer than thus,' insisted Ralegh, handing Manoury a small piece of paper, 'as is here written.'

It was an odd little memorandum in Sir Walter's hand, the same fractured French in which he habitually conversed with Manoury. The doctor later produced the fragment in evidence. It read: '*Ve la M. Mannowry L'acceptance de tout mes trauaus, pertie de mon estat, & de mon fils, mes maladies & doleurs. Ve la C'effect de mon confidence au Roy.*'

Its fractured French urged Manoury to bear witness to

Ralegh's resignation in the face of all his troubles – the loss of his wealth and of his son, as well as the sicknesses and sorrows he suffered – and to his confidence in the King.

King James, meanwhile, was the focus of a solemn ritual of investiture at the Bishop's Palace, raising barons and viscounts to the condition of earls.[9] At one side of the close His Majesty laboured, attired in robes of state but none the less contriving as usual to look flabby and unkempt, while on the other side the adventurer, once the epitome of Elizabethan elegance and high style but now dressed in a nightshirt and pitted with pustules, worked upon Manoury.

'I desire to fly and get myself out of England,' Ralegh said, according to Manoury's record, 'and if you will help me in my escape, it is all in your power, for Sir Lewis Stucley trusts in nobody but you.'[10]

'At your coming to London,' suggested Manoury, 'you should keep yourself close, concealed in the house of a friend of mine in Shire Lane.'

This overture sounded sweet, and Ralegh inclined to go along with it at first. But soon he took courage and told the Frenchman that he had long ago decided on another plan.

'I have already sent Captain King to hire me a barque below Gravesend which will go with all winds, and another little boat to carry me to it,' he confessed, 'for if I hid myself in London I should always be in fear to be discovered by the general searchers there.'

Ralegh knew enough about the capital's busy hive of spies and rummagers and searchers to be justifiably wary.

'But,' he told Manoury, 'to escape I must get leave to go to my own house in Broad Street. Being there, I will handle the matter so that I will escape out of the hands of Sir Lewis Stucley by a back door and get me into the boat. For, thanks to you, monsieur, no one will believe that I can go on foot, seeing me as feeble as I seem to be.'

Ralegh fell silent then and mused for a while.

'Sir, why need you fly?' asked Manoury. 'Your apology and your last declaration, do they not justify you sufficiently?'

'Never tell me more,' Ralegh exploded angrily in English. 'A man that fears is never secure.'

Sir Walter was a man bedevilled by fear. It drove him now as it always had. When so long ago he scratched that line with a diamond on a window pane for his Virgin Queen – 'Fain would I climb, yet I fear to fall' – it was an honest conceit but an incomplete one. Fear drove him to climb in the first place: fear of failure, of exposure, of dishonour, of poverty, of impotence and insignificance. Immediately following her death, he fell, or was pushed by her successor. Then he was crushed by fear. Though afraid to die, he stabbed himself with a blunt knife.

Now he was *in extremis* again, tugged by hope and despair, bounced momentarily out of depression into absurd exhilaration by exercising what little power he had left, the talent to deceive, and enjoying the effect of it on those who had him in their clutches. He veered between impulsiveness and hopelessness, ill-considered action and the inability to act at all. Caution was never his strong suit. A man who can measure fear may be cautious, but one possessed by fear, a desperate man, does not know how to be prudent. That is why Ralegh chose to trust Dr Manoury.

He trusted Stucley, too, to convey his petitions across the close to the lords who attended the King. If he was to escape he had to obtain His Majesty's licence to resort to his own house in London or, as an option, to his brother's house near Salisbury.[11]

His suit for the first was presented to the King by the Vice Chamberlain, and for the second by Mr Secretary, Sir Robert Naunton. Both petitions were supported by Stucley, and by the physicians' assessment of his physical condition. Despite the Privy Council's order to the Lieutenant of the Tower, so recently issued, the King's permit was procured. It gave Sir Walter leave to spend five days regaining his strength and ordering his affairs at his house in Broad Street in the custody of Sir Lewis Stucley before being taken to the Tower.[12] Ralegh was jubilant.

'Hereby one may see that His Majesty does not mean to take your life,' Manoury said, 'seeing that he suffers you to go to your own house to recover your health.'

'No,' said Sir Walter, 'they used all these kinds of flatteries to the Duke of Byron, to draw him fairly to the prison, and then they cut off his head.'

Ralegh maintained that the authorities considered it expedient for a man to die in order to reassure the Spanish and restore the negotiations that his affair had ruptured. Then, so Manoury later testified, he broke forth into most hateful and traitorous words against the King's person, ending with threats and bravado: 'If I can save myself, I will plot such plots as will make the King think himself happy to send for me again, and render me my estate with advantage, yea, and force the King of Spain to write into England in my favour.'

'Sir, if you do escape, what will become of Sir Lewis Stucley?' Manoury asked. 'Will he be put to death on your account, or not? Or will he lose his office and estate?'

'Not to death,' said Ralegh, 'but he will be imprisoned for a while. The King cannot have his lands for they are already assured to his eldest son. As for the rest, it is no concern of mine.'

'But, sir, is it not treason in myself to be aiding your escape?'

'No, for you are a stranger,' said Ralegh, meaning that by definition a foreigner cannot commit treason. 'Nevertheless, you must not be known to have done anything, for then you will be sure to be put in prison.'

It may be that this last warning tipped the balance for

Manoury and turned him again, back towards loyalty to his first master.

'But what if it be discovered that I had any hand in your escape?'

'Why, monsieur,' said Ralegh with a big smile on his pimply face, 'follow me into France – that is your country – and quit all. I will make you amends for everything.'

8

APOLOGY

If the ill success of this enterprise of mine had been without example, I should have needed a large discourse and many arguments for my justification. But if the vain attempts of the greatest princes of Europe, both amongst themselves and against the great Turk, and in all modern histories left to every eye to peruse, have miscarried, then it is not so strange that myself being but a private man, and drawing after me the chains and fetters wherewith I had been thirteen years tied in the Tower, being unpardoned and in disgrace with my sovereign Lord, have by other men's errors failed in the attempt I undertook.[1]

his is how Ralegh began the *Large Appologie for the ill successe of his enterprise to Guiana* that he wrote to the King in secret from his Salisbury lodgings, while apparently weakened by lack of food, diarrhoea and vomiting, suffering vertigo and urinary problems, disfigured by an illness physicians thought terminal, and exhibiting unmistakable signs of madness.

The rational arguments and persuasive passion of his *Apology* are worth recognising, as are the tricks, the bribery, the exultant deceptions he indulged in to get it written. Biographers and historians who give the episode any space at all tend to give it little weight. It is a picturesque scene, peripheral and whimsical, wherein our hero entertainingly outwits his captor. But it was a desperate ploy and a characteristic one.

Sir Walter began by listing princes and commanders who, despite much greater resources than he had at his disposal, failed in their grand designs. His first example is the Holy Roman Emperor Charles V. In his *Discoverie*[2] he had drawn attention to him as the King who had taken 'the maidenhead of Peru and the abundant treasures of Atabalipa'. Add to that mighty achievement the acts of the current Spanish King, and consider 'how many kingdoms he hath endangered, how many armies, garrisons, and navies he hath, and doth maintain'; remember how he could afford to sustain great losses, such as the Armada of 1588, 'yet notwithstanding he beginneth again like a storm to threaten shipwreck to us all'.

'These abilities,' Ralegh wrote, 'rise not from the trades of sacks [sherries] and Seville oranges, nor from aught else that either Spain, Portugal, or any of his other provinces produce; it is his Indian gold that endangereth and disturbeth all the nations of Europe.'

If the Spanish King could keep England from foreign enterprises and from challenging his trade, either by threat of invasion or by besieging us in Britain, Ireland, or elsewhere, then he successfully drives us towards our peril. This had been a central thesis of Ralegh's *Discoverie*, and yet, he writes in his *Apology*, this same Charles V, begetter of Spanish power, now had feet of clay. He also could fail, for he 'returned with unexampled losses (I will not say dishonour) from Algier in Africa'.

Secondly Sir Walter chose to recall the failure of King Sebastião who 'lost himself and his army in Barbary'. Ralegh refrains from mentioning it, for his readers did not need telling, but the centre of the Portuguese King's army on that disastrous

Moroccan crusade was commanded by Sir Lewis Stucley's great-uncle, Thomas.[3] If he had not perished in the desert, Thomas Stucley would have gone on to besiege Ireland with Dom Sebastião's aid, in the hope of winning it from Queen Elizabeth and becoming its king. The tacit implication was that the infamous traitor and Sir Walter's keeper were of the same blood.

Ralegh continued his recital of heroic failures, including his mentors Sir Francis Drake and Sir John Hawkins, and Sir John Norris's loss of 8,000 men at the siege of Lisbon. It was no wonder that his own plans had foundered, since his followers, apart from some forty gentlemen, were inexperienced volunteers, whom families and friends were glad to be rid of, 'the very scum of the world, drunkards, blasphemers, and such like'.

Next, he tackled accusations and slurs that had gained currency in the past year. Most men, he wrote, had believed that he honestly meant to go to Guiana, but that once at liberty 'and in my own power, having made my way with some foreign prince', he would turn pirate and abandon his country. We know that he negotiated with the French before his departure, and that on the voyage he frequently spoke of piratical prizes and the Plate fleet as an insurance policy. But, carefully omitting any reference to dubious plans and dealings, he briskly concluded that 'my being at Guiana, my returning into England unpardoned, and my not taking the spoil of the subjects of any Christian prince hath, I doubt not, destroyed that opinion'.

Having his word disbelieved and his motives mistrusted were occupational hazards for Ralegh. After his first voyage to Guiana in 1595 many suspected that he himself had not crossed the Atlantic at all, but had holed up in Cornwall for eight months until his fleet came back. On his return he wrote his eloquent *Discoverie* partly to allay such doubts. In a revealing letter to

Sir Robert Cecil he commented: 'What becomes of Guiana I much desire to hear, whether it pass for a history or a fable.'[4]

The poet George Chapman accepted its reality and in the same breath made of it a myth worthy of 'Eliza', the Virgin Queen:

> Riches and conquest and renown I sing,
> Riches with honour, conquest without blood,
> Enough to seat the monarchy of earth,
> Like to Jove's eagle, on Eliza's hand.
> Guiana, whose rich feet are mines of gold,
> Whose forehead knocks against the roof of stars,
> Stands on her tiptoes at fair England looking,
> Kissing her hand, bowing her mighty breast,
> And every sign of all submission making,
> To be her sister, and the daughter both
> Of our most sacred maid, whose barrenness
> Is the true fruit of virtue, that may get,
> Bear and bring forth anew in all perfection,
> What heretofore savage corruption held
> In barbarous chaos.[5]

'The country hath more quantity of gold, by far,' Ralegh had written in his *Discoverie*, 'than the best parts of the Indies, or Peru.' The kings of the coastal territories were mostly already Queen Elizabeth's vassals, he says, 'and seem to desire nothing more than her Majesty's protection and the return of the English nation'. Keymis confirmed this on his return, and Thomas Masham, a gentleman aboard the pinnace *Wat* on the third voyage Ralegh sent to Guiana, wrote: 'The people in all the lower part of the country go naked, both men and women, being of several languages, very tractable and ingenious, and very loving and kind to Englishmen generally.' Inland, in the mountains, 'they go apparelled, being, as it seemeth, of a more civil disposition, having great store of gold, as we are certainly informed by the lower Indians, of whom we had some gold'.[6]

The first European navigator who sighted the coast of Guiana was Alonso de Ojeda in 1499 or Vincente Yanez Pinzon in 1500. Two more Spaniards navigated the mouth of the Orinoco in 1531 and ascended it some distance, despite frequent skirmishes with Amerindians, especially on the north bank. In 1591 Antonio de Berrio, governor of Trinidad, descended the Meta river and the Orinoco from the new kingdom of Granada, the home of Cristóbal Guayacunda, to the Orinoco estuary. This gave the Spanish a first foothold in Guiana at the confluence of the Caroni river with the Orinoco, a village visited by Laurence Keymis in both 1595 and 1596 which he described as 'a ranceria [*rancherío*, settlement] of some twenty or thirty houses', San Thomé. In 1595 Ralegh had captured and interrogated Berrio, who tried to dissuade him from his enterprise with dire warnings of disaster. When reinforcements arrived from Spain in 1596, Berrio dispatched 470 men upriver to discover the fabulous city of Manao d'El Dorado. But Amerindians ambushed the expedition, killed 350 of them and sent the remainder back to famine and plague in San Thomé.

That is the crude history, but it is Ralegh's disturbing image of the country which resonates in the mind. Towards the end of the *Discoverie* he wrote:

> Guiana is a country that hath yet her maidenhead, never sacked, turned, nor wrought; the face of the earth hath not been torn, nor the virtue and salt of the soil spent by manurance [cultivation]. The graves have not been opened for gold, the mines not broken with sledges, nor their images pulled down out of their temples. It hath never been entered by any army of strength, and never conquered or possessed by any Christian prince.

In those days he celebrated the innocence and virginity of his South American Eden, even as the imperial threat of penetration and exploitation overshadowed her. Twenty-one years later he had hoped to woo her back, willingly, from the Spanish

usurper. But now, in Salisbury, idealism had been overtaken by
sordid squabbles over money and the disloyalty of men.

In his *Apology* Ralegh complained that a rumour had been put
about by 'a hypocritical thief', the first master of the *Destiny*,
and by 'an ungrateful youth which waited upon me in my cabin',
that he had brought £22,000 from England, in two- and twenty-
shilling pieces, and so neither needed nor cared to discover a
gold mine in Guiana or anywhere else. This gossip spread
through his ship, and through the fleet anchored off Trinidad.
When Ralegh went ashore there was talk of setting sail and
abandoning him to die of starvation, to be eaten by wild beasts
or flayed alive by Spaniards. 'If it can be proved . . . that I had
either in my keeping, or in my power . . . above 100 pieces
when I departed from London, of which I had left 45 pieces
with my wife . . . I acknowledge myself a reprobate, a villain, a
traitor to the King, and the most unworthy man living, or that
ever hath lived upon the earth.'

Next he dealt with the accusations of the captains who ran
away: traitorous Baily at Lanzarote, Woolaston and ungrateful
Whitney in the Indies. It is usually true, he wrote, that men are
the causes of their own miseries, 'as I was of mine, when I
undertook my late enterprise without a pardon'. The whole fleet
knew him to be *non ens* in law, which gave every petty companion the courage to spread defamatory rumours about him.
Implicit in his protest was a covert reproof to the King for
granting him his commission on so faulty a basis.

Then he countered the allegations of delay. The captains
blamed him for procrastination at the Isle of Wight and Plymouth, though the cause was their own inadequate provisioning
and equipping of their ships. He had put into Cork harbour
after a great storm off Scilly had sunk one pinnace and driven
Samuel King's into Bristol. They needed to regroup, he wrote,

and gave examples of naval actions disabled when fleets were split up. 'That we stayed long in Ireland it is true, but they must accuse the clouds and not me.'

He dealt at some length with insinuations of hostile behaviour in the Canaries, and explained that once the governor of La Gomera was sure that his fleet was not a Turkish one come to sack the island, he exchanged presents with the Spanish count and his half-English wife. He had documentary proof: letters from the count which demonstrate his good will, including one addressed to Don Diego Sarmiento de Acuña, the Spanish ambassador – he enjoyed making this point – written as a testimonial to his good conduct.

Men said that he had sailed on to Cape Verde, knowing it to be an infectious place, and so lost many of his men to fever. In fact, he wrote, he came no nearer to it than Brava, one of the Cape Verde Islands, 160 leagues (actually 380 miles) off the coast of Senegal; but, as any English trader knew, there was as little danger of infection there as anywhere else. There were few places in the world near great rivers where people were not subject to fevers at some time of the year. Malaria was rife, he pointed out, at Woolwich in Kent, and down both banks of the Thames.

'But as good success admits of no examination of errors, so the contrary allows of no excuse', however reasonable or just. We can hear the sigh in his voice as he illustrates this fateful principle in the lives of Cavendish and Drake. 'For the rest I leave it to all worthy and indifferent men to judge, by what neglect or error of mine the gold mine in Guiana, which I had formerly discovered, was not found and enjoyed.'

Next he launched into his sad account of the fate of those five companies in five boats which he had sent up the Orinoco. He transcribed the text of the detailed instructions he had given to Laurence Keymis. If they found the mine rich, then it should be defended for all it was worth. If it was not worth holding, 'then shall you bring but a basket or two [of ore], to satisfy his Majesty that my design was not imaginary but true'.

His weakness prevented him being present, he had written, but in any case the companies would only agree to land in Guiana if he stayed with the ships off Trinidad, for the galleons of Spain were expected any day. 'Let me hear from you so soon as you can. You shall find me at Punto Gallo, dead or alive,' he had assured Keymis, 'and if you find not the ships there, yet you shall find their ashes, for I will fire with the galleons ... but run away I will never.' Ralegh added a damning comment: 'That these my instructions were not followed, it was not my fault.'

He described the San Thomé débâcle and his impetuous son Wat's death, together with the ambush that first deterred Keymis from locating the mine. Ralegh quoted Keymis's letter of 8 January, which he received aboard the *Destiny* on 13 February, in full. Keymis had delayed writing it, though wanting Ralegh to have the truth from him, rather than uncertainties from others, and to pass on Wat's last words: 'Lord have mercy upon me and prosper your enterprise.'

Keymis told Ralegh that they had taken the governor's servant – Cristóbal Guayacunda – prisoner. They had found three or four refiners' houses, the best ones in the town, but had seen no coin or bullion. Whitney and Woolaston had only just come upriver – their ships had been stranded on shoals in the Orinoco delta – which meant that Keymis could at last proceed to the mine. He could not have gone earlier because of 'the murmurings, disorders and vexations, wherewith the sergeant major [Sir Walter's young nephew George Ralegh] is perpetually tormented and tired, having no man to assist him, but myself alone'.

Ralegh explained to King James how Keymis returned to the *Destiny* empty-handed, with empty excuses. 'Had he brought to the King but one hundred weight of the ore, though with the loss of a hundred men, he had given his Majesty satisfaction, preserved my reputation, and given our nation encouragement to have returned the next year with a greater force, and to have held the country for his Majesty to whom it belongeth.' Ralegh described how he had refused to condone or excuse Keymis's folly, to which his old friend replied, 'I know then, sir, what course to take', went up to his cabin and killed himself.

Some 'puppies', Ralegh wrote, had suggested that Keymis committed suicide because he had seduced so many gentlemen and others with an imaginary mine. But the captains Parker, Ralegh and King could all testify how Keymis told them that the mine was just two hours' journey from a place on the river-bank where they moored on their return. They were in a hurry to rejoin the fleet – and here Ralegh revealed how aware he was that King James himself had betrayed him to the Spanish – because in San Thomé they had discovered the King of Spain's letters, including the one dated 17 March 1617, before Ralegh's fleet had left the Thames, and a commission ordering troops to come downriver from New Granada and upriver from Puerto Rico to reinforce the Orinoco.

If only they had 'pinched' the governor's servant, Ralegh emphasised, Guayacunda would have directed them to two or three more gold mines, and a silver mine, within four miles of the town. Not only that, but the native lord of Garrapana sent them a great canoe full of fruits and provisions, hoping that an English force would stay to neutralise the Spaniards, and offered them a rich gold mine in his own territory as a reward.

Ralegh's physical condition, as he secretly wrote this *Apology* in Salisbury, was a fraud, but his anguish was real enough. It was a compound of grief and anger and regret that he had come so close to rehabilitating himself and his fortune but had only succeeded in losing his elder son and his last hope in the world.

If his purpose had been to gain his liberty, he wrote, why did he not keep his liberty when he had it? Why did he put his life into obvious peril with his crew by insisting on coming home? Why, if he had intended to turn pirate, did he oppose his mutinous crew and risk being killed or thrown into the sea by refusing to do so?

It would have been a strange fancy, he insisted, to persuade his son and his wife to risk everything – the £8,000 His Majesty gave them for Sherborne, the house Bess sold in Mitcham, and Wat's life – in return for mythical mines. 'Being old and sickly, thirteen years in prison and not used to the air, to travail and to watching, it being ten to one that I should ever have returned . . . what madness would have made me undertake this journey, but the assurance of the mine?'

The Spaniards, Ralegh continued, had set up their wooden town and made a fort, but neither conquered nor made peace with the Guianians. What was more, before the Spanish planted themselves at San Thomé, the Guianians had willingly resigned their territory to Queen Elizabeth, 'who by me promised to relieve them and defend them against the Spaniard'. Although imprisoned for fourteen years, he wrote, adding a year for effect, he had paid for an expedition every year or two to keep them in hope. If the Spaniards' usurped possession gave the King of Spain the right to call himself king of Guiana, then he, Ralegh, might as well declare himself king of Ireland because he had taken possession of Limerick and built a fort there.

'I am persuaded', Ralegh declared to King James, 'that his Majesty, if he had been resolved that Guiana had not been his, would have stayed me.' Either Guiana was the King's or it was not. If it was, he had caused no offence. If it was not, he would have been at fault if he had taken gold out of the mines, even if he had found no Spaniards there. In any case, if England were at peace with the Spanish, why had they tied thirty-six unarmed Englishmen, of Mr Hall's ship of London, back to back and cut their throats after trading with them for a whole month? 'To break peace where there is no peace is impossible.'

The best way for the Spanish ambassador to have prevented his going to Guiana, Ralegh suggested, was to have revealed 'the great practise' which Sir Walter supposedly had with the King of Spain against King James in 1603, 'for which I lost my estate, and lay thirteen years in the Tower', rather than focus on his recent offence in Guiana, to which King Philip had no other title than the sword.

Ralegh pointed out to King James that the Spanish consistently attached the epithet of 'enemy' to the English, for they accused the Indians in Guiana of trading 'with the Flemish and English enemies'. So he came to the end of his *Apology* with a polemical rush and concluded by repeating his most telling point:

> I have said it already, and I will say it again, that if Guiana be not our sovereign's, the working of a mine there and the taking of a town there had been equally perilous to me; for by doing the one I had robbed the King of Spain and been a thief and by the other a disturber and breaker of the peace.

Sir Walter ended his scribbling in a hurry and with huge relief. He handed the heap of paper to Dr Manoury who copied it in a fair hand. His play-acting had bought him the time he needed secretly to assemble a sober and irrefutable case to put before the King. But did he protest too much? Had he and Keymis been as sure of the mines as he pretended? Did he lie about the location of San Thomé?

The Reverend Samuel Jones, preacher aboard the *Flying Joane*, wrote in his letter of 22 March 1618 to the Privy Council: 'At Cayenne, in November last, Sir Walter being somewhat recovered, opened his project for the mine, which upon the plat he demonstrated to be within three or four miles of the town of Sancti Thomae, which he knew to be inhabited by the Spaniards, for he seemed oftentimes in my hearing to doubt whether it were reinforced or no.'[7] We can imagine him unfolding his plat, the plot, map or chart of the Orinoco region, and pointing out to his surviving gentlemen where his hopes were invested. It was a map descended from one drawn on his first voyage in 1595 and refined by the expeditions he sent in the years that followed, a chart pored over by cartographers at Durham House and Sherborne Castle, a plot burned into Ralegh's brain during the long years in the Tower.

Sir Warham St Leger must have studied that map at Cayenne, for he was in overall command of the land force. He would have led the upriver expedition, but he was replaced by George Ralegh after becoming violently ill. Samuel Jones wrote that if Sir Warham had gone up to San Thomé, 'as I have heard himself often say, he had not the particular directions; but in a seeming courtesy Sir Walter had left all things to his valour and judgment'. Now, 'seeming courtesy' was a fine way of delegating unwanted responsibility. The lack of 'particular directions' suggests that neither the map nor Ralegh's instructions were as precise as they had promised to be, and that the intended commander was unhappy that so much was left to his initiative.

Jones maintained that when they approached San Thomé the captains 'desired Captain Keymis first to show them the mine, which Sir Walter had formerly said to be three or four miles nearer than the town'. Then, after they had taken San Thomé, he described how Keymis went out with a small party and returned with ore; but when one of the expedition's refiners tried it, it proved worthless. Finally, after alarms and fatal excursions, he recounted how the prospecting party disappeared upriver for three weeks, for 'whereas the mine was described to be three miles short of the town, they went not only three miles but three score leagues beyond it'. Nothing seemed to be in the right place.

Ralegh first sowed the seed of an idea, that San Thomé was not where he had expected it to be, in the letter he sent to the

King from Plymouth before Stucley arrested him. Then he wrote of 'Guiana, where (without any directions from me) a Spanish village was burnt which was newly set up within three miles of the mine'.[8] In the *Apology* he stated that George Ralegh and Keymis, 'finding a Spanish town or rather a village, set up twenty miles distance from the place where Antonio Berrio had attempted to plant . . . agreed to land and encamp between the mine and the town which they did not suspect to be so near them as it was'. That night the expedition had been attacked by Spaniards whom they pursued to San Thomé, and so had no choice but to take the town.

The truth was that San Thomé had not moved.[9] Ralegh lied about that. A new San Thomé would be established twenty-five miles or so downriver in 1684, but in January 1618 it was still on the Orinoco's south bank, about a league (three miles) downriver from the Caroni's confluence, exactly as Keymis had described it in 1596, newly-built at the landing-place called Morequito where he and Ralegh had disembarked the previous year. They had heard the Caroni's multiple cataracts from there. Ralegh marched up the riverbank to see them and wrote a glittering description:

> there appeared some ten or twelve overfalls in sight, every one as high over the other as a church tower, which fell with that fury, that the rebound of water made it seem as if it had been all covered with a great shower of rain, and in some places we took it at the first for a smoke that had risen over some great town.

Lyrically Sir Walter celebrated the flora and the fauna of the promised land, as well as the rich geology, for

> every stone that we stooped to take up promised either gold or silver by his complexion . . . and yet we had no means but with our daggers and fingers to tear them out here and there, the rocks being most hard of that mineral spar aforesaid, which is like a flint, and is altogether as

hard or harder, and besides the veins lie a fathom or two deep in the rocks.[10]

That was the first 'mine', on the right bank of the Caroni, some three miles upriver from San Thomé, where they would have to dig for ore. A London refiner had tested a sample of hard spar that Ralegh collected and pronounced it rich in gold. But there was a second site too. A chief named Putijma had pointed it out to Ralegh and Keymis from a distance: Mount Iconuri, twenty miles downriver from San Thomé and not more than fifteen miles inland. Ralegh had been unable to endure the march to it. Keymis had not reached it either, though on his second voyage he made another attempt with an Indian guide who showed him how 'without digging they gather the gold in the sand of a small river, named Macawini, that springeth and falleth from the rocks where this mine is'.[11] On that occasion Keymis turned back for fear that the Spaniards might cut off his retreat.

It was to this second mine that Ralegh ordered Keymis to go, in the written instructions he quoted in his *Apology*. Confusion was laid upon confusion because, while Ralegh and Keymis knew of at least two mines, one upriver and one downriver from San Thomé, as well as reports of gold which Keymis pursued much higher up the Orinoco, they had only ever talked publicly of a single mine.

In his letters from the Tower proposing the voyage to Guiana, Ralegh conflates their experience of one site with reports of others. In Guiana, after Wat's death, Keymis had seemed uncertain where to go or what to do. 'Hence,' Samuel Jones wrote, 'it was considered that Keymis himself might be deluded, even by Sir Walter Ralegh, in the ore and the place.'

From far away in London it had been possible to be certain, to simplify the picture and the 'plat', for presentation to those who might release Ralegh from imprisonment and support the expedition. Once in Guiana, uneasily aware of the Spanish presence and embroiled in a struggle to motivate 'the very scum of the world', everything looked much more doubtful. One way of explaining the uncertainty, confusion and failure which dogged the search for 'the mine' was to declare that San Thomé had moved.

To write of a town 'which they did not suspect to be so near them as it was', because it had been set down some twenty miles from where Keymis had last seen it, cleverly explained why the Spanish had surprised the English land force; it excused a conflict that had caused King James political embarrassment. It also furnished a plausible reason for Keymis's apparent disorientation. It compromised access to the gold mine.

Ralegh's letters from the Tower had hinted that it was not going to be simple. He wrote to Robert Cecil, Earl of Salisbury, saying that abundant ore waited to be exploited, 'the mountain being near the river side and of easy carriage thither'.[12] Interestingly, he maintained that he had not valued the sample of ore he brought back because so much had been lying about and because it was so similar to other marcasite or 'fool's gold' that had been picked up. It was by chance that a refiner tried it, he wrote, for he had often come close to throwing it away. The refiner was skilful but poor, and Ralegh confessed that he had promised him twenty pounds if he could find gold or silver in it. The refiner none the less staked his life on the result of his assay and, what was more, Ralegh kept some in reserve for a second trial.

Sir Walter had been willing to stake his own life on the project, if only he was allowed to return to Guiana. 'When God shall permit us to arrive,' he wrote, 'if I bring them not to a mountain near a navigable river covered with gold and silver ore, let the commanders have commission to cut off my head there.'[13]

But it was sixteen years since he and Keymis had seen the

place, he remarked to the Earl of Salisbury, and because the country was desolate and overgrown it would be difficult to find the exact site. That was a good reason to release him to accompany Keymis, he wrote, for two guides are better than one, but added, 'I dare not trust mine own memory and mine own marks for the finding it'. Then he noted details that seem to relate not to the Caroni mine where he found his specimen, but to the Iconuri mine described by the Indian guide: it does not lie deep in the ground, in any rock or hard spar, but 'the gold ore is found at the root of the grass, in a broad and flat slate'.[14]

He had assured the Privy Council, 'I am content to adventure all I have (but my reputation) upon Keymis's memory . . . considering that if Keymis miss of his marks my poor estate is utterly overthrown and my wife and children as utterly beggared.'[15] Just before his release he had reassured his ally Sir Ralph Winwood, 'that I know of the riches of that place not by hearsay but what mine eyes have seen'.[16]

With good fortune in prospect, Sir Walter had been content to tell half-truths. When all was lost, including Keymis his witness, it was just too difficult to disentangle all the tedious facts and make the truth plain. Propped up on a sickbed in Salisbury with a quill in his hand, and feigning extreme weakness, it was easier to lie, single-handedly to move a town twenty miles down the Orinoco. Why labour to tell the complex truth if a simple lie will explain everything? The consummate play-actor not only rewrote the script, but also shifted the scenery.

9

HAIL POWDERED WITH
DIAMONDS

Ralegh's *Apology* was delivered, hot, across Salisbury's cathedral precincts into His Majesty's hands, or into the hands of his councillors. James may even have read it.[1] Sir Walter's petitions were considered and, along with royal permission for Ralegh to return to his wife's house in Broad Street, Stucley received brusque orders to convey him there without delay.

The medical men had given their opinion that Ralegh's startling symptoms were not fatal and that his health would allow him to be moved. On Monday 3 August, or thereabouts, Stucley and his escort installed Sir Walter in a coach and resumed their journey to London.

Dr Manoury pondered Ralegh's offer of fifty pounds a year, and the prospect of accompanying him to France with the unquantified promise of compensation for quitting his life in England. He weighed it up against the probability of Ralegh's escape being foiled and the certainty, which Sir Walter had acknowledged, of his own imprisonment if he was suspected of abetting him.

Ralegh still had faith in Guillaume Manoury, having only a day or two earlier confided his escape plan to him: 'I have already sent Captain King to hire me a barque below Gravesend which will go with all winds, and another little boat to carry me to it.' Meanwhile, in London, Samuel King trusted a Mr Hart, a former boatswain of his, and a man by the name of Cottrell who had been a servant to Sir Walter in the Tower, to turn his master's dreams of escape into reality.[2] Hart owned a Thames ketch lying off Tilbury which he agreed to put at Ralegh's disposal. Everything now depended on extreme secrecy and discretion.

Cottrell and Hart, though, saw a quicker profit in betrayal and contacted William Herbert who had both backed and taken part in the Guiana expedition. Herbert passed the intelligence on to Sir William St John, half-brother to George Villiers, Earl of Buckingham, the King's favourite. In the course of successfully lobbying Villiers for his release from the Tower in 1616, Ralegh had given Sir William St John and an associate substantial gifts of £750 each. 'Sir,' he had said, in offering Villiers profuse thanks, 'you have by your mediation put me again into the world.' Now Villiers's half-brother's mediation was about to put Sir Walter out of the world. The details of his escape route were in the hands of men at the highest level. Neither Captain King in London nor Ralegh in Salisbury had a hint of this. Nor, yet, did Stucley. Manoury was fortunate that his master remained in ignorance for the time being.

From Salisbury Ralegh and his escort travelled eighteen miles to Andover, in Hampshire, where they dined and lodged. 'At Andover,' Stucley wrote later, 'I first discovered he had a design a-hatching.' Manoury ensured that he was the first to expose the game of deception he had played with Ralegh. Now Sir Lewis understood that Sir Walter had used his supposed sufferings and Mr Vice Chamberlain's pity to buy time and win him five days in his London home.[3]

From Andover they continued another thirty-two miles to Hartford Bridge, breaking the journey for refreshment at

Basingstoke. They were moving no faster than before, but in Dr Manoury's account, as edited by Francis Bacon, the mundane particulars of the itinerary now grow sparser, as if the journey's inner momentum was gathering to a climax.

At Bagshot in Surrey, thirteen miles along the road to Staines, they dined. There they were met by Sir William St John, who had ridden from London to warn Sir Lewis about Mr Hart's ketch waiting in the Thames and the wherries that Captain King and Mr Cottrell had organised to ferry Sir Walter downriver to it. This intelligence put Stucley's plans into question. Did the royal licence for Raleigh to be held under house arrest at Broad Street still apply? Should Sir Lewis convey him directly to the Tower instead? No, they must proceed exactly as before. Ralegh must not realise that his plot had been betrayed.

Manoury had not betrayed Ralegh to Stucley before they left Salisbury. It seems, as we have seen, that he voluntarily revealed at least some of Ralegh's ploys to his master at Andover. The official report of his evidence implies that he did, but it makes no mention of St John or the information he brought to Bagshot. So it is more than likely that it was St John's dramatic news which forced Manoury to tell all. Once the plot was exposed, his complicity in it put him in danger. In any case, if Sir Walter's escape plans were blown, Manoury's hopes of a pension and a new life in France were scuppered too.

It was probably at this point on the road to London that Manoury resolved to come clean. Stucley's astonishment can have been matched only by his displeasure at discovering that the French doctor had known and connived at so much. Of course, Manoury may not have immediately confessed to his central role in counterfeiting Ralegh's symptoms. Stucley's response to these revelations was swift: from that moment on he 'used extraordinary diligence in guards and watches upon him'. Ralegh sensed the change of atmosphere, noted how closely observed he was, and grew anxious that his chances of ever eluding his captors were growing slimmer.

Ten miles beyond Bagshot they arrived in Staines, where they lodged for the night. Before supper Ralegh conferred privately with Manoury, unaware of the fact that the Frenchman had turned.

'I perceive all too well, monsieur,' Ralegh said, 'that it is not possible for me to escape by our two means alone. Stucley is so watchful, and sets such strait guard upon me, it will be too hard for us, for all our cunning.'

Manoury must have agreed.

'Therefore,' said Ralegh, 'there is no way but to make him of our counsel.'

Manoury surely smiled, or wept, inwardly at this. Ralegh must have been desperate to risk this ploy. Though Stucley was his kinsman, his loyalty was demonstrably to the King.

'And if we can persuade him to let me save myself,' Sir Walter continued, 'I will give him in hand £200 sterling worth.'

Sir Lewis was greedy; this was Sir Walter's only hope. He was not aware that his cousin could hardly indulge an appetite for gold when the whole court and counsel already knew of his escape plans. He showed a jewel to Manoury. Among the valuables found on Ralegh's person when he was admitted to the Tower was a sprig jewel, or diamond-encrusted spray, mounted with soft stones and a ruby. It was probably this that he put into the physician's hand. Manoury described it as 'made in the fashion of hail powdered with diamonds, with a ruby at the middest'.[4]

'It is worth £150 sterling,' Sir Walter said, 'and besides this jewel he will have £50 in money. I pray you, go tell him so from me, and persuade him to it. I know he will trust you.'

Ralegh knew Stucley well enough to be confident of his avarice. He trusted Manoury too. Over and above that, he trusted Stucley's faith in Manoury. Upon the topmost point of this insubstantial pyramid of faith he balanced his new plot. The town of Staines had been unkind to Ralegh; it was there in September 1603 that he had been indicted for treason. Now this new turn in his fortunes would soon give him another reason to be ungrateful to the place.

Manoury went at once to Stucley's chamber, without deceit, and reported the conversation verbatim. Sir Lewis debated the matter before instructing Manoury to report back to Sir Walter.

'Tell him I accept the offer,' he said. 'Tell him I am content to do as he desires, for I would choose rather to go away with him than tarry behind with shame and reproach.'

However insincere the message was, it hints at Stucley's true feelings. Throughout the journey, especially when they had stayed with Ralegh's kinsmen or friends, he must have suffered looks and words which registered his traitorous status. He, a petty grandee, was leading a great man to his death. Whichever way he jumped now, he could not evade blame. Perhaps he really wished he could flee with Sir Walter. Perhaps, in wild moments, he hoped they might find an alternative escape route. He knew one thing: when Ralegh was gone he would be left behind with shame and reproach for company.

'But, ask him this also,' Stucley told Manoury. 'How does he think I can go with him without losing my office of Vice Admiral, which cost me six hundred pounds? And how will we live after we have fled? And to what place shall we go? And what means will he carry with him, to furnish this intended escape?'

The questions, and the anxiety from which they sprang, seemed genuine. Manoury the go-between carried them to Ralegh's room.

'Tell Sir Lewis this,' said Sir Walter, 'that if he will swear unto me, not to discover me, then I will tell him my whole intent. As to his first point, say that though he shall lose his office, yet he shall be no loser in the matter, for, later, as soon

[119]

as I am gotten into France, or Holland, my wife is to send me a thousand pounds sterling. Tell him I have only a thousand crowns in money and jewels to serve for now in my escape.'

In 1618 £1,000 was the equivalent of more than half a million pounds today; it was a relatively modest amount in Ralegh's scale of values. A thousand English crowns was worth £250, roughly £130,000 in current terms, though Ralegh may have meant French crowns or *écus*, which had a similar value, for at that time it was illegal to carry more than twenty pounds sterling out of the country;[5] wealth had to taken abroad in the form of jewels, French crowns, Spanish pistolets or double-pistolets, 'doubloons', which were worth about thirty-four English shillings, something like £900 today.

After they had supped, Ralegh spoke to Manoury again, regretting the necessity to involve Sir Lewis in their plans.

'Oh, if I could escape without Stucley, I should do so bravely. But it is no matter,' he said philosophically, with a shrug of his shoulders, 'I'll carry him along, and afterwards I'll dispatch myself of him well enough.'

Manoury returned to Stucley and told him what Ralegh wanted him to hear, and what he did not. Then the Frenchman brought the cousins face to face. It was a test of nerve on all sides. Ralegh showed his kinsman the bauble Manoury had spoken about, the jewel like hail powdered with diamonds. Sir Lewis made a fine show of being satisfied with it.

'But, I pray you, cousin,' he said, 'give me a little respite so that I may dispose of my office.'

Sir Walter was not surprised that Sir Lewis asked for time to sell on his vice admiralship to some other Devon worthy before he left the country. It was in character. Manoury sensed that Ralegh had not seen through their pantomime and, happy that his masters were to all appearances of one accord, he wished them good night and went to his bed. The French physician planned to be off to London next morning, at speed.

We do not know the full extent of Manoury's business in the capital, or what reason he gave Ralegh for his departure. Stucley certainly wanted him to ensure that the right people knew the right story, if not the whole one, before he brought his prisoner home to Broad Street. Sir Walter surely commissioned him to visit Lady Elizabeth and to consolidate the arrangements for his escape with Samuel King and his two-faced colleagues.

Early the next day Manoury took his leave of Ralegh.

'Sir, I think I will not see you again while you are in England,' he said, no doubt thinking he would not see him again in this world.

Sir Walter pressed a letter into his hand, addressed to Lady Frances Harris at Radford House near Plymouth, where they had stayed, and from where Ralegh had rowed out towards a French ship but returned to captivity. The letter asked her to deliver an iron furnace to Dr Manoury, with a distillatory, or alembic, of copper that went with it. It was a token of Ralegh's appreciation for all he had done and a means of furthering the physician's chymical endeavours.

'Tell every man you meet that I am sick, monsieur,' said Ralegh, 'and that you left me in an extreme looseness last night.'

That additional piece of misinformation concerning the state of Sir Walter's bowels is, according to the record, the last fragment of conversation the two men exchanged.

Manoury rode ahead to London. He carried Ralegh's letter, which promised him a still when he got back to Devon, and a letter from Stucley which begged an audience with the King. Manoury's priority was to inform His Majesty of Ralegh's conduct on the way from Plymouth to Staines and, no doubt, to impress upon him what a fine job his keeper Sir Lewis Stucley, and naturally he himself, had done against difficult odds. He had a hidden purpose too; he intended to convey intelligence to the French embassy in London.

From evidence later taken from one Robert Mearing at the Tower, it seems that there was a plot to ambush Manoury, or that indeed he was assaulted or intercepted, on his ride to London. 'Being asked whether he ever heard that the French physician was to be set upon by the way, as he came up to London . . . he utterly denieth that he ever heard or knew of any such matter.'[6]

Stucley and the remaining entourage escorted Ralegh onwards at a more leisurely pace. Sir Walter still protested his sickness and regaled Sir Lewis with his symptoms. 'Between Staines and London I added to the knowledge of his purpose a certain notion of his discovered practice,' Stucley reported.[7] After eleven miles they came to Brentford, where they dined at an inn by the river.

Ralegh's next meal was to be with his wife and son at home. But now, as Sir Walter ascended the Brentford inn's stairs, 'there fell out an accident, which gave him great hopes and encouragement speedily to facilitate his intended design for escape'.[8] It was a meeting that seemed for all the world like a chance encounter. It was no accident. It filled Ralegh with optimism, but took him one step nearer the scaffold.

10

HOUSE ARREST

It was impossible for Ralegh to find privacy in that Brentford inn. Stucley's watchful escort were doing their job well; Sir Walter was almost continuously surrounded and the room was guarded. Nevertheless, he was at the top of the stairs when a man approached him. Ralegh later testified that the encounter was quite unexpected; at that moment he had no idea who the gentleman was.[1]

'For as he came on his way to London, in his inn at Brentford, there came unto him a Frenchman named La Chesnay.'[2] The Frenchman greeted Sir Walter with great ceremony and introduced himself as Davide de Noyon, Seigneur de la Chesnée, a nobleman who worked as a translator for Le Clerc, the agent and acting ambassador of the King of France. He had waited for the right opportunity to exchange words with Ralegh. Sir Walter was immediately wary; to be observed at the head of the stairs in furtive conversation with a French official was to be fatally compromised. De la Chesnée said he had something to tell him that would be of great importance to him. Ralegh, by his own account, put him off, saying that just then he was too closely observed for comfort. He asked him to come to his house in London where he would be that evening.

Sir Walter must have believed that something good might come of this contact. He hoped for anything which would make landfall in France easier, or more worthwhile. But doubts clouded every scheme he contemplated. The French physician Manoury had gone ahead, beyond his control. He cannot have entirely trusted Stucley or he would not have been so circumspect about De la Chesnée's sudden appearance.

Ralegh had had dealings with the French before he sailed for Guiana; even King James knew this. Count Des Maretz, the last resident ambassador, had come aboard the newly launched *Destiny* on the Thames to disabuse himself of a current rumour, that Ralegh was about to launch an assault on the port of St Valerie in the Huguenot cause. He had been reassured on that point and, more than that, he alleged that he had heard Ralegh complain vehemently about the abuse he had suffered at James I's hands, and express his readiness to transfer his allegiance to Louis XIII.

Ralegh's trusted friend, Captain Charles Faige of La Rochelle, had gone to France on his behalf, begging the Admiral of France for ships to join his fleet and bear the brunt of the conflict with the Spaniards in the West Indies, and to use his influence to obtain Louis XIII's permission for him to enter a French port on his return. Ralegh had never received the French permit he wanted, no French ships had rendezvoused with his off Guiana, and Faige had absconded, allegedly because he and his companion Captain Antoine Belle of Dieppe did not wish to be associated with the Huguenot elements of Ralegh's fleet.

Faige and Belle had agreed to take charge of four French vessels being armed for Ralegh at Le Havre and Dieppe, but betrayed him by embarking on a business trip to the Mediterranean instead. Their ship was seized by pirates, Faige ended up in a Genoese debtors' prison, and Belle continued to Rome where he confessed his relationship with Ralegh to the Jesuits. Belle's confessor urged him to go to Madrid for his conscience's sake. There, in March 1618, he told his story and handed over the documents for the procurement of French help which Sir Walter had entrusted to him.[3] Thus Ralegh's correspondence, and a map of Guiana intended to guide French ships, fell into Spanish hands.

Ralegh had trusted his French friends, just as he had had confidence in Baily, Woolaston, Whitney, Keymis, Manoury and Stucley. Now, on Friday 7 August, he thought he had only to wait until the evening to learn something to his advantage from De la Chesnée.

The final stage of his journey home was a short one, from Brentford to London, either by horse and coach or by wherry down the Thames to one of the many landing places on the edge of the City, such as Downgate Stairs. From there it was a short step to the Mansion House, then up Threadneedle Street a little way before forking left into Pig Street which, at its junction with Throgmorton Street, became Broad Street.

They arrived late at night, too late for De la Chesnée. There, in Lady Elizabeth's house, were the prized and incidental relics of his life, souvenirs from voyages and campaigns, items that had graced Durham House and Sherborne Castle, books and charts and chymical equipment from his laboratory in the Tower. There he caught up with Bess and Carew after that strange ninety-mile stretch from Salisbury where they had left him. All the while Ralegh was alert, waiting for the Frenchman to arrive. Sir Lewis stayed in the house to keep watch on his cousin as his orders prescribed, but most of the escort dispersed.

Samuel King was in attendance on his master once more, full of the details of the escape route he had arranged with Cottrell and Hart. Back at last in familiar domestic surroundings, Ralegh was resigned to the knowledge that this house was not his destination. His fate was in other men's hands, and he fretted, for the French gentleman did not appear.

Ralegh regarded the escape plan he had contrived with Samuel King, and had subsequently been compelled to share with Guillaume Manoury and cousin Lewis, as his best hope, especially if he could obtain a promise of French co-operation. But he was still preoccupied with his *Apology*; would the King be swayed by it? Some time before his imminent escape he wrote a second, shortened version of it addressed to his most likely advocate on the Privy Council, cousin George, Lord Carew.

'Because I know not whether I shall live to come before the lords I have, for his Majesty's satisfaction, set down as much as I can say', it began, 'either for my own defence or against myself as things are now construed.'[4] But then, admitting that he had no authority from the King to oust the Spanish from Guiana, and that James had no responsibility for, or prior knowledge of, the attack on San Thomé, he stated: 'It is true that though I acquainted his Majesty with my intent to land in Guiana, yet I never made it known to his Majesty that the Spaniards have any footing there.'

Why should he imply that he had kept that knowledge from the King? Every English merchantman who traded in the West Indies was well aware of the Spanish presence in the Orinoco region; Ralegh himself had referred to it more than once in letters to ministers and to the Privy Council. Writing to Sir Robert Cecil in 1611, for instance, he discussed 'those Spaniards which dwell upon the same river' who, since he was there in 1595, had tortured more than a hundred native people to death in the attempt to extract information about the mine's location.[5] Soon afterwards he had urged Cecil and the Privy Council to consult a Captain John Moore who had been buying tobacco and 'came from Orinoco this last spring and was oftentimes ashore at San Thomé where the Spaniards inhabit'.[6]

Ralegh had been frank about the Spanish presence. Why now should he suggest that he had lied by omission? Was it because he knew he had played down the Spanish threat? Or was he bending over backwards to make it clear that he was not ascribing liability to His Majesty? Following this untrue, odd confession, he reiterated the point he stressed in his *Apology*: the English Crown had a legitimate title to Guiana and 'the Spaniards had no other title but force (the Pope's donation excepted)'.

The Pope's donation was a big and contentious issue to enclose in brackets. The year after Columbus discovered America, Pope Alexander VI drew a line of longitude down the Atlantic Ocean a hundred leagues west of the Cape Verde Islands and granted all the newly discovered world west of it to Spain, and all the discoveries east of it to Portugal. The Portuguese disputed it. To placate them, the line was redrawn 270 leagues further west the following year. So on 7 June 1494 at Tordesillas, a small Spanish town on the river Duero, the representatives of Ferdinand and Isabella of Spain and Dom João II of Portugal signed a treaty which shared the expanding globe equally between the two great Catholic sea-going powers. That is how the Portuguese got Brazil. Later, when they were discovering the Far East – the Moluccas, the Philippines and the real Japan and China, rather than Columbus's 'Cathay' or Cuba – the Treaty of Zaragoza drew a corresponding line down the Pacific in 1529 to conclude the half-and-half deal. However much the English, French and Dutch contested it, the Spanish and Portuguese saw the Pope's donation as issuing directly from the hand of God. The New World was divided between them by divine right.

Protestant imperialism was no less ambitious, simply less grandiose. In 1610 Prince Henry's librarian had extolled voyages of colonisation 'for the discovery of strange and foreign lands and nations unknown, whereby the poor people living in darkness . . . may in short time grow to some acquaintance and familiarity with this our Christian world, and in the end come to the saving knowledge of the true God'.[7] So why, Sir Walter asked, should the English bow to Spain's claims when the Dutch and French did not? Just after his return to Plymouth, a French gentleman named Flory set out from there with four ships, three hundred soldiers and an official commission to land, burn and sack all the places in the West Indies that he could conquer, despite the fact that the French King had so recently married a daughter of Spain.[8]

Ralegh had put his argument plainly. All he could add was that he had spent his estate, lost his son and his health, and endured as many sorts of misery as a man could in King James's service. He had committed no hostile act, other than entering a territory belonging to the Crown of England, where his men were set upon and slain by usurping Spaniards. He had returned to England in peril of his life and at the mercy of the King. 'To that grace and goodness and kingliness I refer myself,' he concluded, 'which, if it shall find that I have have not yet suffered enough, it may please add more affliction to the remainder of a wretched life.' Meanwhile he was plotting to ensure that His Majesty would not enjoy that particular pleasure.

All next day there was no sign of De la Chesnée. Nothing was heard of or from him, giving rise to grave doubts in Ralegh's mind.[9] But at eight o'clock on Saturday night, without any prior warning and accompanied by a man with a white feather in his hat, De la Chesnée entered the house and ascended the grand staircase. He introduced his companion as Monsieur l'Agent.

Sir Walter conducted Le Clerc, the acting ambassador, to the far end of a gallery. There the Frenchman embraced him and sympathised with his misfortunes. He expressed his abhorrence of the persecution Sir Walter had suffered at the hands of the ambassadors and agents of Spain, but he spoke so fast that Ralegh frequently had to interrupt him. It was clear that Le Clerc had been surprised at Ralegh's lack of prudence in not giving him advance notice, for he would have wanted to plan his passage with greater secrecy; but the point of his speech was that, if Ralegh had the will to save himself, he would furnish him with a French barque which was waiting on the Thames, ready to take him across the Channel.

Ralegh responded with elaborate courtesy. 'Where is the barque?' he inquired.

'Where is it?' Le Clerc asked De la Chesnée.

'The boat is up the river,' said De la Chesnée, 'but it is fully laden, or at least partly.'

'She will not be of any use to me if she is not already off Gravesend,' replied Ralegh. 'I am already equipped with a little English boat which is waiting for me above Gravesend, and if I find it feasible or possible to escape, I will risk it tonight or tomorrow night.'

A pause followed this announcement.

'Which port are you aiming for?' asked Le Clerc.

'The nearest,' said Ralegh, meaning Calais, although he had doubts about the reception he would get from the authorities on the coast.

'Do not trouble yourself on that score,' said Le Clerc, 'for you are well enough known everywhere by name and reputation. To ensure you a good welcome I myself will send a dispatch which will reach France as soon as you do.'

'I cannot offer to do anything in France which deserves this,' Ralegh said, 'or to serve, unless against the Spanish in the West Indies, but if something happens between the two kings, I will do all that a man can do, whether in England or in France, towards the destruction of that western monarchy.'

Le Clerc did not doubt Ralegh's self-confidence. He assured him that De la Chesnée would keep him company all the way, or go by another route to meet him in France. Ralegh gladly accepted the second option. His English conspirators would convey him to Calais and the French would guarantee him a good reception there.

It is possible that the agent and his colleague remained with Sir Walter into the small hours, for Ralegh is reported as confessing later that Le Clerc was with him on Sunday morning.[10] At length, after more ceremonious words and a promise to remember him, the Frenchmen made to leave. Ralegh wanted Le Clerc to remain unnoticed as he made his exit. So, having led the Frenchmen to the foot of the stairs without coming across anyone, he left them to find their own way out.

Samuel King urged Ralegh to make his getaway at once, before any aroused suspicions could be acted upon. But Sir Walter wanted more time and it was not until the following day that Bess and Carew prepared themselves to say farewell to him. Captain King confirmed the escape plan's every detail. Edward Cottrell was ready with two small wherries, manned by watermen who would row them downriver to their rendezvous with Captain Hart's Thames ketch. All this time Sir Lewis played the part of a trusty co-conspirator playing the part of a dutiful guard. Ralegh prepared a disguise so that no one would recognise him as he rode down to the Thames.

All day Sunday the house filled with visitors, friends from his past life: those who had been faithful to him during his years in the Tower, and those who remembered him in his glory days.

De la Chesnée's curiosity was such that he could not resist returning to see whether Ralegh had already made, or would soon make, his escape. This unwise, unnecessary visit later earned him a stiff rebuke from his master, Le Clerc. But, after dinner, when Sir Walter's chamber was full of people waiting to see him, De la Chesnée entered the house and went boldly in among the crowd. He approached Ralegh directly and asked a simple question.

'Sir, do you stand by your decision to embark tonight?'

'Yes,' said Sir Walter.

De la Chesnée was satisfied.

'I shall prepare to mount my horse,' Sir Walter added, 'as soon as I hear that you have gone.'

With that, Ralegh took his leave of the noble interpreter.

11

FLIGHT

Ralegh had slept, or tried to sleep, in his own bed at Broad Street for just two nights. His Majesty had licensed him to stay there for five to recuperate and order his affairs before entering the Tower. Captain King had tried without success to persuade him to board the Thames ketch on the second night, because the state of the tide had been perfect then. But now, after dark on the third, Sunday 9 August, Sir Walter was ready to go. The ebb would hurry them to Gravesend by first light.

Close friends and curious visitors left the house. Farewells were said. Carew, Bess and Sir Walter looked forward to a reunion in France. Ralegh shrugged on an undistinguished cloak and donned a broad-brimmed hat trimmed, in a style quite foreign to him, with a green ribbon. He carried a cloak bag and four pistols. Over his own neatly-trimmed grey whiskers he fixed a dark false beard.

Having carried off so many grand roles in such superb costumes, it now seemed natural for Ralegh to dress up as if for a bit part in a pantomime. Disguise was the least of it. His major subterfuge had been to exaggerate his real sickness and feign false symptoms so that, from the King downwards, his enemies believed he was too ill and weak to make a bid for freedom. Or so Ralegh assumed.

There was to be no coach for this night ride. Horses stood ready to take the party of four to the Thames: Ralegh, Ralegh's page Robin, Stucley and one of Stucley's sons, perhaps his eldest, John, who had joined his father for this venture. From Broad Street they trotted through alleys and down deserted lanes, cutting unobtrusively across the main thoroughfares of Bishopsgate Street, Leaden Hall Street and Fenchurch Street, until they threaded their way towards Tower Hill and the looming east flank of the Tower of London itself. Beside it the open expanse of river was sliding down to the sea beneath a foggy shroud. They felt the night breeze on their faces, smelt the Thames's stench and dismounted at Tower Dock.

Was it residual bravado, or a refined sense of irony, that led Ralegh to launch himself to freedom from the shadow of this prison? He had spent too much of his life there already and, but for Manoury's recipes, would have been inside at that very moment. At the Tower's foot, on the river's brink, we can hear the echo of suppressed hilarity seeping from Ralegh's Salisbury lodgings: 'We shall laugh well one day, monsieur, for having thus cozened and beguiled the King, his Council and the physicians and the Spaniards and all.'[1]

Samuel King and Captain Hart greeted the escapees. Edward Cottrell had the wherries moored at the foot of Tower Stairs, with watermen at the oars. It was a tense moment. Sir Walter handed two of his pistols to Sir Lewis.

'Have I not distinguished myself thus far as an honest man?' Stucley asked Captain King.

'I hope you will continue so,' was all King said.

Once Ralegh was installed in a wherry, along with Robin and Stucley, King stepped down into the other to join Stucley's son and Captain Hart. The boatmen cast off, pushed their craft into the stream and unshipped their oars. They had twenty-five miles of rowing ahead of them. The tide was flowing fast. A short way upriver, behind them in the mist, they could hear water in spate, cascading down six feet between the massive piers of London Bridge and the timber piles that protected them. When that sound faded, all they could hear was oar blades slicing the river and sucking as they withdrew.

Soon, as they took the slow bend past Wapping and entered Limehouse Reach which turns south around the Isle of Dogs towards Greenwich, Sir Walter became aware of a third presence, a larger wherry, which seemed ominously attached to them, though always maintaining a discreet distance. Alarmed, he confided his suspicions to Stucley, who reassured him that the escape plan was turning out well, and urged the oarsmen to stroke as swiftly as they could for Gravesend.

The name Gravesend took on its sinister aspect. The third boat appeared to shadow them still, a blot of denser black upon the murky glimmer of the water. For long intervals it faded into foggy darkness and allowed Ralegh momentarily to take Stucley's word for it and believe what he had wanted to believe for days, that soon he would be secure on Hart's ketch, sailing out of the river's mouth into the ocean and the Channel, en route for Calais.

They left Deptford behind, and the *Golden Hind*'s carcass rotting in its dock. Soon afterwards, four miles or so into their passage, they passed Greenwich and the palace from which King James had issued his first proclamation denouncing Ralegh and the hostile invasion of San Thomé just two months before. There another wherry overtook them, very close, and Ralegh convinced himself it had come to arrest him. Nothing happened, except the uninterrupted crouch and stretch of the watermen's backs, the splay and flex of their arms, the dip and tug of the oars. Ralegh was badly shaken. Now they were making north again, up Blackwall Reach, then east and south around Blackwall Point.

Ralegh panicked. He needed reassurance. In his need he forgot to consider consequences and asked the oarsmen a straightforward but foolish question.

'Will you still go on,' he shouted at them, 'even if someone calls upon you to stop in the King's name?'

It was their turn to be frightened. They were unaware of the plot or the counterplot and did not know whom they were carrying aboard their craft. They stopped rowing as soon as they understood his question.

'Do not trouble yourselves, row on,' said Sir Walter, quickly improvising a story to explain himself and calm their fears. 'A brabbling matter with the Spanish ambassador, a quarrel, has caused me to go to Tilbury, to embark for the Low Countries.'

The boatmen shipped their oars.

'Row on,' urged Stucley.

'I will give you ten gold pieces for your pains,' said Sir Walter, 'if you will go on.'

The second wherry came to ride alongside them. Captains King and Hart wanted to know what the matter was. King saw at once that Ralegh was, as he dryly put it later, 'not well satisfied'.[2]

'God's wounds,' screamed Stucley. 'Damn me that I should be so unfortunate as to venture my life and fortune with a man so full of doubts and fears.' He played the part well. Then he turned on the watermen. 'You great boobies, I will kill you if you do not row on.' He addressed Sir Walter more calmly. 'There is nothing to fear,' he said. 'There is no such danger as you suspect.'

'He is right,' said Captain King, 'there is nothing to fear.'

After a long delay, the boatmen were persuaded to take to their oars once more. Soon they were approaching Woolwich, where Ralegh's last venture had begun to materialise. In the spring of 1616, through the mediation of the Lord Admiral, the shipwright Phineas Pett obtained the King's permission to lay the keel of the *Destiny* on the galley dock there. Ralegh's proud ship had been launched that December. Two months ago Stucley had arrested her. Now, in a small wherry off the royal dockyard, Ralegh's last Guiana adventure came full circle.

A mile beyond Woolwich, in Gallions Reach, the watermen began to murmur again and rest on their oars. When the other wherry came alongside, their fellows murmured too. Debating and disputing had delayed them too long. The tide was lost, they all agreed. It would soon be on the turn and there was no chance of rowing another fifteen miles to Tilbury and Gravesend by morning.

In midstream the gentlemen conferred. Should they land here at Plumstead and find horses to take them to Gravesend? Stucley discouraged this notion. There were two or three ketches in the river, Captain Hart commented, adding the odd remark that he was not sure which of them was his. At this, Ralegh's suspicions were strongly aroused. He sensed that Captain King's ex-boatswain was not to be trusted.

Sir Walter ordered the watermen to turn back for Greenwich. Almost as soon as they had done so, out of the darkness a voice from the craft that followed in their wake hailed them in the name of the King. It was William Herbert's boat. Ralegh, Samuel King and Robin were appalled. Stucley pretended to be.

Against his better judgment Sir Walter still clung to his belief in his cousin's loyalty. Could they not even now contrive a means of escape, he suggested, so that he could make his way back to his house in Broad Street? Ralegh offered Stucley a way to save himself from suspicion: he could say that Sir Walter had been still in his custody and that he, Stucley, only pretended to go along with him in order to discover his intentions, and seize upon his private papers.

But the third, larger, wherry was manned by more oarsmen than theirs; it would surely overtake them. Stucley did not relish an engagement on the water with pistols and swords. Ralegh resigned himself to imminent capture. No one offered any resistance when the craft approached and escorted them back towards Greenwich.

All at once Ralegh saw Cottrell and Hart's duplicity. They had betrayed him to William Herbert, a distant relative of his on Bess's side of the family. Herbert had invested heavily in the *Destiny*. Through Herbert and Sir William St John, half-brother of the royal favourite Villiers, he was betrayed to the King.

From his pockets Ralegh unloaded the valuables that were to have funded his escape and subsistence in France. For their safe keeping, in Samuel King's words, he 'gave them to Stucley, who all this time not only hugged and embraced him, as it seemed with the greatest tenderness, but made the utmost protestations of love, friendship and fidelity'.

That last traitorous embrace would be Sir Lewis's undoing.

Six miles back upriver, they disembarked at Greenwich, and guards from Herbert's boat surrounded Ralegh and Stucley, Robin and King. Now Sir Lewis revealed himself. He confronted his cousin.

'Sir Walter,' he declared, 'I arrest you in the name of the King.'

Ralegh was confounded, but he simply looked his cousin in the eye.

'Sir Lewis,' he said, 'these actions will not turn out to your credit.'

It was a shrewd prophecy. The party, or at least the major players, resorted to a Greenwich tavern for what remained of the night. The flight was over.

Later, but still early on that Monday morning, 10 August 1618, they were rowed back upriver. Stucley escorted Ralegh to where he had started out from, the Tower of London. Robin the page and Samuel King were taken into custody with him. King had been duped by his ex-boatswain Hart. Sir Walter shared his grief, for he had been betrayed by his old servant, Cottrell, and by his kinsman, Stucley.

'For your part, you should be in no fear of danger,' he assured King. 'But as for me, it is I am the mark that is shot at.'

Stucley conveyed them into the custody of the Lieutenant of the Tower, Sir Allen Apsley, who was expecting Ralegh, and had King James's warrant of 30 July as his authority to detain him. Captain King was soon released, but Sir Walter remained 'in that place under your charge with that liberty as he enjoyed when he was last discharged thence'.[3] It was a poor welcome and poor liberty, compared to the reception and freedom waiting for him across the Channel.

Lady Elizabeth Ralegh discovered what had happened soon enough, for she found herself held under strict guard in her Broad Street house. Access to her was forbidden. By all means the authorities intended to prevent her hiding or spiriting away jewels and other valuables. Whatever wealth remained in the Raleghs' hands would be seized in order to compensate venturers in the Guiana expedition for their losses.

Interrogations lay ahead, and the interminable scratching of nibs on paper that would heap up a mountain of evidence against Sir Walter. But first, a little list. His gaolors compiled an inventory of his personal possessions:

£50 in gold coin.
A wedge of 22-carat gold.
A stobb of coarser gold.
A chain of gold with diamond sparks.
Sixty-three gold buttons with diamond sparks.
A diamond ring of nine sparks.
A naval officer's whistle set with small diamonds.
An ancient silver seal bearing the roebucks from Ralegh's coat-of-arms.

A Symson stone set in gold.

A sprig jewel mounted with soft stones and a ruby.

One ounce of ambergris, pungent flotsam of warm oceans.[4]

One spleen stone from Guiana, for the cure of melancholy.[5]

A lodestone in a scarlet purse.[6]

A diamond ring from his finger, given him by Queen Elizabeth.

A gold-cased miniature of his wife, the Lady Elizabeth, its frame set with diamonds.

Three sea cards or charts of the West Indies which, out of everything, Ralegh was most reluctant to hand over. 'I would not have parted with those,' he muttered, 'for three hundred pounds.'

One plott or map of Guiana and the New Kingdom.

Another plott and description of the river Orinoco.[7]

Five silver-mine samples.

One jacinth seal engraved with a figure of Neptune, and, tied to it with string, a specimen of ore from Guiana.

A idol from Guiana made of copper and gold.

It was agreed that he could keep one sapphire ring which was his personal seal. Sir Lewis Stucley took the rest.

12

TOWER

Moss by unburied bones, ivy by walls,
Whom life and people have abandoned,
Till th'one be rotten stays, till th'other falls;

But friendships, kindred and love's memory
Die, cool, extinguish, hearing or beholding
The voice of woe or face of misery.[1]

hen in turmoil, and given the leisure to write, Ralegh always turned to poetry. Back in confinement now, he must have recalled lines from the verse petition he once wrote to Queen Anne. They give us an insight into his state of mind during his previous stay in the Tower of London, but seem even more appropriate now.

For friends in all are like those winter showers
Which come uncalled, but then forebear to fall
When harmful heat hath burnt both leaves and flowers.

Then what we sometime were they know no more
Whenas those storms of powerful destiny
Have once defaced the form we had before.

It was all about loyalty, the very issue upon which he would presently stand or fall. He brooded upon the constancy or inconstancy of all those friends who had welcomed him home, wholeheartedly or warily. He bemoaned the fickleness of kindred. He mourned the loss of the love he had once enjoyed.

On Wednesday 12 August 1618, Stucley, who had written his *Appollogie* the day before, came to see Ralegh in the apartments of the Lieutenant of the Tower where he was kept for the time being. In Sir Allen Apsley's dining chamber, in front of witnesses, Sir Walter swore that he loved Sir Lewis as well as any friend he had in the world. Or so Stucley reported, though he added that Ralegh 'used an equivocation, as he doth in these things now concerning me'.[2]

After what had just happened it is no surprise that Ralegh was equivocal. He could be a cunning liar, a subtle one who sometimes half meant what he said, or sometimes meant two things at once. Did he embrace his cousin and profess his love ironically, for the benefit of Sir Allen and the others in the room: to show them a mirror image of Stucley's traitorous hugs and protestations off Greenwich, or to stir remorse in Sir Lewis's own heart? Did he hope that Stucley might still help him?

Ralegh was clearly willing to try anything, and anyone who could intercede on his behalf. He considered approaching the King's favourite, 'Steenie', George Villiers, who on the first day of the year had been raised to the rank of Marquess of Buckingham. He had, after all, worked upon His Majesty to obtain Ralegh's release on licence in 1616. But Sir Walter was under no illusions; he knew that he had abused Villiers's trust in attempting to flee; Villiers was even then promoting a Spanish alliance, and his half-brother Sir William St John, with Ralegh's cousin William Herbert, had played a principal part in foiling Ralegh's escape. But the ear of an enemy in high places might be better than nothing. Sir Walter wrote to Villiers on the same day he swore his love for Stucley:

> If I presume too much I humbly beseech your lordship to pardon me, especially in presuming to write to so great and worthy a person who hath been told that I have done him wrong. But, my worthy lord, it is not to excuse myself that I now write. I cannot, for I have now offended my Sovereign Lord … and my very enemies have lamented my loss, whom now, if his Majesty's mercy alone do not lament, I am lost.[3]

What comforted his soul, he wrote, was that in his escape he had no other motive than to serve the King, and to make His Majesty understand that his Guiana expedition had been founded upon a truth, one which he had intended to confirm, or die in the attempt, 'being resolved as it is well known to have done it from Plymouth had I not been restrained'. He wanted Villiers to understand that he planned at all costs to return to the Orinoco with a French ship and find the gold mine.

Had he really been resolved to do this from Plymouth? Through Samuel King he had negotiated with two French captains there, but on the one occasion that King reports – the night-time attempt to escape from Radford House and embark on a ship in Plymouth Sound – it seems that Ralegh held back.

> Hereby I hoped not only to recover his Majesty's gracious opinion but to have destroyed all those malignant reports which had been spread of me. That this is true, that gentleman [Stucley] whom I so much trusted, my keeper, and to whom I opened my heart, cannot but testify … that when we came back towards London I desired to save no other treasure than the exact descriptions of those places in the Indies.

'It was that last severe letter from my lords' – the one the Privy Council sent to Stucley on 23 July – 'for the speedy bringing of me up … that first put me in fear of my life,' Ralegh frankly confessed, 'which strengthened me in my late, and too late lamented, resolution.' Then he concluded his letter with one long, tumbling, almost incoherent sentence of supplication that betrays, as surely as his disciplined poetry, his state of mind.

> If his Majesty's mercy do not abound, if his Majesty do not pity my age and scorn to take the extremest and uttermost advantage of my errors, if his Majesty, in his great charity, do not make a difference between offences proceeding from a life having natural impulsion without all ill intent, and those of an ill heart, and that your lordship, remarkable in the world for the nobleness of your disposition, do not vouchsafe to become my intercessor, whereby your lordship shall bind a hundred gentlemen of my kindred to honour your memory, bind me for all the time of that life which your lordship shall beg for me to pray to God that you may ever prosper and ever bind me to remain your most humble servant,
>
> W Ralegh
>
> From the Tower this 12 of August.

Villiers, however, was keen to please Spain. It is symptomatic of the prevailing climate of appeasement that on this very day angry citizens who had rioted and thrown brickbats at the Spanish ambassador's house in the Barbican were called in for questioning at Westminster City Hall. The protesters, including the father of the boy who had been injured by Don Diego Sarmiento de Acuña's horse, were fined heavily and imprisoned at the King's pleasure.[4]

Ralegh had written to the King, and would again. Now he had written to Villiers. At some point he also wrote a letter to Queen Anne, which has been lost. He may have reminded her of his verse petition, which has survived.

> Cold walls, to you I sigh, but you are senseless,
> Yet senseful all alike as are those friends,
> Friends only of my sometime happiness.

To whom then shall I cry? to whom shall wrong
Cast down her tears or hold up folded hands?
To her to whom compassion doth belong,

To her who is the first, and may alone
Be called the Empress of the Brittanies.
Who should have mercy if a Queen have none?

The Queen, knowing that her word in the King's ear was less effectual than his favourite's, also wrote a note to Villiers:

My kind Dog,
If I have any power or credit with you, I pray you let me have a trial of it, at this time, in dealing sincerely and earnestly with the King that Sir Walter Ralegh's life may not be called in question.

Ralegh had been released from the Tower in March 1616 and since then had enjoyed, or suffered, less than two-and-a-half years' freedom. It was freedom of a sort, though, for all this time he remained unpardoned and therefore dead in the eyes of the law, as he had been since 1603. In that year he was sentenced to death for treason, reprieved at the last minute and made an unsuccessful suicide attempt at almost the same time as his secretary had taken poison.

After that, Ralegh had lifted himself out of his melancholy and made a life for himself within the damp, unwholesome fortress, dreaming always of 'beyond'. At that time Bess and ten-year-old Wat mostly lived inside with him, though she had acquired a house outside the walls, on Tower Hill, near All Hallows. Late in 1604, after a stroke, he wrote to remind Sir Robert Cecil of his miserable condition: 'daily in danger of death by the palsy, nightly of suffocation by wasted and obstructed lungs, and now the plague being come at the next door unto me . . . my poor child having lain this 14 days next to a woman with a running plague sore and but a paper wall between.'[5]

He felt abandoned when Bess, heavily pregnant with Carew,

and his household moved out. Again he wrote to Cecil hoping that, out of respect for his past, or compassion for his present, he would

> save this quarter which remaineth from the ravens of this time which feed on all things ... For mine own time, good my lord consider that it cannot be called a life but only misery drawn out and spun into a long thread without all hope of other end than death shall provide for me, who, without the help of king or friends, will deliver me out of prison.[6]

Cecil considered him to be 'lodged and attended as well in the Tower as in his house'. Ralegh was given the use of the Bloody Tower and the lieutenant's garden beside it. Formerly called the Garden Tower, it was supposed to have been the scene in 1483 of the murder of Edward IV's young sons, the 'Princes in the Tower'. It had been heightened, and a new floor inserted, for Ralegh and his household. When she was not in residence, Bess boldly drove into the precincts in her coach to see her husband. A doctor and a chaplain visited him regularly and three servants lived in. Indians, brought from Guiana in 1595, attended him for talk and instruction. John Talbot, who would die on the second Guiana expedition to Ralegh's grief, became his new secretary and Wat's tutor.

The then Lieutenant of the Tower, Sir George Hervey, invited Sir Walter to dine with him. He allowed him to walk, for the good of his health, on the inner walls and, for the exercise of his mind, to equip an old hen-house in the garden as a still-house or laboratory. A young man called Sampson worked there as Ralegh's technician or 'operator' for twelve years. It was a place in which to pursue chymical interests and indulge his obsession with Guiana ores.

It did not have the views that Durham House's lantern tower above the Thames had offered, but this little shed was an alchemical chamber, a fantastic arena of exploration, a means of escape more sure than the coca leaves he must have chewed in the forests of Guiana or in his ship's shut cabin. Ralegh cured tobacco leaves in his laboratory, distilled strawberry water and concocted his celebrated Guiana balsam or Great Cordial. In February 1605 a son, conceived in his imprisonment, was born and christened Carew in the chapel of St Peter ad Vincula on Tower Green.

Sir Walter was always under suspicion. When Bess went to Sherborne and ordered the armour to be cleaned, it was rumoured that he would escape. The paranoia surrounding the Gunpowder Plot soon embraced him, despite his situation. The Privy Council required him to answer whether he had exchanged letters with Northumberland, the 'Wizard Earl', or had dealings with the French ambassador, both of which he denied. He did admit to seeing the French ambassador's wife, when she visited the Tower with the Lord High Admiral's daughter-in-law to see the lions in the Royal Menagerie and to glimpse the royal prison's most famous occupant. They caught sight of Ralegh because the garden fence was down, hailed him and begged a little Guiana balsam.

Sir George Hervey had been replaced as lieutenant by the less amiable Sir William Waad, who had the broken-down fence replaced with a brick wall for his own privacy. He only succeeded in giving Sir Walter another wall to walk upon, another stage for his public appearances. The people, Waad wrote to Cecil, 'gaze upon him and he stares at them, which he does in his cunning humour that it might be thought that his being before the Lords was rather to clear than to charge him'.[7]

He gained congenial company too: the Earl of Northumberland, convicted of complicity in the Gunpowder Plot, was fined a vast £30,000 and committed to the Tower. The Wizard Earl and Ralegh shared resources and joined forces in philosophical speculations and chymical experiments. The 'great alchymist' Laurence Keymis, Thomas Hariot, and later Walter Warner and

Robert Hues attended them. It is ironic that a small-scale 'School of Night' should be revived within the very Tower. Sir Francis Bacon even proposed that Ralegh and Northumberland's team should officially be set to do experimental work.[8]

Ralegh suffered a more severe stroke in 1606. His physician, Peter Turner, reported his symptoms: 'all his left side is extreme cold, out of sense and motion or numb. His fingers on the same side beginning to be contracted. And his tongue taken in some part, in so much that he speaketh weakly and it is to be feared that he may utterly lose the use of it.' He advised that Sir Walter should be moved out of the dank Bloody Tower to warmer quarters, 'a little room which he hath built in the garden adjoining to his still-house'.

Sir Walter's anxiety, and Bess's fury over Sherborne Castle, had come to a head in 1607. She blamed him for negligence, he blamed her for rash errors and folly; 'what he says is fitter to be related than written'. Their affection was wearing thin under the strain. It became clear that the deed by which Ralegh thought he had transferred the property to Wat was faulty. Missing words allowed King James to take it for his then favourite Robert Carr.

The strain on the Ralegh family was compounded, for Sir William Waad tightened the Tower regime. The Gunpowder Plot had dramatically ended King James's English honeymoon, and Waad responded by restricting access to prisoners and regulating their servants' behaviour. Bess could no longer drive into the Tower in her coach, or lodge there, for cell doors were locked during the day and wives had to leave at night. She was ordered in the King's name to 'resort to her house on Tower Hill or elsewhere with her women and sons'. Ralegh would soon petition that 'my wife might be made again a prisoner with me'.[9]

Meanwhile other relationships comforted him. Her Majesty Queen Anne came visiting to obtain one of his cordials. She was not like the Virgin Queen who had obsessed and tantalised him, but she was the Queen. No longer the slender fourteen-year-old Danish beauty, white-skinned and golden-haired, that James had first met in Oslo – 'our earthly Juno and our gracious Queen' – she had just given birth to, and lost, her seventh and last child, Sophia. Ralegh's medicine helped her. The hypochondriac Anne seemed not to share James's wariness of him. Best of all, when she returned a second time to see him, she brought her eldest son, thirteen-year-old Henry, with her. He grew to admire Sir Walter unstintingly. 'Who but my father', the Prince is supposed to have declared, 'would keep such a bird in a cage?'

How often Ralegh met Henry in person is not known, but from this time the 'traitor' effectively became tutor to the heir to the throne. The 'dead man' wrote widely and deeply for the edification of the prince, and often communicated with him through his cousin Sir Arthur Gorges. He offered Henry his analysis of the balance of power in Europe, *The Present State of Things as they now Stand between the three great Kingdoms, France, England and Spain*, which admits of no realistic option but renewed conflict with Spain. He made grand plans for an unfinished treatise on naval policy, *Art of War by Sea*, the opening chapter of which he developed into a draft *Discourse on the Invention of Ships* which advocates alliance with the Dutch, trade by force in hostile areas, and conquest by seduction of Spanish colonies. In 1612 he wrote *Touching a Marriage between Prince Henry of England and a Daughter of Savoy*, followed by *A Dialogue between a Jesuit and a Recusant: shewing how Dangerous are their Principles to Christian Princes*. At a time when royal irrationality was provoking popular resentment, his fragment, *On the Seat of Government*, stressed his conviction that reason should guide kings to win their subjects' love.

Ralegh's greatest work, which he and his researchers laboured over in order to present a perfect gift to the future king and the nation, was *The History of the World*. In its preface Sir Walter – always Queen Elizabeth's 'Water' in at least one corner of his heart – first declared his 'fidelity towards Her, whom I must still honour in the dust', before drawing lessons from recent European history which demonstrated the immutability of God. Later in the century Oliver Cromwell would enjoy his treatment of 'the strange windings and turnings of Providence'.[10]

The five books proper, containing about a million words, began with the Creation and expounded Greek, Roman and biblical history up until the second century B.C. Ralegh pulled no punches. He had written to counsel Prince Henry, not to curry favour with the King. He satirised monarchs whose qualities many readers ascribed to James himself. King Ninias of Assyria, for example, was 'esteemed no man of war at all, but altogether feminine, and subjected to ease and delicacy'. Ralegh came to terms with himself too. He saw how 'the world's bright glory hath put out the eyes of our minds ... It is therefore Death alone that can suddenly make man to know himself. He tells the proud and insolent, that they are but abjects, and humbles them.' In Book Five, which contains his most sophisticated and insightful prose, he rewrote the struggle between Carthage and Rome; his treatment made a parable of the Punic Wars, a secret history, *une histoire à clef*, which related as much to present politics as to the ancient past.

When James came to the English throne in 1603, he was hailed 'England's Caesar' and his ritual entrance into London was choreographed as a Roman triumph. Alexander Ross, chaplain to Charles I, would write that had Ralegh 'lived in Roman times he would have been a fit man to have accompanied the triumphant chariot, and to have abused the emperors with uncivil language, as the custom was then'.[11] Sir Walter turned accepted history on its head. He took Carthage's part and drew uncomfortable parallels between the Punic Wars and England's protracted conflict with Spain and its Armada, warning Prince Henry that *rapprochement* with the Spanish must spell disaster.

He diminished the Roman hero Regulus, whose name meant 'petty king', and cast himself as the Carthaginian general Hannibal.

'It was for the service of that inestimable Prince Henry,' Ralegh recalled, 'that I undertook this work. It pleased him to peruse some part thereof, and to pardon what was amiss.' *The History of the World* was licensed to be published in 1611, the year that the new version of the Bible, authorised by King James, came out. But typesetting on such a scale took time, and Prince Henry wanted his teacher to expand the book. Ralegh concurred, despite his desire to refocus his mind on Guiana. He was also unwell, and had had another 'bout' with the Privy Council.

They had found him 'as bold, proud and passionate as ever. The lawless liberty of the Tower, so long cockered and fostered with hopes exorbitant, hath bred suitable desires and affections.'[12] His liberty was curtailed. He was close confined for three months. 'For my extreme shortness of breath doth grow so fast on me, with the despair of obtaining so much grace as to walk with my keeper up the hill within the Tower,' he wrote to Queen Anne in a letter about Guiana, 'as it makes me resolve that God hath otherwise disposed of that business and of me who, after eight years' imprisonment, am as straightly locked up as I was the first day.'[13]

Towards the end of 1612, to Ralegh's grief and the dashing of his hopes of regaining Sherborne and preferment through the prince's mediation, Henry contracted typhoid fever after a swim in the Thames.

Who knows how far the *History* might have come if Prince Henry had not fallen mortally ill, though it would never have come up to date.

I know that it will be said by many that I might have been more pleasing to the reader if I had written the story of my own times, having been permitted to draw water as

near the well-head as another. To this I answer that whosoever, in writing a modern history, shall follow truth too
near the heels it may haply strike out his teeth.

That November, in 1612, as the heir to the throne lay dying,
King James absented himself, for he habitually ran away from
sickness and death. Queen Anne sent to the Tower for a phial
of Ralegh's Great Cordial. It had cured her, she believed, and
it would cure Henry. Her insistence on its virtue caused heated
arguments among the physicians and the lords who attended
her son. Ralegh wrote that it was effectual against fever, but
not against poison. It was administered to the prince as a last
resort. He rallied, opened his eyes, uttered something and died.
Taking Ralegh's cue, the Queen believed he had been poisoned.

Ralegh's masterpiece, *The History of the World*, was 'left to
the world without a master' in March 1614. There was no
proper title page and its author was unnamed, for he was 'civilly
dead'. The work had got as far as 168–67 B.C. and closed with
the words: 'O eloquent, just and mighty death! ... thou hast
drawn together all the far stretched greatness, all the pride,
cruelty, and ambition of man, and covered it all over with these
two narrow words, *Hic iacet*.'

Nine months passed before King James learned of the *History*'s subversive nature. He found it 'too saucy in censuring
princes', and had it suppressed. The Archbishop of Canterbury's
agents seized copies from the bookshops. It was given over to
the censors, guaranteeing enormous sales when it came out
again two years later. This book, and Ralegh's other prose works
that touched on monarchy and good government, had a pro-
found and catalytic influence on the critics of the Stuart dynasty
and on the Parliamentarians who temporarily overthrew it.

Henry's death had closed a door on Ralegh's future. In
1616 Ralegh escaped through another to Guiana, but that had
slammed shut. His attempt to flee to France had been foiled to
his great discredit. He was contained again within the stone

walls that held so much of his inner life. All he could do now, in 1618, was to appeal to his enemies, to doubtful friends, and to Queen Anne. But she was increasingly alienated from King James and from his court, and suffered from a constellation of agues: dropsy, gout, poor circulation, loneliness and deepening depression.

Early in 1618 John Chamberlain had noted, 'the Queen is not well, but they say languisheth whether with melancholy or sickness, and continues at Whitehall being scant able to remove'.[14] But as we have seen she did rouse herself to beg her 'kind Dog' Villiers to beg the King 'that Sir Walter Ralegh's life may not be called in question'.

The Great Cordial could save neither of them now. The lords were busy following up Sir Walter's undercover dealings with the French. They planned to interrogate members of Stucley's party, and of Ralegh's Guiana expedition. They debated the best way to gratify King James and Philip the Pious of Spain in disposing of the troublesome knight as quickly and quietly as possible, but with all the appearance of justice. Ralegh's recurrent nostalgic dream of restoring his fortune to what it was during the great days of Elizabeth was empty and, in the present sad state of the kingdom, even his old petition to Anne echoed hollowly in his head.

> If I have sold my duty, sold my faith
> To strangers, which was only due to one,
> Nothing I should esteem as dear as death,
>
> But if both God and time shall make you know
> That I, your humble vassal, am oppressed,
> Then cast your eyes on undeserved woe,
>
> That I and mine may never mourn the miss
> Of her we had, but praise our living Queen
> Who brings us equal, if no greater, bliss.[15]

13

JUDAS

I t had been a long two months, but in the end Sir Lewis Stucley had done a difficult job well. King James had to acknowledge that, though he seems to have half-wished that Ralegh had got away. Maybe His Majesty had calculated that Stucley would be incapable of holding on to so slippery an operator. John Aubrey tells us that the King considered Ralegh 'a coward to be so taken and conveyed, for else he might easily have made his escape from so slight a guard'.[1]

Now James had to do something with him and be seen to do it with princely wisdom and justice. He had promised him to Madrid, where Philip the Pious would exact his people's ritual revenge by executing the impious English pirate and his captains in the Plaza Mayor. James anticipated trouble from the anti-Spanish faction in the Council, the court and the country. Ralegh was an embarrassment. If only he had gone quietly.

Sir Walter was safely in the Tower. Stucley was out in the world, at the mercy of his enemies. After Ralegh's many years out of circulation, followed by a disastrous expedition, it was a wonder he had so many supporters; Stucley had not anticipated that. That he had simply obeyed His Majesty's commands did not persuade the public. That he had implemented his orders with consideration went unregarded. The King and the Privy Council might thank him privately, but the world was against him.

Still, he put in his bill to the Exchequer 'for bringing up out of Devonshire the person of Sir Walter Ralegh, Knight'. For all his trouble, for supervising the arrest of the *Destiny* and the dispersal of its cargo, for the costs incurred in hiring horses and coaches, and for paying members of the escort, including the French physician Dr Guillaume Manoury, for their mounts' stabling and hay and the men's bed and board en route, his charge was £932 6s 3d. It was worth something like half a million pounds in today's terms.

When they heard how Stucley had sworn his love for Sir Walter and embraced him so warmly moments before he turned to arrest him at Greenwich, people within the court and without spoke openly of Stucley's reward as 'thirty pieces of silver'. Sir Lewis was soon universally derided as Sir 'Judas' Stucley.

Stucley needed his blood money. He had inherited the family seat of Affeton Castle in mid-Devon in 1610, but a life of indulgence in London was more to the Vice Admiral of Devon's taste than the care and nurture of his rural inheritance. Within a decade 8,000 acres of the estate had been sold off, and Sir Lewis's son, John, was later compelled to mortgage Affeton for £1,000.[2]

The day after he delivered Ralegh into the hands of the Lieutenant of the Tower, on 11 August 1618, feeling the weight of unjust opprobrium, Stucley sat down to write his own *Appollogie*.[3]

I know full well that all actions of men, of whatever condition, in these censorious times shall be scanned, as already I am informed mine have been in the execution of my Sovereign's late commands. Even since yesterday that I performed the same, committing Sir Walter Ralegh, and some of his adherents and instruments to his intended escape from out of my custody, to the Tower. I have been accused for conspiracy and falsehood towards him.

He wanted to persuade honest men that he had done his duty, obeying orders from above: those of 12 June from the Lord High Admiral, followed by a letter from Mr Secretary, His Majesty's commission to arrest Sir Walter. Even this he had interpreted as flexibly as possible, allowing his cousin time and trust, and earning himself a rebuke from the Privy Council, dated 23 July,[4] chiding him for his delays and excuses.

At Salisbury, he reported, he had done everything possible for Ralegh, as Sir Walter must agree and their lordships too, for he, Stucley, had wearied them with solicitations over and above what good manners required, 'for the accomplishment of all his desires'. He had been a faithful go-between, for Sir Walter never had 'an ill return or negative answer to any request I made in his behalf'.

Rather than catalogue all that happened between Plymouth and London, he simply wrote of his cousin: 'I omit to repeat over the travail, pains, and care I had in all his sickness, and I appeal to his conscience, and the testimony of his own people, whether I declared myself friendly and lovingly or not.' He protested that he could not have pitied those afflictions more if they had befallen his own son, or himself. He presented a picture of familial sympathy.

At Andover, he wrote, he first discovered that Ralegh was hatching a plot. Sir Walter had taken advantage of all his supposed sufferings to win sympathy, to gain Mr Vice Chamberlain's pity and His Majesty's leave to spend five days at home where, instead of ordering his affairs before his committal, he would implement his plan of escape. 'A perfect light whereof I have not yet,' Stucley wrote, 'but credible information I had, as the event hath manifested.'

If Sir Lewis wanted to shed 'a perfect light' on the episode, he would have consulted Dr Manoury and others. But the fact that the *Appollogie* makes no mention of Manoury, nor of Sir William St John, William Herbert, Cottrell, Hart, De la Chesnée and Le Clerc, raises the question of how much Stucley is trying to reveal or conceal. To save his blushes he played down the extent to which he had been gulled. To save his neck he played down how much he had been tempted to go along with Ralegh's plans.

He admitted, 'Sure I am so easy a man, and so good natured did he find me,' that Sir Walter tried to lure him into colluding with his escape. He realised how gross an abuse of His Majesty's goodness Ralegh had intended. Stucley could not but abhor his hypocrisy, and to unmask it effectively he pretended complicity, once he saw that nothing would persuade Sir Walter 'to rectify his affection and judgment'. Between Staines and London, Stucley augmented his knowledge of Ralegh's intentions with the discovery of his secret dealings. In fact, Sir Walter's plans had been not so much 'discovered' as betrayed wholesale to 'cousin' William Herbert by Cottrell and Hart, and carried to Stucley on horseback by Sir William St John, Villiers's half-brother.

The court and the King already knew too much. Stucley had to play it straight from that moment on. Shortly after he learnt that Ralegh's scheme had been uncovered, he wrote, His Majesty sent him an injunction to secrecy, along with a commission to do exactly what he had done. That was his authority, and his excuse. There had been no alternative. The matter had grown to be the King's secret; to reveal it or to disobey would have been 'in me treasonous treachery'.

Sir 'Judas' could not win. No apology could make amends. If he had not protested he would have been damned in any case for betraying his kinsman. But everyone who read his *Appollogie* saw that he protested too much. His tragedy was that nothing could stop him being crushed by Ralegh's fall.

It was almost over for Ralegh, but not for Stucley. On official business the Vice Admiral of Devon visited Lord Admiral Charles Howard, whose relationship with Ralegh had not been untroubled.[5] But when Sir Lewis appeared at his door, he had a vision of his younger self: the Charles Howard who once knelt down to wipe the dust from Sir Walter's shoes with his cloak. Remembering his then unalloyed admiration for Ralegh, he picked up his staff.

'What, thou base fellow!' he bellowed at Stucley. 'Thou, the scorn and contempt of men, how darest thou offer thyself in my presence?'

In his fury he raised his staff and threatened to beat him from the house. Sir Lewis made an undignified retreat.

He was met with insults and threats wherever he went. As Vice Admiral of Devon he dared not return to his jurisdiction for fear of literal or verbal cudgelling, for Devonshire was still the territory of the great Sir Walter Ralegh. He paid court to King James and complained that he went in fear of his life because he had obeyed His Majesty's commands. The King responded as if to a whining boy.

'What wouldst thou have me do?' he asked. 'If I should hang all that speak ill of thee, all the trees in my kingdom would not suffice.'

Sir Lewis could not say what was in his heart, but the King paused as he paced, or shuffled, up and down the audience chamber hanging on to Villiers's arm.

'I have done amiss,' he said.

James knew what he had done, but he also understood where the blame for it would lie. Few of his subjects would trouble to unpick the tangled skeins of betrayal. He glanced at the obedient, fawning supplicant before him and delivered his parting shot.

'Sir Lewis,' he declared, 'Ralegh's blood be upon thy head.'

Sir Walter's last revenge would be still harder for Sir Lewis to bear. At the end of October, when he made his final speech from the scaffold, Ralegh announced that he had forgiven Stucley. There could have been no stronger condemnation.

Stung by Ralegh's last words Stucley resolved to clear his name by issuing a formal petition addressed to the King and thus to his peers at court.[6] Stucley's *Petition* and King James's *Declaration* were both 'Imprinted at London by Bonham Norton and John Bill, Printers to the King's most Excellent Majesty' and published on successive days, four weeks after Ralegh's death.[7] Stucley's *Petition* was not simply a private citizen's address to His Majesty; it was a significant shot in the official propaganda campaign to justify Ralegh's execution by the state.

Stucley did not even write his petition himself. A letter of 4 December gossips that 'Sir L.S.'s pamphlet was penned by Dr Sharpe'.[8] Dr Lionel Sharpe, a Devonshire rector, was violently anti-Catholic and anti-Spanish. He had been chosen to speak Queen Elizabeth's oration to the assembled army at Tilbury in 1588, and later became chaplain to Prince Henry.[9] He began: 'To the King's most Excellent Majesty. The humble petition and information of Sir Lewis Stucley, Knight vice-Admiral of Devon, touching his own behaviour in the charge committed unto him, for the bringing up of Sir Walter Ralegh, and the scandalous aspersions cast upon him for the same.'[10]

The *Petition* runs to seventeen quarto pages. It begins eloquently but grows increasingly clotted with the outbursts of an angry, envious man who, in the anguish of betrayal, and despite Dr Sharpe's shaping hand, intemperately heaps up accusations, slurs and grudges against his kinsman turned enemy:

> I have no pleasure to fight with a ghost; but seeing an angel of darkness did put on him the shape of an angel of light at his departure, to perform two parts most cunningly: first, to poison the hearts of discontented people;

secondly, to blemish me in my good name, a poor instrument of the just desires of the State, with false imputations.

Give me leave, most gracious Sovereign, to speak for
myself, which I do not to insult . . . the dead, but to defend
myself against the false reports of the living, taken from
the dead upon trust, to strike me directly, but through my
sides indirectly, aiming at a higher mark.

Dr Sharpe probably enjoyed this clumsy image: Ralegh's
arrow passing through Stucley to strike at his real target, the
King. 'All men have long known that this man's whole life was
a mere sophistication, and such was his death, in which he
borrowed some tincture of holiness, which he was thought not
to love in his life, therewith to cover his hatred of others in his
death.' Stucley maintained that Ralegh promised him his love
when he was in the Tower, but once on the scaffold he vented
his hatred. 'An uncharitable charity, not much unlike that man's
repentance, who purposing to hang himself, writes his repentance of that sin beforehand in his book, which he did purpose
to commit.' Here he alluded to Sir Walter's suicidal impulse,
and wished Ralegh had given more convincing evidence of a
change of heart than religious words at his death designed to
work upon men's feelings, 'thereby to infuse more warily the
venom of sedition into the hearts of as many as he might', and
to score points against the King by spending 'his malice upon
me your poor servant, who did nothing but execute your just
commands'.

Ralegh's motivation in inviting so many to witness his death,
Stucley claimed, was to leave a legacy of hatred against him, by
which others would destroy him. 'Yea but it was the testimony
of a dying man, now a penitent (as all say), as some say, a saint
. . . yea, but it was the testimony of an enemy, of a perjured, of
a condemned man,' a man, Stucley implied, still full of rage and
bitterness at the death sentence His Majesty had dealt him in
1603.

Stucley justifies his own pure motives and dutiful conduct and compares them to Ralegh's dishonesty and bad behaviour: the pretence of the gold mine; his misconduct in Guiana; his conspiracy with the French and attempted escapes; his past mistreatment of Sir Lewis's father, John Stucley; his disloyal sentiments uttered against Queen Elizabeth; his plot against Essex and his insults on the occasion the Earl's execution; and, in Manoury's hearing, his expressions of disloyalty to King James, when he said 'that if he had escaped, he was like to prove as dangerous a traitor to this Crown, as ever Antonio de Peres was to the Crown of Spain'.

If this was not enough, Stucley alleged that Sir Walter made a promise upon the Bible to his ship's company which he intended to break, an oath considered fateful by Lady Elizabeth Ralegh: 'which perjury, his Lady hath said, was the cause of all his ruin'.

Stucley also claimed that Ralegh had informed him that his one remaining friend in high places, Lord Carew, gave him advice about his escape. Sir Lewis said he no longer believed this, 'but that Ralegh told it unto *Stucley*, yea, and that many times, I will avow it unto death, and take the sacrament upon it'. Here, in expressing this most solemn of oaths, the ventriloquist's lips moved: it was the only time in the *Petition* that Dr Sharpe slipped from first person into third and wrote 'Stucley' instead of 'me'.

More examples of Ralegh's mendaciousness followed in quick succession. 'Certainly perjury was but a peccadillo with this man . . . No Coriolanus heart could be more vindictive than he was unto them to whom he did impute his fault.'

'Yea, but he died most resolutely,' said public opinion.

'Yea, but he was taken most sheepishly,' Stucley replied. 'Never was there man, out of the conscience of his own corruption and guiltiness so cowed at his taking, as he was; trembling and weeping to come before justice.'

'Yea but he gathered his spirits afterwards, and died resolutely.'

'Even so hath many a Jesuit died at Tyburn ... But with this difference, that they died in hope of false martyrdom, and this with a desire of false popular fame.'

'But he died like a saint too.'

'He hath before very much called his saintship into dispute by the carriage of his life.'

Stucley's *Appollogie* had little effect and his *Petition* only served to add to the scorn and contempt in which the world held him. His tract simply helped to shift liability from the King to himself. In it everyone could read his mean spirit, his petty grudges and his vindictive attempts to deface a great corpse for the sake of his own meagre complexion.

The King blatantly had betrayed Ralegh and made Stucley his scapegoat. Sir Lewis had been faced with an impossible choice: either to obey his king and betray his kinsman, or be loyal to his cousin and incur His Majesty's wrath.

Sir 'Judas' became *persona non grata* throughout England. London society was intolerable to him. Even thirty pieces of silver – or £932 6s 3d – were not sufficient to service Stucley's debts. Five months after he was paid for delivering Ralegh to the Tower he and his son were accused of clipping coin.[11] To clip, or pare away the edges of the coin of the realm, was, in Macaulay's words, 'one of the ... most profitable kinds of fraud'.[12] He was condemned on the dubious testimony of a servant, one Guillaume Manoury. However, perhaps because the King knew in his heart how much he owed Stucley, he was given a royal pardon.

'Judas' Stucley was now Vice Admiral of a county loyal to Ralegh. His home there, Affeton Castle, could not defend him from his detractors. His aunt, Mary Grenville, took pity on him and persuaded her son Sir Barnard Grenville to offer him sanctuary on their property, Lundy Island, eleven miles off the coast of north Devon.

The island's name comes from the Norse, *lunde*, which means puffin. It is a little plateau of lumpy land, three miles by half a mile, slung between sheer granite cliffs which stand three to four hundred feet above the Bristol Channel. It is inaccessible, except for where, in a small section of Devonian slates at the south-east end, the sea has bitten a small cove, sheltered by tiny Rat Island. A notorious haunt of Algerian and Spanish smugglers and privateers, Queen Elizabeth had once threatened to confiscate the island from the Grenvilles for maladministration; a naval force was sent to cleanse it. Anciently a royal warren, its granite castle of 1244 had been paid for by the sale of rabbits. Sir Lewis Stucley exiled himself there, to live among rabbits, puffins and outlaws.

He lost his mind too, and it was said he wandered about the island raving. Some conclude that he suffered from guilt-induced dementia.[13] In the summer of 1620, less than two years after Sir Walter was beheaded, Camden notes that 'Stucley, who betrayed Ralegh, has in some manner died mad'.[14] He had fought with a ghost and lost. His corpse was shipped to the mainland and buried at the market town of South Molton. Even in death, he did not quite get home to his castle of Affeton or the church[15] where his ancestors lay.

14

INTRIGUES AND
INTERROGATIONS

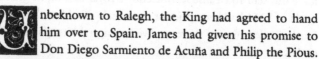nbeknown to Ralegh, the King had agreed to hand him over to Spain. James had given his promise to Don Diego Sarmiento de Acuña and Philip the Pious. Between August and October of 1618 the Lords of the Privy Council gathered, elicited, extracted and subpoenaed as many fragments of information as they could from which to construct a narrative to present to the King. It would be issued in his name and offered to his subjects as *A Declaration of the Demeanor and Cariage of Sir Walter Raleigh, Knight, aswell in his Voyage, as in, and sithence his Returne; And of the true motives and inducements which occasioned His Majestie to proceed in doing justice upon him, as hath bene done.*[1] It had to make sense of what was already known, and it had to be a consistent story which justified His Majesty's submission to the Spanish authorities.

The Privy Council's first recorded examination took place at the Tower. The name of the man they interrogated appears nowhere else. His evidence implies that he was aboard the *Destiny* off Trinidad but he is not listed among the ships' masters or captains of land forces who accompanied Ralegh to Guiana. He has no place in Ralegh's journal of the voyage or in any of his letters. There is no record of what he did on the voyage or what he felt at the time. We do not know whether or not he travelled from Plymouth to London with Ralegh under Stucley's escort. It is clear that he was a member of the Guiana expedition and a close prisoner in the Tower from the day Sir Walter was brought there. Perhaps he was one of those who waited in captivity to be transported to Madrid with Ralegh.

We have notes of the answers he gave to the Privy Council, or to be exact – and we can be exact because their names are subscribed to his deposition – to five of its members: the Archbishop of Canterbury, George Abbot; the Lord Chancellor, Sir Francis Bacon; the Lord Privy Seal, the Earl of Worcester; the Master of the Rolls, Sir Julius Caesar; and the Privy Councillor and ex-Chief Justice, Sir Edward Coke, who, along with Secretary Naunton, formed the special commission of enquiry. How much of this man's evidence was noted down and how much was ignored we do not know. He may have lived long and done much, but he entered recorded history and exited from it again on this particular day, Friday 4 September 1618. His name was Robert Mearing.

'I thought the French physician, Manoury, was true to me,' Ralegh told Mearing on the morning Stucley delivered him into the Tower, 'but now I see that he aggravated Sir Lewis Stucley against me; for everything he told me about Sir Lewis he told Sir Lewis as if I had spoken it against him.' Then, continuing to pace up and down the Lieutenant's dining-chamber, Sir Walter added, 'I have heard that Sir Lewis sent Manoury to the King.'

Mearing remembered that conversation clearly enough. He also recalled how Cristóbal Guayacunda was brought to Ralegh at Trinidad. Sir Walter had first spoken to him on the deck of the *Destiny* in the hearing of the ship's company. After that they had many conversations in the cabin and elsewhere. Guayacunda talked about the gold mine, Mearing said, and Sir Walter berated

Laurence Keymis and his party for not interrogating him about it.

'If you did not know where it was,' Ralegh had said, 'you had Spaniards who could have told you, as well as the Indian. There were but two means to get the information from him, using him well or using him hardly, and you tried neither.'

Asked why he had not revealed the mine to them, Guaya-cunda replied that he had no reason to. 'You killed my master and my friends,' he said, 'and made a drudge of me, and set me to grind corn, and you took away my fine clothes and did not respect me.'

The Lords asked Robert Mearing how he had known what was said, seeing that he did not understand the language. He explained that Sir Walter had interpreted it in his hearing, and in the hearing of many others.[2]

Five days later, on Wednesday 9 September, the Lords interrogated the French agent's interpreter, Davide de Noyon, Seigneur De la Chesnée.[3] He conceded that he had indeed seen Ralegh three times, first at Brentford, eight miles from London, and twice at Ralegh's house in Broad Street. He had simply been enquiring about a certain Frenchman (meaning Manoury) who had made the journey from Plymouth with Sir Walter. His visits had no other purpose. There was no talk of any other matter. He had no knowledge of any boat prepared for Ralegh's flight, nor of his intention to retire to France. He had never spoken about anything to do with making an escape attempt.

The Lords did not believe De la Chesnée. They committed him into the custody of Mr Edmond Doubleday, a Justice of the Peace for Middlesex, who was required to keep the French-man in his house. De la Chesnée was not allowed to confer with anyone or send or receive any messages or letters without Doubleday's knowledge.[4]

The next day, at the request of the Spanish agent, who wished to deflect English anger, a proclamation was issued remitting the fines and imprisonment imposed upon the rioters at the house of the Spanish ambassador.[5]

At the same time the lords wrote to Sir Thomas Wilson, Keeper of the State Papers, a man who had learned espionage in Walsingham's service and had been rewarded with a pension for his work as a government spy on the Bye and Main plots in 1603. His Majesty had ordered that a trusted person be planted upon Ralegh, and the Privy Council 'thought fit to make choice of you for that purpose'.[6] Sir Thomas was to report to the Tower where Sir Allen Apsley, the Lieutenant, would provide him 'with diet, lodging, and all other things necessary'. There was no need to give such an old hand instructions, other than to keep Ralegh a close prisoner and not allow anyone access to him except in his hearing, and then only those who brought him meals and other necessities. 'And whatsoever you shall observe worthy of advertisement to acquaint us with it from time to time as becometh you.'

Sir Thomas wasted no time. He was in place within twenty-four hours. His coming 'bred a wonderment' among officers of the Tower who exclaimed that Sir Walter's days would be short, as if Sir Thomas had been a messenger of death. He wrote to Mr Secretary, Sir Robert Naunton, that same Friday evening: 'I can say little yet to any purpose.'[7] He had found Ralegh lying on a bed in the Wardrobe Tower. When Apsley introduced them, Ralegh said, 'You are welcome. Let the King do even what he will with me, for never man was more desirous to die.'

There were two windows, Sir Thomas wrote, from either of which he considered letters might be thrown to close confederates. Ralegh had a man, also a prisoner, who attended him to dress his sores. This was Ralegh's old page, Robin. Sir Thomas asked whether this servant should be replaced with a man of his own. He also wished to know if he should admit the apothecary and surgeon who were due at eight the next morning. For himself, he begged the lords to write to Apsley about his accommodation: 'one poor bare-walled prison chamber ... both for my men and myself right over Sir W.'s lodgings.'

On his copy of the letter he also noted that there had been a heated argument about the keys. Apsley had told him that it was contrary to his oath to relinquish them and that keepers never had their own keys, but were locked up at night with their charges. Next day Sir Thomas wrote a second letter to Mr Secretary, explaining that he would not take absolute charge of Ralegh until he had keys.[8] He had asked for better lodgings too, he said, and traipsed about the Tower all day looking for a place, but Northumberland, the 'Wizard Earl', and Lady Shrewsbury had the best accommodation. There was a Brick Tower, Sir Thomas wrote, the Master of the Ordnance's lodging, which the Lieutenant was happy for him to use, but when Apsley asked Northumberland for it 'he answered he could not spare it, for his son must lie there when he cometh, which seems strange to me, that he, having all the King's fairest lodgings must possess that also which is so far off for his son, who is so seldom here'. The noblest prisoner in the Tower, Ralegh's old friend, still exercised enormous influence.

Sir Thomas next asked that Ralegh be moved to the chamber above his, so that he would hear when he or anyone with him stirred, and, because it was so high, his prisoner would be unable to convey letters or anything else from it. But Ralegh flatly refused to leave his cell unless they carried him out by force.

Sir Thomas gave the Privy Council an ultimatum: Apsley must be issued with a warrant, either to house them all in the Brick Tower or to remove Sir Walter to the upper chamber, 'otherwise I dare take no charge of him'. He asked again whether Robin, the page who had attended Ralegh for so long, should be replaced by a man who could be trusted to supervise 'the going out and coming in of his linen apparel and other things' at times when he, Sir Thomas, was writing or otherwise employed.

Before he had finished penning this letter, Ralegh sent to speak with him. He had remembered a door at the entrance to his chamber where there was a convenient lodging for Sir Thomas, if the Lieutenant was agreeable. Apsley showed it to Sir Thomas, who found it very convenient, but still felt that Ralegh should be shifted. Sir Walter was suspiciously reluctant to leave his cell, as if a move would spoil arrangements he had secretly contrived and deprive him of access, via the windows, to two blind passages.

Meanwhile Ralegh wallowed in misery. His afflictions were too much to bear. A stitch under his right side had made it hard to breathe. His physician, Dr Guyn, and his brother, the King's apothecary, had applied poultices that were too strong; they excoriated his flesh, causing holes in his side which ulcerated, but even after these had healed he was left with a great swelling which was beginning to form an abscess. He thought it would soon burst. His liver was swollen too, he said, so that he would need no other death.

Sir Thomas suspected that he was exaggerating and discussed his condition with Dr Guyn, who confirmed Ralegh's symptoms but not his prognosis. Sir Thomas also learnt, from an officer, that with the help of Robin, Ralegh had caused his own problem by treating himself without a doctor's advice in order to create a wound where there was none before.

For all his pining and groaning, Sir Thomas noted that if he got Ralegh talking about his late voyage or former actions, he responded immediately with as much heartiness and cheerfulness as the soundest and strongest man.

'Why would you want to escape if you had no design for France?' Sir Thomas had asked Ralegh.

'I proposed to escape before ever I met the Frenchman,' said Ralegh, 'because I understood that the Spaniard would be satisfied with nothing but my life. I thought I should be welcome in France because I had offended the Spaniard.'

'The King, as you know, is so merciful,' said Sir Thomas, 'that he will forgive you and do you good if you reveal the plans the French had for you, or anything else that may do the King service.'

'If I had in my heart or knowledge anything that might do the King service,' said Ralegh, 'I would write it to him this very night.'

Sir Thomas noted that he said this with protestations that might convince a credulous man, or a mere child unaware of his cunning. Sir Allen Apsley, the Lieutenant, came into the cell at that point and interrupted their conversation with enquiries about the finances of the Guiana voyage.

For the next couple of days Sir Thomas pursued his quarry with quiet questions and a seemingly sympathetic ear. Ralegh told him how Northampton and Suffolk had plotted to be rid of him when King James came to the throne in 1603. He reminisced about his long years in the Tower. He was frank about his recent escape plans, proposing to go to France so that, if Prince Charles's Spanish marriage did not come off, there would be a French one, and he would be well placed. In any case he felt that Queen Anne would in time procure his pardon and recall him to England.

'Was Stucley acquainted with your purpose?' Sir Thomas enquired.

'Yes,' said Ralegh, 'but as we were journeying up we met with Sir William St John and cousin William Herbert. Stucley went out of the coach and spoke to them, and when he got back in he told me that my plans were betrayed and I was but a lost man.'

Then Ralegh accused Stucley of slandering him, by claiming that he had offered him ten thousand pounds to assist in his escape and by maintaining that Lord Carew and Lord Doncaster were ready to help him reach France.

'If only you would reveal all you know,' said Sir Thomas, 'the King will forgive and favour you.'

'How can I be assured of that?' said Ralegh. 'When all is told, he will say, the craven was afraid for his life or else he would not have told it, and therefore no God a mercy.'

From this outburst, Sir Thomas concluded that he did have something to tell. But Ralegh later said: 'I know nothing worth the revealing.'

The next day Ralegh was deep in misery once more. Sir Thomas assured him of God's mercy and spoke of those who had suffered as grievously as flesh and blood could bear, yet had been restored to felicity. Ralegh was not to be fobbed off with easy comfort.

'The Romans are to be praised', he said, 'for bravely killing themselves, rather than meeting a base death.' He commended those suicides of ancient and recent times who had chosen death with courage: Socrates, for example, and the Wizard Earl's father, who had killed himself in the Tower. 'Some divines hold that a man may do it,' he added, 'to avoid shame or for other respects, and yet die in the favour of God and be saved.'

Sir Thomas grimly noted that, having argued with him for argument's sake, he had no fear that Ralegh would summon up that Roman courage, even though he lacked the Christian armour that should defend him from it.

Apsley wanted to remove Ralegh's array of drugs and medicinal compounds from the room.

'If I choose to kill myself,' said Sir Walter, 'I have only to run my head against a post.'

His drugs remained in place.

'Has Sir Lewis Stucley misreported you,' Sir Thomas asked later, when he judged it a good moment, 'in saying that you told him that the French agent had provided a barque for your escape?'

'I never said a word about the French agent,' Ralegh replied, 'for I do not know what man he is. But I had polite conversation with the French gentleman De la Chesnée, and told Sir Lewis that he had promised me a barque. I told him so to encourage him to come with me, so that if the other barque failed, he might have two strings to his bow. I told him that De la Chesnée had assured me of it, which was not true, but I said it to reassure him.'

'Why then,' said Sir Thomas, 'should De la Chesnée come to meet with you, to your stair at Brentford, and afterwards to your house, at a third time, at the very time of your escape?'

Ralegh was taken aback at this mention of three visits. He was sure that no one had seen either De la Chesnée or Le Clerc on the second occasion. Sir Thomas was watching his reaction, and observed how he often answered questions with questions in order to get more out of the replies than Sir Thomas intended to give away. Ralegh asked why he spoke of three visits from the Frenchman, but Sir Thomas was not to be drawn.

'De la Chesnée was never with me but twice,' said Ralegh. 'I wondered at his coming to me at Brentford, and also to my house, for he knew I was under guard at both places.'

On 16 September, at eight o'clock in the evening, a man called François de Vertou, alias De la Forest, who worked for the French agent, met Dr Manoury by chance. Among other things, Manoury informed him that there was a man of quality, a knight though not a Privy Councillor, who had tried to bribe him to accuse the agent, Le Clerc, of having had dealings with Sir Walter Ralegh. Manoury said he refused to level such an accusation. The gentleman had pressed him about it on three separate occasions. The last time, he tried to persuade him that he, Manoury, had already told him about Ralegh's meeting with Le Clerc and that it was essential he stick to the story.

De la Forest had reported this conversation to Le Clerc the following day. Le Clerc sent for Manoury at once, and the physician confirmed what he had told De la Forest but would not name the gentleman concerned.

'Was he Sir Lewis Stucley?' Le Clerc asked.

'No,' said Manoury.

The Lords had employed Sir Thomas Wilson to worm information out of Raleigh with sympathy and subtlety but, as the spy confessed, Sir Walter was too cunning to be caught. They compiled a list of straightforward questions that they would put to Ralegh, and to the other witnesses they called, as follows:

Did Sir Walter really intend a mine in Guiana, or only pretend it to abuse the state and attract followers?

Did he appear to know that the country of Guiana near the mine was inhabited by Spaniards?

Was the assault on San Thomé intended and directed by him, or was it attacked incidentally by those who were sent to discover the mine?

Did he have any commission or aid from France?

Did he intend to make for France at the end of the voyage?

What would his employment be there?

Who was most intimate with him during the voyage?

The next day, William Herbert, Sir Walter's cousin and a close friend of Villiers's half-brother Sir William St John, was examined before the Lords at Whitehall.[9]

'Sir Walter was sincere about the mine, I believe,' Herbert said, 'though he had not seen it himself, but took Keymis's word for it. Keymis told me that Sir Walter never went to the mine.

'Both Ralegh and Keymis knew that the country was inhabited by Spaniards, and that San Thomé, near the mine, was a town of Spaniards.

'Regarding the attack, I can say nothing of Sir Walter, because he was not there when the orders were given. But the Spanish attacked us first, at night, within half a mile of the town, while we were consulting whether to set upon the town or go forward. Even before the captains and officers consulted, there was much discussion among the private gentlemen as to whether our commission authorised us to assault the town.

'At dinner in Plymouth Sir Walter spoke quite openly about a commission he had which he said he would show us at the Canary Islands. He did not say whether it was a French one, or ever show it as far as I know. The captains' gossip had it that it was a French commission.

'Captain Whitney was most intimate with Ralegh on the voyage,' Herbert said, 'but he went to Newfoundland, and is now gone for the straits.

'I never heard anything from Sir Walter himself about French ships, but the captains understood that two of them should have joined us, and that Captain Faige, a French soldier who was often in Ralegh's company and parted from him at Plymouth, should have come with them.'

Herbert had already proved his loyalty to the Crown by manning the wherry that finally caught up with his cousin. George Ralegh, Sir Walter's nephew, also turned against his uncle. They, and the other captains implicated in the assault on San Thomé, volunteered evidence not only to add weight to the case against Sir Walter, but to recoup as much of what they had invested in the voyage as possible, and to save their own skins. They had no wish to be dispatched to Madrid to share Ralegh's fate.

Captain Roger North was next.

'I think Ralegh did not believe there was a mine. Keymis behaved confidently until we took San Thomé, but after that his errors were so gross that it all seemed extremely unlikely. The Moors who came over to our side, never said anything about a mine. Later, I heard Sir Walter say that if there had been a mine we could not have profited from it at that time, but that he had meant to bring back a sample of its ore to save his credit with the King and with you, my Lords, which was his chief desire.

'Ralegh expostulated vehemently with Keymis in public, but was soon private with him in his cabin, and ate and drank with him as before. He gave Sergeant Major George Ralegh bitter words too, but told him not to take offence, for his anger was only for show.

'Ralegh clearly knew Guiana to be inhabited by Spaniards,' North declared 'for before we left London he said he knew where we might make a saving voyage in tobacco; and on the passage itself he said we might be sure of forty thousand pounds weight, or worth, I am not sure which, of tobacco if we could surprise the town.

'Our land forces disembarked, on George Ralegh's orders, five miles short of the town at four o'clock in the afternoon. Wat Ralegh was very forward. Indian guides led us along the track to the town while the boats continued up the river. The first shot that landed among us came out of the wood at eleven o'clock at night.

'I have heard that Sir Walter had a commission from France,' North said. 'Captain Faige, who took a liking to me, told me in great secrecy at Plymouth that he was to go to France and then rendezvous with Sir Walter at sea; he showed me a letter from a port in Normandy, which I took to be Newhaven or Dieppe, saying that two ships were ready for him.

'After Keymis's death I heard Ralegh say – and I think Captain Pennington was present at the time – that he would make for France, for he was unsure how events would be interpreted in England. Clarke, the gunner's mate on the *Destiny*, told me that Ralegh assured those of his crew who were determined to stay at sea that he would not bring his ship to England.'[10]

Captain John Chudleigh was questioned on the same day.

'I urged Sir Walter, who was then lying sick unto death in his cabin, in the presence of Captain Pennington, to appoint a chief over us in case he died, and give orders regarding the mine. But Sir Walter refused, and told us to agree a chief amongst ourselves, for he could not assign his commission. He claimed he had a French commission which would do us good against the Spaniard.

'While we waited off Trinidad, nine or ten weeks, Sir Walter never spoke encouragingly about the mine, but repeatedly tried to persuade us to sail to the Caribbean Islands instead, abandoning the men who searched for the gold.'[11]

Sir Thomas Wilson got his way. He evicted Ralegh's page, Robin, and replaced him with his own man, possibly a relative, Edward Wilson. A better lodging had at last been requisitioned in the Brick Tower. Northumberland's son would have to find another place to stay on his rare visits. 'I have been wholly busied in removing this man,' Sir Thomas wrote of Ralegh, 'to a safer and higher lodging, which though it seems nearer heaven, yet is there no means of escape from thence for him to any place but hell.'[12]

In the move Sir Thomas was able to examine all his captive's trinkets and take an inventory of them. There was nothing of value, but for the sapphire seal ring Stucley had allowed Ralegh to keep. 'As for the dear diamond which is spoken of, he saith he had never any such of Queen Elizabeth's giving.' Did they suppose that Ralegh was still concealing a valuable stone given him by the late Queen, which he had in addition to the diamond ring already listed in Stucley's inventory? 'The things that he seems to make most reckoning of are his chemical stuffs, amongst which there are so many spirits of things that I think there is none wanting that I ever heard of, unless it be the spirit of God.'

All the while the old spy kept the closest watch on the man himself and the cunning words he uttered.

'What kind of man is the French agent?' Ralegh asked him. 'Is he a wise fellow or no?'

Sir Thomas could not tell whether Ralegh really wanted to find out, in order to know if he had confided in a reliable accomplice, or whether he intended to make him believe he had never had dealings with Le Clerc.

'Sir, why do you ask me this question?' Sir Thomas responded. 'You know him better than I.'

'As I am a dishonest man, I do not,' Sir Walter protested.

By that evening, Sir Thomas had convinced him that his masters knew all about the French connection. When confronted with the intelligence Stucley had fed them, Ralegh realised that Le Clerc had not after all gone unobserved at his house as he had hoped. What could he do but admit to the meeting? He told Sir Thomas that De la Chesnée had brought the French agent to his house, though for some reason he said they came not on Saturday night but on Sunday morning.

'What conference did you have with him?' said Sir Thomas.

'About that I will write to the King,' said Ralegh, adding, 'if I may have leave.'

Sir Thomas told him he would soon know, for he had already written to the court to get permission. Not long afterwards Sir Allen Apsley, the Lieutenant, returned with the King's reply.

'His Majesty is pleased to give you leave to write unto him,' he said, 'provided you write no trivial or delusory or dilatory things; for if you do, assuredly you must look for no favour but for death.'

Ralegh glimpsed light here: the chance of something other than death.

'You have so lost your reputation for truth that no man believes any word you say,' Apsley continued, and concluded with a story. 'There was once a king who had been so much deluded with false tales and dealing by a subject of his who, as he said, had always fed him with nothing but smoke, and that therefore he should die with smoke.'

Ralegh was famous for lies, then, and smoke. He may have

puffed at his pipe as he listened to this brief fable from the real King, the one who had written a *Counterblast to Tobacco.*

'I will write nothing to his Majesty but truth, and such things as will be material,' Sir Walter answered. 'I will write it this afternoon.'

Sir Thomas allowed Ralegh to have pens and such like only when he was present to supervise him. 'You must write it tomorrow,' he said, 'for I have business to attend to this afternoon.'

Sir Thomas was off to visit Lady Carew, who was in town. Her husband was Ralegh's confidant, Lord George Carew, the cousin Sir Walter had implicated in his escape plot, according to Stucley.

Lady Carew told Sir Thomas she believed the French agent had no commission to deal with Sir Walter, but might have obtained one, or done it on his own iniative. She had sources she would not name, but discussed Le Clerc's contacts on the court's fringes, mentioning a particular Frenchman, whose name, sadly, is missing or illegible in Sir Thomas's surviving report to Naunton.[13] She reported Queen Anne as saying she would much prefer a French marriage to a Spanish one for Prince Charles, despite all the Spanish lady's gold. She said Le Clerc had told her that if Sir Walter went to France he would be welcome. She had asked what Ralegh would do there and the agent had replied, '*Il mangera, il boyera, il faira bien.*' He will eat, he will drink, he will do well.

The following day Sir Thomas Wilson was delighted when Sir Walter wrote and signed a declaration to the King which told the story of his meetings with De la Chesnée and of his conference with Le Clerc. He added that he did not wish to conceal anything that was true from His Majesty, and confessed that when he wrote to Villiers on 12 August he had smuggled out a little note with the man who had brought his bed from Broad Street to his cell. The note warned De la Chesnée that

Stucley had informed the authorities about his visits and the offer of the French ship, but not, he hoped, about Le Clerc. It was up to them how to respond, the note went on, but if the coming of Le Clerc was not found out by other means, it would not be discovered through him, for he would deny everything.[14] Now, in the hope of the King's mercy, he had admitted it all.

A correspondence soon ensued between Secretary Naunton and Sir Thomas, concerning this mercy that the spy had dangled as bait in front of Sir Walter's eyes. Suddenly the King and his advisers, who had betrayed Ralegh to Spain, were having scruples about the morality of inducing him to confess with spurious promises of clemency. A little casuistry was required to calm the royal breast. Naunton reassured the King that Sir Thomas would not have given Ralegh a firm promise of mercy, although he might have said that confession was his only way to get one. That, Naunton said, was not the same as 'assuring him of your Majesty's mercy', but simply 'the ordinary method used in examining of prisoners'.

For now, Sir Thomas penned an obsequious letter which was dispatched by messenger with Ralegh's at seven o'clock on 18 September. 'According to your Majesty's commandment,' it began, 'I have employed the uttermost of my poor discretion to work out what I could from this arch-hypocrite,' and ended, 'The king of heaven preserve your Majesty from having many such dangerous subjects.'[15]

Sir Walter also wrote to Bess on this most trying day, and sent the note by his keeper, Edward Wilson. It was to accompany a box of cordials from his laboratory which he wanted her to have, for he was concerned about her health. Sir Thomas consulted Secretary Naunton concerning the spirits. Naunton considered that there was no danger in sending to her, but that what she sent in return should be watched. Nevertheless, Sir Thomas kept the box until he had asked the apothecary to identify the spirits. The apothecary could not: 'No man in the

world knows what they are,' he pronounced, 'unless he had
seen the extraction of them.' Still, Bess received the note: 'I am
sick and weak. This honest gent, Master Ed Wilson, is my keeper
and takes much pain with me. My swollen side keeps me in
perpetual pain and unrest. God comfort us.'[16]

Bess sent Mr Wilson back at once with her reply:

> I am sorry to hear among many discomforts that your
> health is so ill, 'tis merely sorrow and grief that with wind
> hath gathered into your side. I hope your health and com-
> forts will mend and mend us for God. I am glad to hear
> you have the company and comfort of so good a keeper.
> I was something dismayed at the first that you had no
> servant of your own left you.[17]

That same day Dr Manoury dined with Le Clerc, De la
Forest and a number of other French gentlemen. The agent
declared that he was obliged to Manoury for having revealed
the plot against him and Manoury confirmed the details of it
before them all. After the physician had left, and the allegations
had been formally noted and witnessed, Le Clerc instructed De
la Forest to find Manoury the next morning and remind him
to stick to what he had promised. Le Clerc ordered De la Forest
not to ask Manoury what that was; he would tell him himself
in due course.

The following day De la Forest and Guillaume Manoury
were both interrogated. De la Forest told the lords that Sir
Walter had committed a great folly by returning to England. If
he had gone to France he would have been well received and
rewarded with a big pension. He could have had letters of
recommendation to whomever he wanted, to the Lords of the
Council of France. Le Clerc, he said, was angry that Ralegh had
come back to England, and believed he was lost.

Without coercion, De la Forest described to the lords how
he had met Dr Manoury by chance and learned how a certain
gentleman had urged him to inform against Le Clerc. He said

that when Le Clerc asked Manoury if the mysterious gentleman was Sir Lewis Stucley, Manoury had said no.

Manoury was nervous about the consequences of what he was embroiled in, but he answered the Lords' questions. He spoke about the gentleman who, three times on the terrace at Whitehall, had pressed him to accuse Le Clerc. This gentleman had offered him no recompense for informing on the French agent, Manoury said, but only told him he would serve King James by doing so. He and the gentleman had agreed that their conversation had never happened, and Manoury had undertaken not to give him away.

But now Manoury told the Commission that this gentleman was indeed Sir Lewis Stucley. The French agent had not promised him a reward for revealing this, other than in terms of general favour and the satisfaction of serving Louis XIII. He had originally thought it impertinent, he said, to trouble the agent with the matter, but at dinner the previous day Le Clerc had asked him to repeat the allegations in front of witnesses. He had told Le Clerc that the Lords of the Council – whom he was now addressing – would be angry with him. Le Clerc had replied that his King would recompense him.

De la Chesnée, who had been held incommunicado in Justice Doubleday's house, was brought before the Lords a second time. Confronted with Ralegh's admission and Manoury's evidence he was compelled to confess that what he had denied just a week ago was in substance true. He also admitted that he had received a little note from Ralegh, informing him that he had been captured and no longer needed the barque, as well as something else he could not understand for the note was badly written. He said all this without coercion or, as the lords put it to the King, any 'insinuation of promise, menace or torture, but . . . by the evidence of truth itself appearing in Sir Walter Ralegh's letter to His Majesty which had been shown unto him'.[18]

Wilson was instructed to get Ralegh to tell him the names of his servants or friends who saw the coming and going of Le Clerc and De la Chesnée, and then to write them down.

'No one saw the French agent come,' said Ralegh. 'As to De la Chesnée, several people were in the parlour when he passed through, but I know not whether any one noticed him.'[19]

The King, who had been hunting at Havering, was informed that De la Chesnée had come clean about the French agent's improper behaviour. It was an international scandal. After grave diplomatic and legal consultations with His Majesty's Advocate General and other highly-placed lawyers about the Crown's relationship with France, it was resolved that Le Clerc himself should be summoned for questioning.

The Lords charged Le Clerc with what they knew, but he vehemently denied it. It would, he protested, have offended not only them, in whose country he resided, but also his master, King Louis, if he had committed so grave an error. They let him stew a little, then confronted him with De la Chesnée. The agent glared at his interpreter. It was an intolerable loss of face. De la Chesnée repeated his story. Le Clerc confessed. The lords declared that he had clearly violated the law of nations and must therefore relinquish his benefits and privileges. They banned him from court, ordered him to keep to his house and forbade him to engage in negotiations or public duties. The King refused him audience and sent word that he would never see him again. In response, the English ambassador in France, William Becher, was confined to his residence, as a protest. He was quickly recalled to London and diplomatic relations with France were broken off.

A letter from James I to Louis XIII was drafted at once and sent from Hampton Court.[20] It is written in grandiloquent diplomatic French, but it boils down to an angry complaint about 'the bad behaviour of your Agent Le Clerc, resident in our Court'. It outlines how Ralegh had 'perpetrated insupportable cruelties against the Spaniards to the rupture of the peace and amity between the two Crowns of Spain and ourselves' and how, as soon as he had been taken prisoner in London, 'your Agent at 8 pm, being an ungodly hour for a public servant, and without having asked any leave from us, went to find him'.

Le Clerc made and signed a declaration on 16 October,[21] ten days before he was recalled to France. He had learned, it stated, that while King James was in Salisbury, Sir Walter Ralegh was there as well, and had declared that if he reached France he would render a great and signal service to King Louis. Knowing that Sir Walter was returning to London for five days to order his affairs, Le Clerc said that he looked for an occasion to see him in his house. He admitted that he approached him one night, and that Ralegh took him to the end of a gallery where they conferred.

How did Le Clerc first find out about what had happened in Salisbury, about Ralegh's vow to serve France, or about the five days' grace he was granted? He learnt these things from Manoury. In response he despatched De la Chesnée to Brentford so that he could bump into Sir Walter 'by chance'.

Dr Guillaume Manoury is the key to all this. He has been written off as a minor character, a foreign quack with a bit part in Ralegh's downfall. But he was a skilful French physician who had – in common with Ralegh, Keymis, Hariot, Northumberland and the rest – a serious interest in alchemy and distillation. Shared interests made Ralegh believe he could trust him. Hence the letter Sir Walter handed him when they parted, addressed to Lady Harris at Radford House, Plymouth, requesting her to give Manoury the alembic or distillatory of copper.

Manoury assumed the role of an accomplished double agent. In Salisbury he had dared to play Stucley and Ralegh off against each other. When Stucley sent him ahead from Bagshot to London, he not only took the story of Ralegh's deceptions to the King, but went to the French embassy with news of Ralegh's projected escape and of the notable service he would offer Louis of France against Philip of Spain.

Manoury kept his cover at first. But it seems he slipped up, after Ralegh was in the Tower, by intimating to Stucley that the French agent was involved. Sir Lewis later approached him on the terrace at Whitehall to induce him to pass on what he knew to the lords. Manoury had baulked at that. He pretended he had not pointed the finger at Le Clerc. Stucley had returned twice more to try and persuade him that he had, and should. Of course, they both agreed that these conversations never happened.

Was it by chance that Manoury met and informed De la Forest about the English machinations that threatened Le Clerc? When the agent put it to him point-blank, he at first denied that Sir Lewis was the gentleman who had tried to 'corrupt' him. There is no knowing what promises of reward or insinuations of menace and torture the Lords offered, but when they interrogated him he revealed that the mysterious gentleman was Stucley.

Did Manoury regret Le Clerc's disgrace, and Ralegh's fate? Did he reckon it just, on his warped scale of values, that Sir Lewis was universally scorned as Sir 'Judas'? He must have weighed up the two English knights and found Stucley woefully wanting. It may have gratified him that his evidence would shortly help to convict Sir Lewis and his son of clipping coin. It was a capital offence, but a rather petty crime when compared to Sir Walter's grand and grandiose intrigues.

15

LAST JUDGMENT

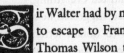ir Walter had by now refined his excuses for attempting to escape to France. Up to this point he had told Sir Thomas Wilson that he wanted only to save himself until the storm was blown over, until Queen Anne or his friends had procured his pardon. But on 21 September he confided in him, as if Sir Thomas were his confessor, that he had hoped to sail in the *Destiny* from Plymouth to France and then on to Guiana with two pinnaces to find the gold mine he had missed because of his sickness. Even if he remained on French soil, he said, Spanish fears of what he might do to Spain would persuade King Philip to write to King James to recall him home and pardon him. 'This', wrote Sir Thomas, 'is his last dream.'[1]

That night the King came in person to the Tower. The purpose of his visit is unclear. We know that Sir Thomas was anxious about a jealous feud that had sprung up between him and Sir Allen Apsley, the Lieutenant, that would make 'his friends near the King rather to put gall than sugar to any thing that shall come from me'. There were doubts about Sir Thomas's credibility, as well as about his presumptuous offers of mercy to Sir Walter.

His Majesty urged the spy to get more out of Ralegh concerning his business with the French: not just about the recent plot, but about Faige and La Rochelle, his so-called French commission and his plans to take the Spanish plate fleet. Ralegh was compliant: 'If His Majesty desires to know former matters,' he offered, 'I can say much more. Pray bring me paper and ink.'

Sir Thomas then 'conjured him by all means I could' to write down everything that King James ought to know.

'I will do it,' said Sir Walter, 'but in no hope to save my life, for the more I confess the sooner I shall be hanged.'

He sat down there and then and confessed on paper to his royal master that he had always shrunk from speaking the whole truth for fear of giving pain and trouble to those who had supported him, but that now he would tell everything.[2]

He admitted that Captain Faige had suggested he approach the French ambassador Des Maretz to obtain letters to the Duke of Montmorency, the Admiral of France, from whom he received a commission at Faige's hand. He did not tell everything. He was as vague as ever about the nature of this commission. After that he simply reiterated what the King already knew.

> And to tell the truth to your Majesty, I resolved to make the effort to save myself as best I could, seeing that my enemies in the kingdom have great power to do me harm.
>
> I pray you humbly, therefore, to pardon and have compassion on me, and if it may please your Majesty to grant me life, even in prison, I will disclose things which will be very useful to the State, and from which great wealth and advantages will result, while my death can give nothing but gratification to those who seek it with such vindictiveness and anxiety, contrary to the natural disposition of your Majesty, who has always been inclined to goodness and clemency.
>
> And these alone are all the hopes I have in this world, causing me to pray God to give your Majesty as much happiness as I desire for myself, I am, Sir, your Majesty's most humble and most unhappy subject and vassal,
> W Ralegh.

Sir Walter did not invest much in these last hopes. On 26 September he told Sir Thomas about his interrogation before the Lords and the questions they had asked.

'I hope I have not long to stay here,' Sir Thomas told him that night. He had come like the messenger of death; his exit presaged death's entrance.

'When you are gone,' said Ralegh, 'I shall be delivered to the secular power as they call it, and yet, if the Spanish match hold, it is not good policy to have me put to death, for I have a great many friends in England and my death will but procure the King envy.'

He had already talked to Sir Thomas about his own great kindred, 'naming the greatest and almost all in the west country of note and a great number more of great families and great lords in England, how they were allied to him and his wife'.[3]

After supper, Apsley's servant told Sir Thomas that his master could not come that night. Sir Thomas climbed to Ralegh's chamber to pass on this news. Ralegh knew why the Lieutenant stayed away: he was discussing his fate. 'I am resolved for my death,' he said. He declared that though he had praised wilful self-murder before, he now detested the idea of suicide and would be executed in public where he could speak. Then he discussed Stucley's predicament, and added: 'I desire to die in the light, not in darkness, so that I may make known what some men are.'

Two days later Sir Walter bemoaned the fact that he had revealed what Le Clerc had said to him.

'What have I done?' he said. 'Nothing but hurt myself more.'

'Why?' asked Sir Thomas.

'I have procured more enemies by this means.'

'What enemies?'

'Why, do you think Le Clerc has no friends? And shall I not lose them all?'

'Who do you mean?' said Sir Thomas.

Ralegh said nothing, but the spy understood that he meant a certain noble lady to whom Lady Carew had alluded. She whose name must not be spoken was, of course, Queen Anne.

'It is reported in town', said Sir Thomas, 'that the Queen has begged your life.' Sir Walter grunted. 'And I hear it said,' continued Sir Thomas, 'that when the King visited him a little before his death, the late Bishop of Winchester told the King that he never expected to see His Majesty again and would therefore beg but one thing of him, and that was the life of an old gentleman who had incurred His Majesty's grievous indignation. Yet because he had been so dearly respected by that noble Queen, his predecessor, and for many other reasons, he begged that he would save his life and let him die in peace and not come to an untimely death. But,' said Sir Thomas, 'the party who reported this did not know whether the King granted it or no.'

The bishop, James Montague, had died of dropsy at Greenwich, shortly after expressing this last wish that Ralegh's life be spared. The feeling was, as one gentleman wrote to another on 3 October, that 'Sir Walter Ralegh's business trouble the Lords much. The King had a disposition to have hanged him, but it could not handsomely be so; it is likely now he shall live as long as he can by nature.'[4]

Sir Thomas tried to ingratiate himself with Ralegh to the end, while still regaling the King with how he confronted Sir Walter's cunning with his simplicity and openness. He wrote his last letter concerning Ralegh to His Majesty on 4 October.[5] He says that Sir Walter, 'finding his subtlety encountered by my simplicity', had first tendered him fair promises and small presents, but seeing those did not work, tried to woo him with flattery and offered to tell him all he wanted to know, as if he was his confessor. But it was openness, he writes, that made Sir Walter confess what he now regrets admitting. However, Wilson was of the opinion that he could get nothing more out of him, and summarised all the intelligence he had extracted, and the lies Ralegh had repeated. 'By telling a lie often in one fashion, [he] believes himself at length that it is true.'

The old spy suggested to the King that it was time he abandoned his role of keeper in the Tower to get on with his job as Keeper of the State Papers, 'wherein I shall spend my time better for your Majesty's service than I can do here with this arch-impostor'.

Sir Thomas stayed on in the Tower for another ten days, but there is a premature sense of ending, as if everyone involved is engaged in mopping-up operations, ordering papers, making things tidy before the inevitable, banal finish. Ralegh was doing the same, but he was determined that his end would be far from anti-climactic. He wrote a note,[6] a sort of codicil to his will, about practical matters. The first item involved contested leases, one in County Cork and another in Dorset, where his old enemy and ex-bailiff John Meere was claiming the lease of a parcel of Sherborne land. Ralegh protested before God that he never made the lease in the first place.

Next he desired his wife, if she was left to enjoy her goods, to help the relatives of his friends Christopher Hammond and John Talbot who both died – 'to mine inestimable grief' – on the voyage to Guiana. He urged Bess to help Hammond's wife and to relieve Talbot's mother too, for having no son to support her he feared she would otherwise die.

The final paragraph concerned Sir Lewis Stucley. It stated that Sir Lewis sold all the cargo of tobacco at Plymouth. Ralegh had given him a fifth part of the most of it, also a roll of tobacco for 'my Lord Admiral', and a roll for himself. Stucley had taken ten gold pieces from Ralegh on the Sunday that they took a wherry down the Thames on their abortive escape attempt. He pretended to borrow the money, Ralegh claimed, to send his men into the country, whereas in fact he sent them downriver to join William Herbert and the arresting party. If Ralegh could not punish him for treachery, he might get him for fraud. 'I desire', he wrote with concealed fury, 'that he may give his account for the tobacco.'

He replied to a letter Bess had written him about the *Destiny*'s tangled finances. The ship had been arrested and confiscated by the Crown, but Ralegh still owed money on it. 'You have a note what the ship cost, in which every particular is set down and it is signed by Master Herbert.' Cousin William Herbert had a quarter share in the *Destiny* and now, after playing his part in foiling Sir Walter's escape, was reclaiming his money. 'As I remember the ship and her furniture doth amount unto £7,000 or near it . . . And as I do remember Master Herbert hath disbursed towards his fourth part eleven hundred pounds. You say that he demands twelve and it may be true.' From memory he detailed further obligations to his captains and gentlemen. 'There is a paper book which Samuel King kept of all the particulars of the ship and to whom the money was paid.' Then, before initialling the letter, he warned Bess about the shockingly firm, neat signature she would find at the foot of the documents. 'My son whom I have lost,' he wrote, 'hath also signed that note, inventory and agreement between me and Master Herbert. Your desolate husband, W R.'[7]

Lady Ralegh was eventually awarded £2,250 for the *Destiny*, William Herbert got £750, later withheld to compensate the Spanish for tobacco taken or burnt at San Thomé. The King's shipwright, Phineas Pett, had built the ship for £2,500 of which Ralegh had paid £500 in advance; according to Pett's own account he never recovered the balance, though other creditors got at least some satisfaction.[8]

In a postcript to this letter of 4 October Sir Walter asked for some notebooks. 'There is in the bottom of the cedar chest some paper books of mine. I pray make them up altogether and send them me. The title of one of them is *The Art of War by Sea*. The rest are notes belonging unto it.' He had some time now to revert to writing, and planned to augment and revise this work.[9] He also begged a phial of medicine for dysentery. 'There is amongst the little glasses the powder of steel and pumice for to stay the flux. If you can find it now, for I have a grievous looseness and fear that it will turn to the bloody flux.' He also requested a fresh supply of the herb *Stachys betonica*, a remedy for rupture, to treat the swelling in his side. 'Send some more bitony.'

Iron, pumice and betony: none of them was a remedy for all diseases, and certainly not for the deep ills that afflicted Ralegh.

On 15 October some relief arrived from Spain: orders from Philip III that spared Ralegh the indignity of execution in Madrid's Plaza Mayor, and relieved James I of the English resentment that would surely have been provoked by such a demonstration of Spanish vengeance. James could again look forward to a Spanish match for Prince Charles, and to the Infanta's dowry.

That same day, Secretary Naunton wrote to Sir Thomas Wilson expressing His Majesty's pleasure at the care and vigilance he had shown in the safe-keeping of Sir Walter, and relieving him of that duty. A postscript announced that Lady Ralegh's house arrest was ended; she was to be allowed her liberty.[10]

Sir Edward Coke presented the recommendations of the Privy Council's special commission to the King on 18 October.[11] The Lords gave it as their opinion that Ralegh, being attained of high treason at Winchester in 1603, could not be judged for any offence committed since. They therefore presented His Majesty with two options.

The first was to deliver the warrant for Ralegh's execution to the Lieutenant of the Tower and, because so much time had elapsed since Ralegh was sentenced to death, to publish a printed narrative of his recent crimes, to publicise them and to justify the King's actions – although, they added reverently, 'your Majesty is not bound to give an account of your actions in these cases to any but only to God alone'.

The second option, to which they inclined, was to bring Sir Walter before 'the whole body of your Council of State, and your principal Judges, in your Council-Chamber; and that some of the nobility and gentlemen of quality be admitted . . . to hear the whole proceeding'. His Majesty's Council would charge Ralegh with his acts of hostility, depredation, abuse of his commission, impostures, attempts at escape and other misdemeanours. After he was charged, they advised, Sir Walter himself should be heard and, if necessary, confronted. Then the Lords and judges could publicly advise the King as to whether a warrant for his execution should not be issued upon his old attainder and death sentence.

The King's response to this advice was clear. He wanted more than a warrant for Ralegh's execution and a printed narrative of his crimes to be issued, but he disliked the notion of a public hearing before the Council. 'We think it not fit, because it would make him too popular, as was found by experiment at the arraignment at Winchester, where by his wit he turned the hatred of men into compassion for him.' His Majesty had no desire for a repeat of that towering performance of 1603.

'We have therefore thought of a middle course,' the King wrote. Ralegh should be called before those who had already examined him. The examinations should be read. He should then be heard. Others who were with him on the voyage should confront him. The Attorney General and Solicitor General should bring the charges, but the French should not be mentioned except in passing when referring, for instance, to his proposed escape in a French barque. 'And then after the sentence for his execution which hath been thus long suspended, a declaration be presently put forth in print, a warrant being sent down for us to sign for his execution.'[12]

On the reverse side of his draft reply to his Privy Councillors, the King noted points of evidence which he thought should be emphasised: 'Wherein we hold the French physician's confession very material, as also his own and his consorts' confession, that before they were at the Islands he told them his aim was at the [Spanish] Fleet, with his son's oration when they came to the town, and some touch of his hateful speeches of our person.'

Politically the King could not have made a worse decision. His Council was confident in its case and wanted it heard in public. His Majesty wanted it *in camera*. Their show trial became his secret trial. Out of fear, James guaranteed that justice would not be seen to be done.

Ralegh cannot have known exactly what was in store for him, but he sensed there was no escape. In his letter to the King from Plymouth he had written: 'My mutineers told me that if I returned for England I should be undone, but I believed more in your Majesty's goodness than in their arguments.' Now he knew their arguments were sound. Mercy was an unreliable commodity. To the King's favourite, Villiers, he had recently bemoaned his plight, 'if His Majesty do not pity my age and scorn to take the extremest and uttermost advantage of my errors'. But His Majesty would neither pity an old man nor resist capitalising on his every mistake.

Sir Walter received a summons to appear before the Privy Council on 22 October. Even on the eve of the hearing courtiers believed that James would spare the old grandee's life and keep him in the Tower in return for information.[13] They knew that he could give incriminating evidence against the likes of the Earls of Suffolk and Salisbury, and everyone acknowledged that

the author of the *History of the World* and many another treatise
still had invaluable advice to impart.

By the next morning the stage-managers had done their
work. The script was written as far as possible. The one player
whose improvisations the Lords feared would step not on to
the stage of a public arena but into a chamber packed only with
trusted servants of the Crown. Sir Allen Apsley had Ralegh
conveyed from the Brick Tower to confront the Council and
the state's lawyers *in camera*.

The proceedings were ponderous and protracted. The
Attorney General got to his feet and charged Sir Walter under
three heads:

1. Faults before his going on this last voyage.
2. Faults committed in the course of his voyage.
3. Faults committed since his voyage.[14]

Having dilated on these, he presented the court with Sir
Walter's impostures or deceptions, which, according to his reckoning, numbered four:

1. He never intended to discover a mine.
2. He intended to start a war between the Kings of England
   and Spain.
3. He abandoned his company and put them all in danger.
4. He behaved unfaithfully to the King and his company.

As to the first imposture, the Attorney General said that
Ralegh carried no miners or tools; he did not order his men to
seek the mine; he wanted only one piece of ore to blear the
King's eyes; challenged, he had once said that he must promise
something as an inducement to his men; his own son's words
had revealed all, when he urged on the soldiers to plunder San
Thomé: that, he had shouted, was the mine they sought for.

To the second, San Thomé belonged to the Spaniards; Sir
Walter's company assailed it at his direction; he had a com-

mission from the French King to do so; and when the town was taken with little profit he resolved to re-victual and set upon the Spanish fleet.

To the third and fourth, Ralegh assured his company that he had a commission to do as he did; he said he would no longer put his head under the King's girdle; he put it to a vote of his company whether he should return to England or not; he would have departed, after his son was killed, and abandoned his poor company; and he would have given all his ships to the company if he had but one to carry him into some other country. All in all, he was now unworthy of His Majesty's continued favour.

The Solicitor General now rose up, declaring that if Ralegh's actions beyond the sea had demonstrated his lack of love and duty, his actions at home since showed his lack of fear and duty.

1. His intention to fly before he was arrested.
2. His endeavour to fly after his arrest.
3. His imposture to deceive the King and State.
4. His vile and dishonourable speeches, full of insolence to the King.

The Solicitor General discussed the treasonable implications of flight; how Ralegh had ships and money ready for his escape; how he tried to corrupt both Manoury and Stucley, his keeper; how he feigned sickness and madness at Salisbury, persuading Manoury to abet him and saying that he would laugh heartily one day that he had so prettily abused both King and state; that at Mr Drake's house he cursed and said his trust in the King had undone him; and that near Sherborne he had claimed that the King had taken his property from him unjustly. The Solicitor General concluded, like the Attorney General, that Ralegh was no longer worthy of His Majesty's favour.

The select crowd in the chamber held its breath. Sir Walter had made his entrance with a spark of his old energy, but as he sat and listened to the lawyers his pain was palpable; his sickness was visible beneath his thin, pale skin. Arteries pulsed at his temples and his hair was almost white. He stood and opened his mouth. His right arm was slack and his fingers quivered with the tell-tale signature of the palsy. His voice was not loud, but his tongue was as eloquent as ever.

He did not address either the Attorney General or the Solicitor General at first. With his words, though not his eyes, he addressed King James.

'I verily think,' he said, 'that his Majesty doth in his conscience clear me of all guiltiness of my fault in the first year of his reign.'

Some of the company recognised echoes of his passionate defence at Winchester fifteen years before.

'I have heard that the King said he would not want to be tried by a jury of Middlesex.'

His hearers did not know whether to laugh, or gasp at his daring.

'In the second book of Macabees,' Ralegh said, 'Archelaus has this speech, "That had he been among the Scythians he had not been condemned".'

The Lords saw that their interrogations had not tamed him. But, apart from sidelong glances, they kept their composure and metaphorically rubbed hands at hearing him condemn himself by his impertinence.

'My old physician in the Tower, Dr James Turner, told me this: that Justice Gawdy, who sat upon the bench that tried me then, declared upon his death bed', and here Sir Walter looked about the chamber, fixing one and another briefly with his gaze, 'that the justice of England was never so depraved and injured as in the condemnation of Sir Walter Ralegh.'

He pronounced his own name with gravity, as if he stood outside himself and surveyed his own being, as the onlookers were compelled to do, wondering that he had outlived the great days of Elizabeth and survived so long in a narrower, meaner age.

'Now I shall answer Mr Attorney's objections. I did intend a mine. I carried refiners with me, and tools that cost me £2,000, and I trusted Captain Keymis, in whom the refiners also believed, to find the mine. The force I sent was not intended to invade San Thomé, but to keep between its inhabitants and the mine, in case the Spaniards should interrupt my men in their search and labour.

'I did not abandon my men, as that privateer Sir John Ferne hath reported' – here Ralegh implied that the commander of the *Flying Hart* was no more to be trusted than a pirate – 'nor planned to go away and leave them in the West Indies. As to Mr Attorney's other charges, I deny them.'

He paused, but only to give his audience false comfort before resuming.

'Though with regard to the Mexico or Spanish plate fleet I should say that, when I left England for Guiana, some of the leading ministers and members of the Privy Council,' and he darted meaningful looks here and there, 'those disinclined towards Spain and extremely averse to the alliance with that Crown – among them I may mention the late Mr Secretary, Sir Ralph Winwood – these Councillors advised and persuaded me to take every opportunity of attacking the fleets or territories of the Catholic King Philip, so as not only to generate distrust between the two Crowns, but even to give cause for a rupture.'

When he paused the chamber creaked and buzzed with uncomfortable stirrings and breathless mutterings.

'Moreover, Monsieur Des Maretz, the late French ambassador at this court, promised me not only permission to withdraw to France, but likewise, in case of any need, he guaranteed me the protection and favour of his most Christian Majesty, King Louis.'

Even the most cynical of those who sat before him marvelled at Sir Walter's nerve.

'To Mr Solicitor's objections I say this: that I made no attempt to escape until I was arrested by Sir Lewis Stucley. I have already confessed that I tried to escape after that.' Here he broke into Latin, and admitted that he had pretended to be more ill and mad than he was. 'I confess it, but I excuse myself, seeing that I followed the biblical example of David who, when he fled from Saul to the court of King Achish of Gath, found himself in mortal fear and feigned himself mad.[15]

'I confess also that I did say that my confidence in the King had deceived me. But I deny that I used any other ill speeches against his Majesty.'

It was hard to object now, seeing that Ralegh so transparently had good reason to doubt his confidence in the King.

Captain St Leger and Captain Pennington made their entrance. It was not the *coup de théâtre* that the lords had planned, and certainly not the *coup de grâce* for which they had hoped, since Ralegh's confession had already defused, or rather thrown back at the Privy Council's feet, the impact of their words.

'Yes, as these gentlemen will witness,' said Sir Walter, 'I did talk of taking the Mexico treasure fleet if the mine failed. It was but discourse at large. As the world knows, I did not take it.'

The masque could not reach its climax. At last, Ralegh was escorted back to the Brick Tower. The Lords and their King were not a little shaken. There was much righteous indignation and much looking over shoulders. They knew they must confer and be certain that the last act of Sir Walter's play followed their direction.

Two days later, on 24 October, the Privy Council sent a message to the cell in the Brick Tower where Sir Walter lay. His Majesty, it said, had decided that he must be punished by execution, and so he should prepare himself for death.[16]

Ralegh wrote to the King to assure him that he was not one of those who glory in wickedness and malice.[17] For all his errors, he said, his heart was in the right place. There had always been those who had risen again after a civil death, he insisted; such men were still alive, and believed to be honest.

> I take it (under your Majesty's gracious pardon) for a liberty *malentendu*, to be removed out of this steady Tower into a rolling ship, to change the diet of soft bread and fresh meat for hard biscuit and salt beef, to drink unsavoury water instead of wine and beer and to disorder an aged worn and weak body with watching, travel and distempered heat of the Indies, besides a world of other harms and hazards. For the rest (most renowned sovereign) I most humbly beseech your Majesty to conceive that I never had any hidden or dishonest intention in this point.

Ralegh wrote one more letter from the Tower.[18] Since it was first published in 1660 it has been assumed that it was sent to King James, but in it Sir Walter expressed feelings that he would not have addressed to His Majesty. It was Her Majesty Queen Anne who had tried, repeatedly if ineffectually, to help him; it is probable that this letter is his *adieu* to her.

> May it please your Majesty:
> My sad destiny hath been such that I could never present your Majesty but with a prospect upon my complaints and miseries, instead of doing you services which might have been acceptable to you. I have not spared my labour, my poor estate and the hourly hazard of my life, but God hath otherwise disposed of all, and now end the days of my hope. I must nevertheless, in this little time which I am to live, acknowledge and admire your goodness and in all my thoughts, and even with my last breath, confess that you have beheld my affliction with compassion. And

I am yet in nothing so miserable as in that I could never meet an occasion wherein to be torn in pieces for your Majesty's service.

I, who am still your, etc.

16

SCAFFOLD

On the morning of 28 October Sir Walter Ralegh was roused from a feverish sleep. He left his cell, walked down the stairs of the Brick Tower and boarded a coach which carried him through the gates of the Tower of London. Leaving London Bridge to the south and St Paul's to the north, he crossed the Fleet Ditch and made along the Strand, past the great residences and palaces of friends and enemies, including Durham House where he and his company had once studied astronomy, alchemy, mathematics and map-making, and dreamed of Virginia and Guiana.

When he descended from the coach outside Westminster Hall, those who watched were dismayed to see how demoralised, ill and unkempt the great hero looked. A former servant of his cried out when he saw his old master's tangled white hair.

'Let them comb it that are to have it,' Ralegh told him. 'Peter, dost thou know of any plaster to set a man's head on again when it is off?'

He was brought to the King's Bench bar. The writ was delivered to the judges and intoned. Sir Henry Yelverton, the Attorney General, made the opening speech.[1]

'My Lords, Sir Walter Ralegh, the prisoner at the bar, was fifteen years since convicted of high treason ... and then received the judgment of death, to be hanged, drawn and quartered. His Majesty of his abundant grace hath been pleased to show mercy upon him, till now that justice calls unto him for execution.'

The Attorney looked at the sick, dishevelled prisoner.

'Sir Walter Ralegh hath been a statesman, and a man who in regard to his parts and quality is to be pitied. He hath been as a star at which the world hath gazed; but stars may fall, nay they must fall when they trouble the sphere in which they abide.'

The Clerk of the Crown, Mr Fanshaw, read out the conviction and judgment and ordered the prisoner to hold up his hand. Sir Walter raised it. It shook. He was asked what he could say for himself, why execution should not be awarded.

'My Lords,' said Ralegh, 'my voice is grown weak by reason of my late sickness, and an ague which I now have; for I was now brought hither out of it.'

'Sir Walter,' said Sir Henry Montague, the Lord Chief Justice, 'your voice is audible enough.'

'Then, my Lord, all that I can say is this: that the judgment which I received to die so long since, I hope it cannot now be strained to take away my life.'

Ralegh said he presumed that His Majesty's commission, which gave him the power of life and death over his men, had discharged him of that judgment. He undertook a journey, he continued, to honour his sovereign and enrich his kingdom with gold.

'Of the ore whereof this hand hath found and taken in Guiana; but the voyage . . . had no other success but what was fatal to me, the loss of my son and wasting of my whole estate.'

The Lord Chief Justice cut him off. He insisted that talk of his voyage was immaterial, nor was he pardoned by his commission for in law, in the case of treason, a pardon required a specific form of words and was not implicit.

Ralegh bowed to the Lord Chief Justice's opinion and threw himself upon the mercy of the King, 'who I know is gracious; and, under favour, I must say, I hope he will be pleased to take commiseration upon me'. He paused. 'As concerning that judgment which is so long past, and which I think there are some here who can witness, nay his Majesty was of the opinion that I had hard measure therein.'

'Sir Walter Ralegh, you must remember yourself,' said the Lord Chief Justice. 'You had an honourable trial, and so were justly convicted . . . You might think it heavy if this were done in cold blood, to call you to excution; but it is not so, for new offences have stirred up his Majesty's justice, to remember to revive what the law hath formerly cast upon you.' He looked benignly upon the prisoner. 'I know you have been valiant and wise, and I doubt not but you retain both these virtues, for now you shall have occasion to use them. Your faith hath heretofore been questioned, but I am resolved you are a good Christian, for your book, which is an admirable work, doth testify as much.'

He said he would not presume to offer Ralegh counsel, but he would, like the good Samaritan, pour into his wounds the oil of comfort, though, because he was a minister of the law, mixed with vinegar.

'Fear not death too much, nor fear death too little,' he went on. 'Not too much, lest you fail in your hopes; not too little, lest you die presumptuously. And here I must conclude with my prayers to God for it, and that he would have mercy on your soul.' He raised his eyes to the assembly. 'Execution is granted.'

Ralegh seemed happy now. He looked on and relished his own self-possession.

'My Lord, I desire thus much favour,' he calmly requested, 'that I may not be cut off suddenly, for I have something to do in discharge of my conscience, and something to satisfy his

Majesty in, something to satisfy the world in, and I desire I may be heard at the day of my death.'

Sir Walter now addressed himself to a higher court.

'And here I take God to be my judge, before whom I shall shortly appear; I was never disloyal to his Majesty; which I will justify where I shall not fear the face of any king on earth. And so I beseech you all to pray for me.'

King James signed the warrant. At the heart of its long-winded legalese, it declared that His Majesty did 'pardon, remit, and release Sir Walter Ralegh of and from such execution of his judgment to be drawn, hanged and quartered . . . and instead thereof, our pleasure is, to have the head only of the said Sir Walter Ralegh cut off, at or within our palace of West-minster.'

The days Ralegh had begged, in order to satisfy the King and the world, were not granted. This time the master of pro-crastination could win no delay. The time of his death was fixed for the next morning. Sir Allen Apsley delivered Ralegh to the Sheriff of Westminster who was to conduct him to the Abbey Gatehouse and the custody of its keeper, Master Weekes. On the way he met an old friend who asked what the news was. Sir Walter told him to be sure and rise early the next morning if he wanted a good view of his execution.

Joiners and labourers set to work, building the scaffold in Old Palace Yard. It was the stage for Ralegh's last act. Around it they erected bleachers to accommodate spectators. Letters for places began to change hands like tickets.

The King's haste to kill Ralegh was, John Aubrey says, a cautious policy. Speed of execution would allow little time for seditious ferment to brew. The following day was auspicious; Thursday 29 October was the Lord Mayor's Day when 'pageants and fine shows might draw away the people from beholding the tragedy of one of the most gallant worthies that ever England bred'.[2] That was the theory. In practice, a multitude would be at leisure to attend the solemn ceremony before moving on into the day's festivities, Sir Walter's wake.

On its eve, though, Ralegh was locked inside the Gatehouse. All afternoon he heard the sawing, hammering and shouting outside. As the solid framework for his death was constructed, his resolve stiffened. He wrote a statement, in case he might be silenced too soon. He focused on what must be done. There was no more uncertainty, no more ambiguity, and no more anxiety for so short a future. Or just one small worry, that his ague would disable him at his last public appearance; his fever was an intermittent one and usually assailed him at the very hour when he was due to stand beside the block. He longed to be free of it at nine the next morning, for soon afterwards he would be free of everything.

The Dean of Westminster, Dr Robert Tounson, came solemnly to administer spiritual comfort. When he began to encourage him against the fear of death, Ralegh made so light of it that Tounson was astonished.

'The dear servants of God,' said the Dean, 'in better causes than yours, have shrunk back and trembled a little.'

'I do not deny it,' Ralegh responded, 'but I thank God I never feared death. And much less now, for it is but an opinion and imagination.'

Tounson must have pricked up his ears at this.

'This manner of death may seem grievous to others,' Sir Walter said, 'yet I had rather die this way than of a burning fever.'

So he went on, with too much confidence and cheerfulness for the Dean's taste. Tounson tried to instill some gravity into their conversation. 'Do not flatter yourself,' he said, 'for I fear this extraordinary boldness of yours stems from some false ground. If from an humour of vain glory or carelessness or contempt of death, or senselessness of your situation, you are much to be lamented. Heathen men set as little store by their lives as you do, and seem to die bravely.'

'Sir,' replied Ralegh, 'I am persuaded that no man who knows God and fears him can die with cheerfulness and courage unless he is assured of the love and favour of God unto him. Other men may make shows outwardly, but they feel no joy within, as I do.'

The Dean, marvelling at this very Christian performance, left him until the morning.[3]

Ralegh's concern turned to his family. Bess visited him that evening in his cell, where they talked and clung to one another.

'The Lords', she said, 'have granted me the disposing of your body.'

'It is well, Bess, that thou mayst dispose of it dead, that hadst not always the disposing of it when it was alive.'[4]

Soon after midnight he said farewell and she left him. He turned to poetry. He had never been shy of reusing old lines in new poems; now he took the last stanza of the love poem he had written for Bess long ago, 'Nature, that wash'd her hands in milk . . .', and added a final couplet to make it his funeral song.[5]

> Even such is time, which takes in trust
>   Our youth, our joys and all we have,
> And pays us but with age and dust;
>   Who in the dark and silent grave
> When we have wandered all our ways
> Shuts up the story of our days.
>   And from which earth and grave and dust
>   The Lord shall raise me up, I trust.[6]

He settled himself down to sleep for three hours or so. At about four in the morning his cousin Charles Thynne came to visit him and made a sad entrance into his cell. Ralegh tried to cheer him up and joke with him.

'Sir, take heed you go not too much upon the brave hand,' Thynne advised, 'for your enemies will take exception at that.'

'Good Charles,' said Sir Walter, 'give me leave to be merry, for this is the last merriment that ever I shall have in this world.'

Thynne nodded and Ralegh reassured him.

'But when I come to the sad part, thou shalt see, I will look on it like a man.'[7]

Dean Tounson returned to celebrate communion with him, and afterwards Ralegh was very happy.

'I hope to persuade the world that I die an innocent man.'

'Be careful what you say,' said the Dean, 'for in these days men do not die in this manner innocent. Your pleading innocency is an oblique taxing of the justice of the realm.'

'Yes,' Ralegh said with some irony, 'justice has been done, and by course of law I must die. But you, sir, must allow me to stand upon my innocence.'

Sir Walter ate his breakfast heartily, and smoked his pipe, just as he had notoriously smoked one during Essex's execution. As Tounson noted afterwards, he made no more of his imminent death than if he had been about to set out on a journey.[8]

Ralegh dressed himself for the voyage, not in the shabby clothes he had been wearing, but in the fine costume that people expected of him, that he expected of himself: a crisp white ruff, a tawny or hair-coloured doublet, a black embroidered waistcoat under it, black cut taffeta breeches, ash-coloured silk stockings, a wrought black velvet gown and a fine pair of shoes. On his finger he placed a ring with a diamond, one noted by a clerk after his death as 'Given him by the late Queen'. His hair was combed and on his head he wore a lace nightcap, and on that, when it was time to go out, he would put his hat.

A cup of excellent sack was brought to him, and when some-one asked how he liked it, he smiled and quoted the fellow who, stopping to drink at St Giles's bowl on his way to the gallows at Tyburn, said, 'It is good drink if a man might tarry by it.'

Dean Tounson and two sheriffs escorted him out into the chill morning, surrounded by sixty guards.[9] As they approached the scaffold in Old Palace Yard they met a gentleman, Sir Hugh Beeston, brandishing the letter that guaranteed him a good place. Unfortunately the sheriff had left his spectacles at home and simply thrust the paper in his pocket. The eager Beeston was shoved aside.

'Farewell, Sir Hugh,' said Ralegh. 'You must make what shift you can for a place. For my own part I am sure of one.'

A bald old man in the crowd gave Sir Walter his blessing.

'Do you want ought of me?' asked Ralegh.

'Nothing but to see you, sir, and to pray God to have mercy on your soul.'

'I thank you, good friend,' said Ralegh, taking his nightcap from beneath his hat, 'and I am sorry I have no better thing to return you for your good will, but take this nightcap, for you have more need of it now than I.'

The party ascended the scaffold. A brazier burned there, but Sir Walter refused to warm himself at it, perhaps for fear it might bring on the heats of fever. He saluted the lords who stood at the windows about the yard and others whom he could see in the yard, including Lord Sheffield on horseback.

'Silence!' cried an officer.

Ralegh removed his hat. 'My honourable good Lords, and the rest of my good friends that come to see me die,' he began in a quiet but firm voice. He asked the crowd to bear with him, for he was in the third day of an ague and whether he would escape it on this day he did not know. He realised that the lords who stood in a window, some distance from the scaffold, could not hear him. 'I will strain my voice, for I would willingly have your Honours hear me.'

'Nay,' Lord Arundel called, 'we will rather come upon the scaffold.'

So the Lords Arundel, Northampton and Doncaster came down from the window and climbed up to the scaffold where Ralegh greeted them, satisfied that key witnesses would hear him clearly. As he resumed, his noble friends, and many another spectator, attended to every word he spoke in his Devonshire brogue.[10]

'As I said, I thank God heartily that he hath brought me into the light to die, and hath not suffered me to die in the dark prison of the Tower, where I have suffered so much adversity and a long sickness. And I thank God that my fever hath not taken me at this time, as I prayed God it might not.'

He announced that he would refute 'two main points of suspicion' and began by countering the accusations concerning his dealings with the French.

'But this I say, for a man to call God to witness to a falsehood at any time is a grievous sin ... But to call God to witness to a falsehood at the time of death is far more grievous and impious ... I do therefore call God to witness, as I hope to see him in his kingdom, which I hope I shall within this quarter of this hour ... I did never entertain any conspiracy, nor ever had any plot or intelligence with the French King, nor ever had any advice or practice with the French agent, neither did I ever see the French hand or seal, as some have reported I had a commission from him at sea ... Neither, as I have a soul to be saved, did I know of the French agent's coming till I saw him in my gallery unlooked for.'

Secondly, he dealt with the slur of disloyalty to King James. In his *Petition* Stucley justified bringing Ralegh to the Tower, 'upon just reason, believing the disloyal and dishonourable words spoken by such a proud vassal against your sacred person to Monsieur Manoury'.

'But,' said Ralegh, 'my accuser is a runagate Frenchman ...

This fellow because he had a merry wit, and some small skill in chemical medicines, I entertained rather for his taste than his judgment . . . Therefore by the same protestation I have already made, I never did speak any disloyal, dishonourable, or dishonest words of the King, neither to this Frenchman nor to any other. If I did, the Lord blot me out of the Book of Life. Nay, I will protest further, I never in all my life thought any such evil of his Majesty in my heart. Therefore methinks it seemeth something strict that such a base fellow should receive credit against the protestation I make upon my salvation.'

Of Manoury's charge against Raleigh, Captain Samuel King later wrote, 'I must protest till my last hour, that in all the years I followed him, I never heard him name his Majesty but with reverence. I am sorry the assertion of that man should prevail so much against the dead.'[11]

Next, Sir Walter turned penitent: 'I confess I did attempt to escape, I cannot deny it . . . I desired to save my life.' Captain King maintained that, when Sir Walter heard what a storm his enemies had brewed at court, he began to regret the neglected opportunity and, in discussion with him and Lady Ralegh, blamed no one but himself.[12]

'And I do likewise confess that I did dissemble and feign myself sick at Salisbury,' Ralegh continued, 'but I hope it was no sin. David, a man after God's own heart, yet for the safety of his life did make himself a fool and did let the spittle fall upon his beard, and it was not imputed to him as sin.'

Now Ralegh turned to address the subject of Sir Lewis Stucley; 'he is my countryman and kinsman, and I have this morning taken the sacrament of Master Dean and forgiven both Stucley and the Frenchman. But that they are perfidious I think I am bound in charity to speak, that others may take warning how to trust such.'

Stucley, he said, had accused him before the Lords of sharing his escape plan with Lord Carew, and with Lord Doncaster who now stood with him on the scaffold. 'It was not likely that I should acquaint two Privy Councillors of my purpose; neither would I tell him, for he left me six, seven, eight, nine or ten days to go where I listed, while he rode about the country.'[13] His keeper, he said, also claimed that he had boasted that those lords 'would meet me in France, which was never my speech or thought'.

Stucley averred, in his *Petition*, that Ralegh 'did abuse their honourable names, to seduce me, and to draw me to his purpose'.

Ralegh went on, 'He accused me that I showed him a letter, and that I should give him £10,000 for my escape.'

'Concerning the shewing of a letter to me about money,' Stucley remonstrated, 'his wife if she were put to her oath, can tell whether it were so or no.'[14]

'But cast my soul into everlasting fire,' Ralegh urged, 'if I ever made him an offer of £10,000 or £1,000 but merely I showed him a letter, that if he would go with me, his debts should be paid when he was gone.'

Raleigh paused before resuming. 'But Sir Lewis Stucley did me a further injury, which I am very sensible of . . . In my going up to London we lodged at Sir Edward Parham's house, an ancient friend and follower of mine.'

'Whom,' said Stucley in his *Petition*, 'he thought to be a Papist, to be a fit subject of suspicion, which he meant to cast upon his friend.'[15]

There, Ralegh declared, Stucley suggested to him that he had been poisoned. 'I know it grieves the gentleman there should such a conceit be held; and for the cook who was suspected, having been once my servant, I know he will go a thousand miles to do me good.'

Sir Walter consulted his notes. 'Well, thus far have I gone. A little more, and a little more, I will have done by and by.'

He next recounted the humiliating story of the mutiny on

the *Destiny*. The King's *Declaration* tells the same story in reverse:[16] that it was Ralegh who wanted to stay at sea and go after treasure ships while the majority of his crew voted to return to England; that following their show of hands he pretended to agree, but soon offered them the *Destiny* in return for putting him aboard a French ship.

'It was told the King that I was brought perforce into England,' said Sir Walter, but he named Captain Parker and others who would testify to what really happened: how he did not attempt to escape to France, but that the mutineers threatened his life if he landed them in England.

'I hear likewise there was a report that I meant not to go to Guiana at all, and that I knew not of any mine, nor intended any such matter but only to get my liberty, which I had not the wit to keep. But as I will answer it before the same God I am shortly to appear before, I endeavoured and hoped for gold, for gold for the benefit of his Majesty, and myself, and of those that ventured and went with me, with the rest of my countrymen.'

The *Declaration* stated that young Wat, as he led his soldiers against San Thomé, cried, 'Come on my hearts, here is the mine that ye must expect, they that look for any other mine are fools.' As for pickaxes, mattocks and shovels, 'it is true he carried some small quantity for a show' but nowhere near enough, which he excused by saying that his men never saw them unpacked, and that in any case the mine was not more than a foot and a half underground. 'For this mine,' the *Declaration* added, 'was not only imaginary, but moveable.'[17]

'But Keymis,' Ralegh asserted, 'that knew the head of the mine, a wilful fellow, would not discover it when he saw that my son was slain, but made himself away. But I am glad that my Lord of Arundel is here,' Ralegh said, turning to where Arundel stood on the scaffold, 'for his Lordship and divers others being with me in the gallery of my ship at my departure,

I remember your honour took me aside and desired me faithfully and freely to resolve him in one thing, which was whether I intended to return home or no, whatsoever fortune I had, I there told his Lordship and gave him my hand, that whatsoever succeeded, if I lived, I would return.'

'And so you did,' declared Arundel to the crowd, 'it is true, I do very well remember it, they were the very last words I spake unto you.'

'Another opinion was raised of me, that I would have gone away from them and left them at Guiana.' But he listed the names of worthy men, including George Ralegh, who would vouch for the fact that he never intended that.

Stucley affirmed that Sir John Ferne had the testimony of sixty persons to prove the opposite. 'O barbarous cruelty, to leave so many gentlemen, when he had secretly heard that his son was dead, to the mercy of their enemies, without hope or means to return.'[18]

Next, Ralegh examined in detail the suspicion that he had left England with £16,000 in his hands, and that the voyage was simply about getting gold in that way. He protested that this accusation was based upon a misunderstanding of the accounts and that he had not taken a penny more than one hundred pounds.

'Other reports are raised of me touching that voyage which I value not: as that I would not allow the sick persons water enough. Those that go such voyages know that these things must be done in order and proportion; if it had been given out by gallons to some that were sick, all had perished.'

His notes reminded him to deal with one much older grievance and he said he would borrow a little more of Mr Sheriff's time to speak of an imputation that made his heart bleed: that he was a persecutor of Essex; that he stood in a window and puffed out smoke in disdain when he suffered. Stucley accused him of repeating that Essex 'died like a fool, and like a coward, so persecuting his ghost and insolently trampling in his ashes'.[19] Ralegh now said that he wept when Essex died.

'I confess indeed I was of a contrary faction, but I knew my Lord of Essex was a noble gentleman ... and my soul hath been many times grieved that I was not nearer unto him when he died, because I understood that he asked for me at his death, to be reconciled unto me.'

Those were all the points he thought it good to speak of. In a moment he would render up his account to God and, he protested, what he had spoken was true and he hoped he would be believed.

'And now I entreat you all to join me in prayer, that the great God of Heaven, whom I have grievously offended, being a great sinner of a long time and in many kinds, my whole course a course of vanity, a seafaring man, a soldier, and a courtier – the temptations of the least of these were able to overthrow a good mind and a good man; that God, I say, will forgive me, and that he will receive me into everlasting life.

'So I take my leave of you all, making my peace with God.'

The Sheriff asked everyone to leave the scaffold. Ralegh prepared himself for death, giving away his hat and some money to attendants from the Gatehouse. Then he saluted the Lords by him, and gave special thanks to Arundel for his company.

'I entreat you, my Lord,' Ralegh said, 'to desire the King that no scandalous writing to defame me may be published after my death.'

He embraced him.

'I have a long journey to go, and therefore will take my leave.'

He took off his gown and his doublet. The crowd saw how much taller, straighter and younger he suddenly seemed, and how serene his face.

'Pray, Master Headsman, show me the axe.' The executioner

hesitated, Ralegh added, 'I prithee, let me see it. Dost thou think that I am afraid of it?'

Taking it in his hands, he tested the edge with his fingers, smiled to himself and addressed Mr Sheriff.

'This is a sharp medicine, but it is a physician that will cure all my diseases.'

He went to and fro, three times asking those at each side of the scaffold to pray heartily to God to help and strengthen him. The executioner got to his knees before him and begged his forgiveness. Laying his hands upon the man's shoulders, Sir Walter freely absolved him.

The executioner spread out his own cloak on the planking so that Ralegh's black velvet one should not be spoiled.

Ralegh lay down on the cloak, but some objected that he should not lie with his head to the west. Dean Tounson pointed out that he should lie with his face to the east, for our Lord's rising. So Sir Walter rose to his feet, turned about and knelt down again.

'So the heart be right,' he declared, 'it is no matter which way the head lieth.'

He refused to be blindfolded.

'Think you I fear the shadow of the axe, when I fear not the axe itself?'

He had told the headsman that after some short meditation he would stretch out his hands. At that signal he should do his office. Ralegh bent his head and lay down. To observers he seemed as free of apprehension as if he had been present as a spectator rather than a victim. He stretched out his hands. The executioner did not move. He stretched out his hands again. Then he urged him: 'What dost fear? Strike, man, strike!'

The executioner took off his head at two blows, though Sir Walter did not stir after the first. The executioner lifted up the head and showed it on all sides, but could not bring himself to utter the conventional formula, 'This is the head of a traitor.'

The crowd was greatly moved at the sight, and at the gush of blood from Ralegh's neck which they took to show how strong he was, and how many years he might have lived.

Someone in the crowd cried out, 'We have not such another head to cut off.'

It was put into a red leather bag. The body was covered by his velvet cloak. Both were carried away in Bess's black mourning coach.

EPILOGUE

Lady Elizabeth Ralegh wrote to her brother Nicholas[1] almost at once: 'I desire, good brother, that you will be pleased to let me bury the worthy body of my noble husband, Sir Walter Ralegh, in your church at Beddington, where I desire to be buried. The lords have given me his dead body, though they denied me his life. This night he shall be brought you with two or three of my men. Let me hear presently. God hold me in my wits. E.R.'[2]

What Bess and young Carew, Robin the page and Samuel King, 'Judas' Stucley and Guillaume Manoury, Cristóbal Guayacunda and De la Chesnée each felt at the moment the axe fell, surviving written words can only begin to tell us. They suffered the instant in their different ways. It changed their lives. De la Chesnée died the same day. Camden noted that he, 'who had acted to free Ralegh, departed this life with him'.[3]

The Spanish agent in London reported the news of Guattaral's death to King Philip in Madrid. 'Ralegh's spirit never faltered,' he wrote, 'nor did his countenance change.' Then he added in cipher, 'The death of this man has produced a great commotion and fear here, and it is looked upon as a matter of the highest importance, owing to his being a person of great parts and experience, subtle, crafty, ingenious, and brave enough for anything.'[4]

The great commotion seemed to die down. As Dean Tounson wrote ten days later, 'This was the news a week since, but now it is blown over, and he almost forgotten.'[5] But he was not, for the commotion rumbled on and on. There were young people in the crowd who watched Sir Walter Ralegh die at the King's command and never forgot it. They knew, whatever the man's faults and vanities had been, whatever part the play-actor had performed upon the scaffold's stage, that they had witnessed a great spirit betrayed and snuffed out by meaner ones: by James, yearning for a Spanish match and Spanish money, by Stucley, Herbert and other relatives and creditors with big debts and mixed motives. They sensed that His Majesty had not been wise enough, or good enough, in Ralegh's own words, 'to make a difference between offences proceeding from a life having natural impulsion without all ill intent, and those of an ill heart'.[6]

Three men of future importance watched Ralegh die and learnt a radical lesson from what they witnessed. Twenty-six-year-old John Eliot was profoundly moved and recorded:

All preparations that are terrible were presented to his eye. Guards and officers were about him, the scaffold and the executioner, the axe and the more cruel expectation of his enemies. And what did all this work on the resolution of our Ralegh? Made it an impression of weak fear to distract his reason? Nothing so little did that great soul suffer. His mind became the clearer, as if it had already been freed from the cloud and oppression of the body.

Eliot was a friend of Buckingham, who in 1622 would appoint him to Stucley's old position as Vice Admiral of Devon. But Eliot became disillusioned with the royal favourite and with the Stuart notion of kingship. In 1629 he helped draw up resolutions that would condemn Charles I's customs levies and religious policy. When the King ordered the adjournment of Parliament, Eliot had the Speaker held down in his chair until the motions were passed. For his pains he was committed to the Tower where he died.

John Hampden, aged twenty-four, was Oliver Cromwell's cousin, Eliot's friend and a fellow Puritan critic of the Crown. He led the opposition to Charles I's levy of ship money, one of the issues that sparked the Civil War. A colonel in the Battle of Edgehill, he was mortally wounded in 1643 during a skirmish with Royalists at Chalgrove Field.

In the course of the Long Parliament, Hampden became principal lieutenant to thirty-five-year-old John Pym. Pym, who had also watched Ralegh die, was the architect of Parliament's victory over Charles I in 1646. Ralegh would have approved of his passion, and especially of his argument that 'to endeavour the subversion of the laws of this kingdom was treason of the highest nature'. The radical inference, which challenged the theocratic tenet of divine right, was that the King could betray his subjects and so commit treason against the realm.

All three men saw Ralegh's beheading as a shocking instance of kingly injustice. It was a catalytic moment for the Puritan revolution. Richard Polwhele, an eighteenth-century West Country historian wrote, 'I shall only hint, that the execution of this great man, whom James was advised to sacrifice to the advancement of the peace with Spain, hath left an indelible stain on the memory of that misguided monarch.'[7] As the twentieth-century historian G.M. Trevelyan commented, 'the ghost of Ralegh pursued the House of Stuart to the scaffold'.[8]

Bess's first wish for her husband's body was not fulfilled. Either her brother did not grant her request or she changed her mind. Ralegh's headless corpse was buried, not at Beddington church in Surrey, but south of the altar in St Margaret's, Westminster. Bess had her husband's head embalmed and preserved it in its red bag. It was kept in a cupboard and displayed to visitors who revered his memory until her death twenty-nine years later at the age of eighty-two.

Carew inherited his father's head and kept it by him until he was killed in 1666. He too was buried in St Margaret's and the embalmed head was interred with him. But that was not the end, for in 1680 Carew's remains were disinterred and reburied at West Horsley in Surrey, where he had a house. Sir Walter's head, which for almost fourteen years had lain close to the body from which it was severed, was separated from it then for good.

Witnesses to Ralegh's death, Stucely had noted regretfully, said that 'he died like a soldier and a saint'.[9] His head might have become a holy relic. But the Protestant, increasingly Puritan, ethos of England prevented it. In any case he was not a saint. As he himself confessed at the end of his speech from the scaffold, he was 'a great sinner of a long time and in many kinds', but numerous people thought of him as the last great Elizabethan hope, a martyr who might have been a saviour. He had his Judas, after all, one who sourly observed that he had 'borrowed some tincture of holiness', and – echoing Berowne's line in *Love's Labours Lost* that follows King Ferdinand's phrase 'the School of Night': 'Devils soonest tempt, resembling spirits of light'[10] – claimed that 'an angel of darkness did put on him the shape of an angel of light at his departure'.[11]

The mythologising began early. It was Dean Tounson's nephew, Thomas Fuller, who gave us the couplet scratched on a pane by Sir Walter and Queen Elizabeth, as well as the story of Ralegh's 'so free and seasonable tender of so fair a footcloth', his new cloak thrown for her across plashy ground.[12]

His image – the icon that survives in many heads – is an outdoors one, a glitteringly costumed and accoutred courtier, a knight in silver armour on horseback in France or Ireland, a flamboyant seaman on board ship at Cadiz or on the Islands voyage, a gentleman plotting his lands at Sherborne, sitting to parley with the lords of Guiana, standing to gaze at the falls and overfalls of the river Caroli with lyrical wonder, or poised high on the boards of a temporary scaffold. But Raleigh spent most of his days indoors, at court, without and within the portal of Queen Elizabeth's privy chamber, in his study at Durham House and at Sherborne, and, for between a fifth and a quarter of his life, imprisoned in the Tower, confined in successive apartments or closeted in his shed of a laboratory, refining, distilling and compounding his balsams, elixirs and cordials.

Most tellingly, he was a writer, bent over books and papers. It was his valuable library of four hundred books on history, science, alchemy and divinity, together with his own manuscript treatises, sea-charts, plotts, globes and expensive scientific instruments, that the spy and Keeper of the State Papers, Sir Thomas Wilson, urged the King to take possession of, since they were of 'small use to Sir Walter's wife'. Lady Elizabeth clung to them on Carew's behalf.

Ralegh's written works flourished during the Commonwealth. His *Discovery of Guiana* and its vivid depictions of a new Eden gave old England a mission. His *History*'s lessons in tyranny and the sovereignty of God inspired the republicans John Milton and Oliver Cromwell in England[13] and, a century and more later, the revolutionaries in America.

In his *Instructions to his Son* he addressed Carew:

> I feel no more perturbation within me to depart this world than I have done in my best health to arise from table when I have well dined and thence retire to a pleasant walk ... Public affairs are rocks, private conversations are whirlpools and quicksands ... Thy adventure lies in this troublesome bark; strive, if thou canst, to make good thy station in the upper deck.

In his *Treatise of the Soul* it was as if Sir Walter was his own critic, standing in the wings and watching his last performance; not just the final speech in Old Palace Yard, but the twenty weeks and two hundred and fifty miles that led up to it, Ralegh's last and longest journey: 'We are all in effect comedians in religion, and while we act in gesture and voice divine virtues, in all the course of our lives we renounce our persons and the parts we play.'

NOTES

Many of the primary sources for this story are printed in:

Robert H. Schomburgk (ed.), *The Discovery of the Large, Rich, and Beautiful Empire of Guiana* by Sir W. Ralegh (London, 1848), referred to below as 'Schomburgk'.

V.T. Harlow, *Ralegh's Last Voyage* (London, 1932), referred to below as 'Harlow'.

Agnes Latham and Joyce Youings (eds.), *The Letters of Sir Walter Ralegh* (Exeter, 1999), referred to below as '*Letters*'. Numbers refer to the letter, not the page.

William Oldys and Thomas Birch (eds.), *The Works of Sir Walter Ralegh, Kt., now first collected: to which are prefixed the lives of the author*, 8 vols (Oxford, 1829), referred to below as *The Works*.

Primary sources not collected in the above volumes are referred to in the text and/or Notes, of which the most notable are:

Stucley, Sir Lewis, *Sir Lewise Stukelyes Appollogie*, August 1618 (BL, Ashmole, 830, 29).

Stucley, Sir Lewis [Dr Lionel Sharpe] *The Humble Petition and Information of Sir Lewis Stucley, Knight Vice-Admirall of Devon, touching his own behaviour in the charge committed unto him, for the bringing up of Sir Walter Raleigh, and the scandalous aspersions cast upon him for the same* (London, 1618; BL 1093.b.77).

Samuel King, *Captain Samuel King's Narrative of Sir Walter Ralegh's Motives and Opportunities for conveying himself out of the kingdom. With the manner how he was betrayed. MS,* two sheets fol. 1618. This manuscript has been lost but is quoted in *The Works*, Vol. I, p. 513.

Abbreviations:
APC – Annals of the Privy Council
BL – British Library
CSPD – Calendar of State Papers Domestic
PRO, SP – Public Record Office, State Papers

1. DESTINY

1 Contemporary street song (PRO, SP12/278/23):

Little Cecil trips up and down:
He rules both Court and Crown,
With his brother Burleigh clown,
In his great fox-furred gown.
With the Long Proclamation
He swore to save the nation –
Is it not likely?

Ralegh doth time bestride:
He sits 'twixt wind and tide,
Yet uphill he cannot ride,
for all his bloody pride.
He seeks taxes in the tin,
He polls the poor to the skin,
Yet he swears 'tis no sin –
Lord, for thy pity.

2 In what would become Venezuela, but which was then Guiana, along with the whole coast between the Amazon and Orinoco.

3 Letter from Ralegh to Sir George Villiers, 17 March 1616 (in *The Works*, I, p. 468); *Letters*, 212.

4 BL, Cotton Titus C7, f. 94.

5 CSPD 1611–18, 374, 425.

6 See J.A. Spedding, *Gentleman's Magazine*, April 1858, and Bacon (ed. Spedding), *The Letters and the Life of Francis Bacon* (London, 1868–74).

7 Later Count de Gondomar (1567–1626), Galician diplomat and Spanish ambassador to England, 1613–18 and 1620–22; he exercised great influence over James I and laboured to arrange the marriage of Prince Charles and the Infanta.

8 Letter from George Lord Carew to Sir Thomas Roe, December 1616 (in [ed. J Maclean], *The Letters of George Lord Carew to Sir Thomas Roe, 1615–1617* [London, 1860]).

9 Yonge *Diary of . . . 1604–1628.*

10 See Sir Thomas Wilson's report to James I, 4 October 1618 (PRO, SP14/103/16).

11 *Newes of Sr Walter Rauleigh . . . sent from a gentleman of his fleet (R.M.) . . . November 17, 1617.*

12 Letter from Ralegh to Sir William St John, 19 March 1617 (National Library of Wales, Aberystwyth, Bute L3/5) in Ralegh's hand; *Letters*, 214.

13 Letter from George Lord Carew to Sir Thomas Roe, March 1617.

14 *Newes of Sr Walter Rauleigh . . .*

15 Letter from Ralegh to Monsieur de Bisseaux, the French ambassador to England 1611–12, 14 May 1617 (Archivo General de Simancas, Vallodolid, Legajo de Estado 2598, no. 65); *Letters*, 215.

16 See *Sir Lewise Stukelyes Appollogie*

... August 1618. (BL, Ashmole, 830, 29), printed in Brushfield 'Raleghana').

2. BESS'S EYES

1 Letter from Ralegh to Lady Ralegh, 14 November 1617 (best transcripts: Bradford District Archives, Hopkinson 19, f. 82 and BL, Harleian 39, f. 371); *Letters*, 217.

2 *Sir Walter Ralegh's Journal of his Second Voyage to Guiana* (BL, Cotton MSS, Titus B8, f. 153) in Schomburgk, pp. 177–208.

3 Letter from Laurence Keymis to Sylvanus Scorie, 18 November 1617 (from a contemporary copy in Cambridge University Library MSS, Ee. 5–2, 3), printed in Harlow, pp. 160–1.

4 APC, January 1618–June 1619, pp. 7–8, 55–6.

5 It was aboard Captain Janson's ship that Captain Alley, suffering from vertigo, returned to England.

6 Neither Captain Alley nor Lady Elizabeth, or even the aspiring king of the Indians himself could have imagined that the name of Walter Ralegh would still be remembered there after almost four hundred years. Missionaries in present-day French Guiana report that in the folk memory Guattaral still lives.

7 *News of Sr Walter Rauleigh* was published in London in 1618.

8 Ralegh, *The Discoverie of the Large, Rich and Bewtiful Empyre of Guiana* ... (London, 1596); see Schomburgk.

9 Letter from Ralegh to Sir Ralph Winwood, 21 March 1618 (Somerset Record Office, DD/ M1, 18/82, *HMC*, 7th Report, App. p. 592); *Letters*, 218.

10 Letter from Ralegh to Lady Ralegh, 22 March 1618 (BL, Addit. 34631, ff. 47–8); *Letters*, 219.

11 Letter from Captain Charles Parker to Captain Peter Alley, 22 March 1618 (BL, Harleian 39, f. 351).

12 Samuel Jones, *A true and brief Relation of Sir Walter Raleigh his late voyage to Guiana*, c. 22 March 1618 (MS copy in library of Corpus Christi College, Oxford).

13 Letter from Laurence Keymis to Ralegh, 8 January 1617, quoted in Ralegh's *Appologie*, of which various versions exist in the Bodleian Library, Oxford.

14 The official examination of Captain Roger North by the lords at Whitehall, which followed up his initial reports, took place on 17 September 1618 (BL, Harleian, 6846, f. 63).

15 *A proclamation declaring his Majesties pleasure concerning Sir Walter Rawleigh, and those who adventured with him*, 9 June 1618 (Library of Queen's College, Oxford, 79 A 5, no. 49, p. 95).

16 From Ralegh's poem, 'Nature, that wash'd her hands in milk', to whose last stanza he added a couplet on the eve of his execution.

3. AN INEVITABLE ROCK

1 Fray Pedro Simon, *Noticias de las Conquistas de tierra firme en las Indias Occidentales*. Much of what we know of the Indian and of the Spanish view of Ralegh's Guiana expedition is contained in Simon's narrative and in documents stored in the Spanish National Archive at the castle of Simancas in Castile, and in the Archivo General des Indias at Seville, some of which were not rediscovered until two

and a half centuries after the event.

2 See also discussion in *Letters*, p. 361, n. 1.

3 James Howell, *Epistolae Ho-Elianae* (London, 1645).

4 *A proclamation declaring his Majesties pleasure concerning Sir Walter Rawleigh, and those who adventured with him*, 11 June 1618 (see Chapter 2, note 15).

5 Letter from Ralegh to George Lord Carew, c. 11 June 1618 (contemporary Spanish translation in Archivo General des Indias, Seville); *Letters*, 220.

6 Letter from Ralegh to King James, 16 June 1618 (Centre for Kentish Studies, U269/1 O0147), written by a clerk, addressed and signed by Ralegh in a shaky hand; *Letters*, 221.

7 Miniature belonging to the Duke of Rutland. It was said to have been cased in a locket together with a portrait of Wat.

8 *Sir Walter Rauleigh's stabb*, contemporary MS, printed in Hutchins, *History of Dorset*, Vol. IV, pp. 217–19.

9 Howell, *Epistolae Ho-Elianae*.

4. COUSIN LEWIS

1 According to Anthony Wood (*Athenæ Oxoniensis*, 1691–92), Lewis Stucley became a gentleman commoner of Broadgate Hall in 1588, aged fourteen.

2 *Sir Lewise Stukelyes Appollogie* ... August 1618 (BL, Ashmole, 830, 29); in Brushfield, 'Raleghana'.

3 *Devon & Cornwall Notes & Queries*, Vol. XXXVII, part III.

4 Captain Samuel King's account is preserved in *The Works*, Vol. I, p. 513.

5 Bacon (for James I), *A Declaration of the Demeanor and Cariage of Sir Walter Raleigh* ...

6 Sir Walter Ralegh's Will, 8–10 July 1597 (Sherborne Castle, Dorset); *Letters*, Appendix 2, pp. 381–6.

7 Thomas Fuller, *The Worthies of England* (London, 1662).

8 Letter from Ralegh to Master Richard Duke, 26 July 1584 (Devon Record Office, 2850/Z/Z3) in Ralegh's hand; *Letters*, 13.

9 APC, January 1618 – June 1619, p. 220.

5. THE CHYMIST AND THE SOUL

1 Bacon (for James I), *A Declaration of the Demeanor and Cariage of Sir Walter Raleigh* ...

2 As shown in Chapter 4, previous narratives have located 'Mr Drake's house' in or near Plymouth. Geography and chronology again confirm that this is impossible, for Mr Horsey's house was ninety miles from Plymouth, at Clifton Maybank in Dorset. The party aimed to dine there, presumably at the customary time, about noon. Even with a dawn start they could not have travelled so far before dinner. On the other hand, if it was only 'four miles or thereabouts' from Mr Drake's to Mr Horsey's, as the *Declaration* states, it is inconceivable that Stucley would have allowed them to journey such a short distance before stopping to dine. Accepting that Mr Drake's house was in Musbury and that 'four' was a slip of the pen for 'twenty-four' makes sense of an otherwise impossible itinerary.

3 Where direct or reported speech has been recorded in primary sources with some degree of authenticity, as here in the *Declaration*, it has been possible

to reconstruct dialogue, taking no more liberties, and maybe fewer, than a dry account would take.

4 *Elizabethae, Angliae Reginae Haeresim Calvinianam Propugnantis Saervissimum in Catholicos suie Regni edictum ... cum Responsione ...* (1592), Commonly known as the *Responsio*. For its text and the issues surrounding it, see Ernest Strathman, *Sir Walter Raleigh, A Study in Elizabethan Scepticism* (London, 1951).

5 (Robert Persons et al.) *An Advertisement written to a Secretary of my L. Treasurer ...* (Antwerp, 1592). See Strathman, note 4, above.

6 Did Marlowe's rival Shakespeare aim to please his patron the Earl of Southampton and his friend Essex by satirising Ralegh's 'school' in *Love's Labours Lost*, first performed in 1594? Shakespeare's character Armado may be a caricature of Sir Walter, though possibly, and more obviously, 'Don Adriano de Armado, a fantastical Spaniard' is a side-swipe at Adrian Gilbert, regarded by his enemies as a verbose buffoon. There is no hard evidence Shakespeare had Ralegh's 'school' in mind, but, taking the hint from the play, scholars long ago dubbed his coterie the School of Night. When Lord Berowne, besotted with dark Rosaline, cries,

'No face is fair that is not full so black,'
King Ferdinand responds,
'O paradox! Black is the badge of hell,
The hue of dungeons and *the School of Night* –
A beauty's crest becomes the heavens well!'

7 John Dee, *To the Kings most excellent Maiestie* (petition to James I) (London, 1604).

8 'Examinations taken at Cearne', 21–8 March 1594 (BL, Harleian, 6849, ff. 183–90).

9 There is controversy about the Cerne giant's age. In the thirteenth century, Walter of Coventry mentions three Dorset abbeys at Shaftesbury, Milton and Cerne, and writes of worship of the god Helith, but does not mention the figure itself. Dr Richard Pococke saw it in 1754 and thought it to be Hercules, known locally as the Giant or Hele. In 1764 William Stukeley (related to Sir Lewis Stucley's descendants) called it 'a primitive Hercules'. On the hill top is an earthwork, the Trendle, called the Frying-pan by local folk, for they knew the giant as Beelzebub, the prince of devils or lord of the flies who appears in mummers' and miracle plays wielding a club and a frying-pan. F.J. Harvey Darton put forward a case (in *English Fabric* [London, 1938]) for its being cut in the 1640s, by Civil War dissidents, the Clubmen. However, Thomas Gerard of Trent described the giant Helith in his *Survey of Dorsetshire* (mss 1622, published 1732) so it is probable that he dominated the hill in Ralegh's time.

10 Letter from Ralegh to Sir Robert Cecil, 14 April 1594 (Hatfield, CP 26/25) in Ralegh's hand; *Letters*, 69.

11 Letter from Ralegh to Sir Robert Cecil, 20 September 1594 (Hatfield, CP 28/40) in Ralegh's hand; *Letters*, 80.

6. OSMUND'S CURSE

1 Bacon (for James I), *A Declaration of the Demeanor and Cariage of Sir Walter Raleigh ...* pp. 46–7.

2 Sir John Harington, *Nugae Antiquae* (ed. 1779), Vol. I, pp. 105–6.

3 Ibid.

4 Hutchins, *History of Dorset*, Vol. IV, p. 273.

5 William Crowe, *Lewesdon Hill* (1788).

6 Typical of glass in Oxford colleges, the panel is now reset in the west window of St Katherine's Chapel in Sherborne Abbey.

7 Hutchins, *History of Dorset*, Vol. IV, pp. 247–8.

8 Now a relict chancel.

9 Poyntington is now in Dorset.

10 The house was then almost one hundred and fifty years old and is, according to Pevsner, the most complete late Perpendicular courtyard house in Dorset, with stone-mullioned, arched windows, twisted hexagonal chimneys and, above the gateway, the room traditionally regarded as that which the Raleghs occupied on the night of 26 July 1618.

11 Letter from Ralegh to Sir Robert Carr, 2 January 1609 (BL, Harleian, 6908, etc.); *Letters*, 197.

12 Letter from Ralegh to the Earl of Salisbury, c. 16 July 1605 (Hatfield, CP 109/9) in Ralegh's hand; *Letters*, 189.

13 Letter from Ralegh to Sir Robert Cecil, 25 September 1601 (Hatfield, CP 88/62) in Ralegh's hand; *Letters*, 145.

14 Letter from Ralegh to the Western Assize judges, 3 March 1602 (Centre for Kentish Studies, U269/1); *Letters*, 156.

15 Probable forgery of letter from Ralegh to John Shelbury, 3 January 1609 (PRO, SP14/43/7); *Letters*, 198.

16 Letter from Ralegh to the Lords Buckhurst and Cecil and Sir George Hume, c. 14 February 1604 (Hatfield, CP 109/15) in Ralegh's hand; *Letters*, 177.

17 C. Wanklyn, *Lyme Regis, A Retrospective* (London, 1922).

18 Letter from Don Diego Sarmiento de Arcuña to Philip of Spain, 22 October 1617, translated from the original at Simancas and printed by Hume in *Sir Walter Ralegh*; see also Harlow, p. 153.

19 Sir John Harington, *Nugae Antiquae*, (1799), Vol. 1, pp. 104–5.

20 Sir Thomas Wilson's report to Sir Robert Naunton, *A Relacon of what hath passed and bin obserued by me since my coming to Sr Walter Rawley uppon Fryday 11th Sept, 1618*, 16 September 1618 (PRO, SP14/99/12 i); in Harlow, pp. 266–71.

7. IMPOSTURES

1 Letter from Ralegh to Sir Robert Cecil, 26 November 1595 (Hatfield, CP 36/44) in Ralegh's hand; *Letters*, 89.

2 Arthur Throckmorton's diary entries for May 1595, quoted in Rowse, *Ralegh and the Throckmortons*, p. 195.

3 We have already observed that the account in *A Declaration of the Demeanor and Cariage of Sir Walter Raleigh* is based upon Manoury's evidence to Privy Councillors and, though much of it is corroborated by Ralegh himself, it is inevitably biased.

4 Bacon (for James I), *A Declaration of the Demeanor and Cariage of Sir Walter Ralegh* ... pp. 47f.

5 Camden, *Diary (1603–1623)*, entry for 20 July 1618.

6 *Sir Walter Raghleys Large Appologie for the ill successe of his enterprise to Guiana* (Bodleian,

MS Eng. Hist. d. 138 etc);
collated and printed in Harlow,
pp. 316–34.

7 APC, January 1618–June 1619,
p. 239.

8 Bacon (for James I), *A
Declaration of the Demeanor and
Cariage of Sir Walter Ralegh* . . .
p. 55.

9 William Camden, *Annals*, entry
for 2 August 1618.

10 Bacon (for James I), *A
Declaration of the Demeanor and
Cariage of Sir Walter Ralegh* . . .
pp. 57f.

11 His brother Carew was based at
Portland Castle in Dorset, but his
brother's brother-in-law, Thynne,
had Longleat in Wiltshire.

12 *Sir Lewise Stukelyes Appollogie* . . .
August 1618 (BL, Ashmole, 830,
29); in Burshfield, 'Raleghana'.

8. APOLOGY

1 *Sir Walter Raghleys Large
Appologie for the ill successe of his
enterprise to Guiana* (Bodleian,
MS Eng. Hist. d. 138 etc.);
collated and printed in Harlow,
pp. 316–34. See also, *His
Apologie*, printed in *Judicious and
Select Essayes and Observations* . . .
(London, 1650).

2 Ralegh, *The Discoverie of the
Large, Rich and Bewtiful Empyre
of Guiana* . . . in Schomburgk.

3 John Izon, *Sir Thomas Stucley,
Traitor Extraordinary* (London,
1956) and my treatment of the
story in: Paul Hyland, *Backwards
Out of the Big World: A Voyage
into Portugal* (London, 1996).

4 Letter from Ralegh to Sir Robert
Cecil, 10 November 1595
(Hatfield, CP 36/4) in Ralegh's
hand; *Letters*, 86.

5 George Chapman, *De Guianá,
Carmen Epicum*, written in the
months between Ralegh's voyage

of 1595 and Laurence Keymis's
return to Guiana the following
year; it is included, together with
a short Latin poem by L.K.
admiringly addressed to Thomas
Hariot, *Ad Thomam Hariotum
Matheseos et universae philosophie
peritissimum*, in Laurence Keymis,
*A Relation of the Second Voyage to
Guiana* . . . (London, 1596).

6 Thomas Masham, *The third voyage
set forth by Sir Walter Ralegh* . . .
printed in *Hakluyt's Collection of
the Early Voyages, Trade and
Discoveries of the English*, Vol. IV
(London, 1811).

7 Samuel Jones, *A true and brief
Relation of Sir Walter Raleigh his
late voyage to Guiana*, in Harlow,
pp. 232–7.

8 Letter to King James, 16 June
1618 (Centre for Kentish Studies,
U269/1 O0147); *Letters*, 221.

9 See also the discussion in Harlow,
pp. 61ff., and in Nicholl, *The
Creature in the Map*, pp. 174ff.

10 Ralegh, *The Discoverie of the
Large, Rich and Bewtiful Empyre
of Guiana* . . . in Schomburgk.

11 Keymis, *A Relation of the Second
Voyage to Guiana* . . .

12 Letter from Ralegh to Robert
Cecil, Earl of Salisbury, c. July
1607 (Hatfield, CP 124/121) in
Ralegh's hand; *Letters*, 192.

13 Letter from Ralegh to John
Ramsay, Viscount Haddington,
c. July 1607 (Hatfield, CP 103/
49) in Ralegh's hand; *Letters*,
193.

14 Letter from Ralegh to Robert
Cecil, Earl of Salisbury, 1611
(privately-owned transcript)
headed in Ralegh's hand; *Letters*,
205.

15 Letter from Ralegh to the Privy
Council, before July 1611 (BL,
Harleian 39, f. 350); *Letters*,
206.

16 Letter from Ralegh to Sir Ralph

Winwood, early 1616 (Bradford District Archives, Hopkinson 19, f. 81) seventeenth-century transcript; *Letters*, 211.

9. HAIL POWDERED WITH DIAMONDS

1 It is not known whether James I ever read Ralegh's *Apology*. Winton, in *Sir Walter Ralegh*, states categorically that the King never saw the document, at least in Ralegh's lifetime.
2 Lacey, *Sir Walter Ralegh*.
3 *Sir Lewise Stukelyes Appollogie*... August 1618 (BL, Ashmole, 830, 29); in Brushfield, 'Raleghana'.
4 Bacon (for James I), *A Declaration of the Demeanor and Cariage of Sir Walter Raleigh*...
5 Fynes Moryson, *An Itinerary* (London, 1617).
6 The examination of Robert Mering (Mearing) at the Tower, 4 September 1618 (Addit. MSS, 19398, f. 61), printed in The *Letters and the Life of Francis Bacon* (ed. Spedding), Vol. VI, p. 416; and in Harlow, p. 255.
7 *Sir Lewise Stukelyes Appollogie*.
8 Bacon (for James I), *A Declaration of the Demeanor and Cariage Sir Walter Raleigh*...

10. HOUSE ARREST

1 *Déclaration faicte au Roy par le Sieur Raleigh prisonnier en la Tour*, 18 September 1618, part of a bundle of papers forwarded to Louis XIII by James I; see Harlow, pp. 287-8.
2 Bacon (for James I), *A Declaration of the Demeanor and Cariage of Sir Walter Raleigh*...
3 *Anthony Belle's examination at Madrid, taken by Diego Brochero, translated by S.R. Gardiner in his article 'The Case against Sir*

Walter Ralegh', *Fortnightly Review*, Vol. VII, pp. 609-10.
4 Letter from Ralegh to Lord Carew, July/August 1618 (Bodleian, Carte 77, ff. 41-2); *Letters*, 222; the Cotton MSS version is in Harlow, pp. 250-3.
5 Letter from Ralegh to Robert Cecil, Earl of Salisbury, 1611 (privately-owned transcript) headed in Ralegh's hand; *Letters*, 205.
6 Letter from Ralegh to the Privy Council, before July 1611 (BL, Harleian 39, f. 350); *Letters*, 206.
7 Edward Wright, *Certaine Errours in Navigation* (London, 1610).
8 Louis XIII had married Anne of Austria in 1615.
9 Ralegh's *Déclaration*... (see note 1)
10 Letter from Sir Thomas Wilson to Sir Robert Naunton, 17 September 1618 (PRO, SP14/103/25); in Harlow, pp. 271-2.

11. FLIGHT

1 Bacon (for James I), *A Declaration of the Demeanor and Cariage of Sir Walter Ralegh*... p. 55.
2 A lost manuscript, *Captain Samuel King's Narrative of sir Walter Ralegh's Motives and Opportunities for conveying himself out of the kingdom. With the manner how he was betrayed.* MS. two sheets, fol. 1618. Quoted in *The Works*, Vol. I, pp. 513f. I have used this source, together with fragmentary narratives, reported speech and hints contained in letters, in Stucley's *Appollogie* and *Petition*, in James I's *Declaration*, and in later accounts of the episode. There are inconsistencies in the primary sources which I can only resolve by inference and guesswork.

Secondary interpretations have tended to ignore or misconstrue the geography of the Thames and have therefore telescoped what must have happened. By adding up what is known and unravelling it, I have reconstructed the events of the night of 9–10 August 1618.

3 Letter to the Lieutenant of the Tower, 30 July 1618, in Harlow, pp. 254–5.

4 A grey waxy secretion of the intestine of the sperm whale found floating in tropical seas, strong smelling and used in perfumery.

5 'A kinde of greene stones, which the Spaniards call *Piedras Hijadas*, and we use for spleene stones.' Ralegh, *The Discoverie . . . of Guiana* in Schomburgk.

6 A 'way-stone' of magnetic iron oxide used by mariners to point towards the pole star, or lodestar.

7 Ralegh wrote to George Villiers, Marquess of Buckingham, 12 August 1618 (Bodleian, Tanner 74, f. 126) to say that Stucley 'cannot but avow it that when we came back towards London I desired to save no other treasure than the exact descriptions of those places in the Indies'; *Letters*, 223.

12. TOWER

1 From Ralegh 'A Petition to Queen Anne' in *Everyman's Poetry: Sir Walter Ralegh* (ed. Dodsworth).

2 Stucley, *The Humble Petition and Information of Sir Lewis Stucley . . .* (BL, 1093. b. 77), p. 11; and at Hartland Abbey, bound in the volume *Sir Lewis Stucley's Vindication 1618*.

3 Letter from Ralegh to George Villiers, Marquess of Buckingham, 12 August 1618 (Bodleian,

Tanner 74, f. 126) in Ralegh's hand; *Letters*, 223.

4 Camden, *Diary (1603–1623)*, entry for 12 August 1618.

5 Letter from Ralegh to Robert Cecil, Lord Cranborne, late 1604 (Hatfield, CP 109/13) in Ralegh's hand; *Letters*, 184.

6 Letter from Ralegh to Robert Cecil, Lord Cranborne, winter 1604–5 (Hatfield, CP 102/24) in Ralegh's hand; *Letters*, 185.

7 Quoted in Rowse, *Ralegh and the Throckmortons*, p. 252.

8 Bacon suggested this in a note concerning his plans for a 'great renewal' or scientific renaissance. See Francis Bacon (ed. Graham Rees), *Instauratio Magna* (Oxford, 2000).

9 Letter from Ralegh to Sir Walter Cope, 5 October 1611 (Pierpoint Morgan, New York, REIII.EI-1.46) in Ralegh's hand; *Letters*, 209.

10 S.C. Lomas (ed.), *The Letters and Speeches of Oliver Cromwell* (New York, 1904), Vol. II, p. 54.

11 Alexander Ross, *The History of the World . . . being a continuation of the famous history of Sir W. Raleigh* (London, 1652).

12 Northampton to Rochester (Robert Carr), 12 July 1611 (PRO, SP14/61/26).

13 Letter from Ralegh to Queen Anne, after 11 July 1611 (PRO, SP14/67/126) in Ralegh's best italic hand; *Letters*, 207.

14 Chamberlain, *The Chamberlain Letters* (ed. McClure Thomson).

15 Last three stanzas of 'A Petition to Queen Anne' (see note 1 above).

13. JUDAS

1 Aubrey, *Brief Lives*.

2 (John Stucley) *Affeton Castle: A Lost Devon Village*.

3 *Sir Lewise Stukelyes Appollogie* . . .
August 1618 (BL, Ashmole, 830,
29); in Brushfield, 'Raleghana'.

4 Letter from the Privy Council to
Sir Lewis Stucley, 23 July 1618
(APC, January 1618–June 1619,
p. 220).

5 Ralegh had once celebrated
Charles Howard's command
against the Spanish Armada, but
the Lord High Admiral had not
always repaid his old comrade
with true friendship.

6 *The Humble Petition and
Information of Sir Lewis Stucley*
. . . (BL, 1093.b. 77); and at
Hartland Abbey, bound in the
volume *Sir Lewis Stucley's
Vindication 1618*. Stucley's
Petition is a remarkable document
not included in Harlow's *Last
Voyage* or any other modern
volume. Writers on Ralegh have
largely ignored it. Even Brushfield
('Raleghana' 3) treats it
dismissively, though the
conclusions he comes to regarding
its counter-productive effect are
accurate enough.

7 Stucley's *Petition* was published
on 26 November 1618 followed
by King James's *Declaration* on
the 27th.

8 Letter from John Chamberlain to
Sir Dudley Carleton, 4 December
1618, *The Chamberlain Letters*
(ed. McClure Thomson).

9 See DNB, and Strong, *Henry,
Prince of Wales*.

10 *The Humble Petition and
Information of Sir Lewis
Stucley* . . .

11 See DNB.

12 Thomas Babington Macaulay, *The
History of England* (London
1855), Vol. IV, p. 620.

13 See, for example, Lamplugh
Lundy: Island without Equal.

14 Camden, *Diary (1603–1623)*,
entry for 20 August 1620.

15 Affeton Castle (now a remnant
gatehouse, extended and restored)
was until the Civil War a fortified
manor house. It stands to the
west of the village of West
Worlington in whose church of
St Mary are the Stucley family
memorials.

14. INTRIGUES AND INTERROGATIONS

1 Published in London on 27
November 1618, the day after Sir
Lewis Stucley's *Petition*.

2 The minutes of this evidence, and
later depositions relating to it, are
printed in Bacon (ed. Spedding),
*The Letters and the Life of Francis
Bacon*, Vol. VI, p. 416 *et seq.* and
in Harlow, p. 255 *et seq.*

3 Printed in unnaccented French,
from an early seventeenth-century
copy (Bodleian, Carte MSS, 112,
f. 272 *et seq.*), in Harlow,
p. 286.

4 Ibid., p. 285. APC, January
1618–June 1619, p. 251.

5 Camden, *Diary (1603–1623)*,
entry for 10 September 1618.

6 Printed in Harlow, p. 260; PRO,
SP14/99/7.

7 Ibid., p. 261; PRO, SP14/99/9.

8 Ibid., p. 262; PRO, SP14/99/9 i.

9 Ibid., p. 256; BL, Harleian 6846,
f. 61.

10 Ibid., p. 257; BL, Harleian 6846,
f. 63.

11 Ibid., p. 259; BL, Harleian 6846,
f. 58. Each examination bears the
signatures of the six councillors
and the examinate.

12 Letter to Secretary Naunton
(CSPD, James I, Vol. XCIX, no.
25); Harlow, p. 271.

13 PRO, SP14/99/59 ii; in
Harlow, p. 276.

14 Letter from Ralegh to James I, 18
September 1618, not included in
the *Letters*, but printed, in the

French translation sent to Louis XII, in Harlow, pp. 287–8.

15 Ibid., p. 272. Letter from Sir Thomas Wilson to James I (PRO, SP14/99/48).

16 Letter from Ralegh to Lady Elizabeth Ralegh, 18 September 1618 (PRO, SP14/99/9), or perhaps an extract from a letter, copied for Sir Thomas Wilson; *Letters*, 224.

17 This reply is copied on the same sheet as Ralegh's letter (see note 16).

18 Privy Council minute, 17 September 1618 (APC, January 1618–June 1619, pp. 261–3).

19 PRO, SP14/99/62.

20 Lettre du *Roy d'Angleterre au Roy sur la trahison de Walter Ralegh*, September 1618; Harlow, p. 291.

21 Printed in Harlow, p. 291, confusingly, as if it was a continuation of Guillaume Manoury's evidence, but ending 'Signé, *le clerc*'.

15. LAST JUDGMENT

1 PRO, SP14/103/59 i; printed in Harlow, pp. 275–6.

2 Letter from Ralegh to James I, c. 25 September 1618, translation from a Spanish copy in the Archivo General de Indias at Simancas, printed in J.A. St John, *Life of Sir Walter Ralegh* (London, 1868), Vol. II, pp. 331–3; *Letters*, 226 (but there dated 4 October 1618).

3 Sir Thomas Wilson's notes (PRO, SP14/99/77); in Harlow, p. 279.

4 Letter from Sir E. Harwood to Sir Dudley Carleton, 3 October 1618 (PRO, SP14/103/14).

5 PRO, SP14/103/16, 4 October 1618; in Harlow, pp. 282–4.

6 PRO, SP14/103/37, c. 4

October 1618; in Harlow, p. 284.

7 Letter from Ralegh to Lady Ralegh, 4 October 1618 (PRO, SP14/103/22), from a copy taken by Sir Thomas Wilson; *Letters*, 225. Wat's formal signature on surviving documents, 'Waltherus Ralegh filius', is indeed firm and neat.

8 *Autobiography of Phineas Pett* (ed. W.G. Perrin) (London, 1918).

9 Only fragments of *The Art of War by Sea* survive. On 2 November 1618 Sir Thomas Wilson advised that the manuscript be seized.

10 PRO, SP14/103/36.

11 Draft in Sir Edward Coke's handwriting; in Bacon (ed. Spedding), *The Letters and the Life of Francis Bacon* Vol. VI, pp. 361–2; and Harlow, pp. 295–6.

12 Ibid., Vol. VI, pp. 363–4, from the Fortescue Papers. The manuscript was almost certainly a rough draft. Also in Harlow, pp. 296–7.

13 PRO, SP14/103/14.

14 A fragmentary, curtailed record of the proceedings exists in the form of notes taken by Sir Julius Caesar. (Lansdowne MSS, 142, f. 396). An alternative view is that of the Venetian ambassador, Piero Contarini, whose observations of the proceedings, dated 26 October 1618, were dispatched to the Doge and Senate in Venice (Calendar of State Papers, Venetian, 1617–19, no. 570, p. 339).

15 See I Samuel 21: 10–15.

16 Camden, *Diary (1603–1623)*, entry for 24 October 1618.

17 *Letters*, 227, pp. 375–6, from a seventeenth-century transcript of a part of a letter written between 24 and 28 October 1618.

18 Letter from Ralegh to (?) Queen Anne, date unknown; *Letters*,

228. Its content places it in late October 1618. John Donne (ed.), *Collection of letters made by Sir Tobie Mathews* (1660) describes it as a letter to James I, but its sentiments suggest not. Edwards, in *The Life of Sir Walter Ralegh*, questions the letter's authenticity, but Latham and Youings (*Letters*) believe that it is not a forgery and suggest, very plausibly, that it was addressed to Queen Anne.

16. SCAFFOLD

1 Francis Hargrave, *Complete Collection of State Trials* (London, 1776–81), Vol. VIII, App. 4; and William Cobbett (ed.), *Complete Collection of State Trials* (London, 1809), Vol. II, col. 33.

2 Aubrey, *Brief Lives.*

3 Letter from Dean Tounson to Sir John Isham, 9 November 1618, printed in Walterus de Hemingburgh, *Historia de rebus gestis, Edward I, etc.*, (ed. Thomas Hearne) (Oxford, 1731), p. clxxxiv.

4 Newsletter from Chamberlain to Carleton, 7 November 1618 (PRO, SP14/103/73).

5 See end of Chapter 2.

6 Ralegh's poem 'Ev'n such is time' in *Everyman's Poetry: Sir Walter Ralegh* (ed. Dodsworth), p. 45.

7 Letter from John Pory to Dudley Carleton, 7 November 1618 (PRO, SP14/103/74).

8 See note 3.

9 Apart from sources noted above, there are several notable accounts of Ralegh's execution: Anon. 'The effect of Sir Walter Ralegh's speech, written in the hearing of him, before he was beheaded', transcribed in the handwriting of William Sancroft, Archbishop of Canterbury (Bodleian, Tanner 299, no. 9); letter from Thomas Lorkin to Sir Thomas Puckering, (printed in Arthur Cayley *The Life of Sir Walter Ralegh* [London, 1805], Vol. II, App., pp 78–82); dispatch from Ulloa, the Spanish agent to King Philip (translated by and printed in Hume, *Sir Walter Ralegh*, pp. 414–16); Sir Thomas Overbury, *The Arraignment and Conviction . . . of Sir Walter Raleigh* (London, 1648).

10 John Aubrey, 'he spake broad Devonshire until the day he died'.

11 A lost manuscript, *Captain Samuel King's Narrative of Sir Walter Ralegh's Motives and Opportunities for conveying himself out of the kingdom. With the manner how he was betrayed*, MS, two sheets, fol. 1618; *The Works*, Vol. I, p. 513.

12 Ibid.

13 *The Humble Petition and Information of Sir Lewis Stucley . . .* (BL, 1093. b. 77), p. 12; and at Hartland Abbey, bound in the volume *Sir Lewis Stucley's Vindication 1618.*

14 Ibid., p. 12.

15 Ibid., p. 14.

16 Bacon (for James I), *A Declaration of the Demeanor and Cariage of Sir Walter Raleigh . . .* pp. 39–40.

17 Ibid. pp 34–5.

18 *The Humble Petition and Information of Sir Lewis Stucley . . .* p. 13.

19 Ibid. p. 9.

EPILOGUE

1 Sir Nicholas Carew. Elizabeth Ralegh's youngest brother Nicholas Throckmorton had been adopted, after their father's death, by their childless uncle Sir Francis Carew of Beddington in Surrey, taking his name and inheriting his estates.

2 Printed in its original form
('. . . let me berri the worthi
boddi of my nobell hosban . . .')
in Harlow, p. 315.

3 Camden, *Diary (1603–1623)*,
entry for 29 October 1618.

4 Ulloa to Philip III, in Hume, *Sir
Walter Ralegh*, pp. 414–16 and
Harlow, pp. 314–15.

5 Letter from Dean Tounson to Sir
John Isham, 9 November 1618
(see note to Chapter 16).

6 Letter from Ralegh to George
Villiers, Marquess of Buckingham,
12 August 1618 (Bodleian,
Tanner 74, f. 126) in Ralegh's
hand; *Letters*, 223.

7 Polwhele, *The History of
Devonshire*, Vol. II, pp. 220–1.

8 G.M. Trevelyan, *History of
England* (London, 1926),
p. 389.

9 *The Humble Petition and
Information of Sir Lewis Stucley
. . .* (BL, 1093. b. 77); p. 2; and
at Hartland Abbey, bound in the
volume *Sir Lewis Stucley's
Vindication 1618*.

10 William Shakespeare, *Love's
Labours Lost*, IV, 3: 253.

11 *The Humble Petition and
Information of Sir Lewis Stucley
. . .* p. 16.

12 Thomas Fuller, *The Worthies of
England* (London, 1662).

13 Christopher Hill, *The Intellectual
Origins of the English Revolution*
(London, 1965).

SELECT BIBLIOGRAPHY

Aubrey, John, *Brief Lives*, (ed. Oliver Lawson Dick) (London, 1949).

Bacon, Francis (for James I) *A Declaration of the Demeanor and Cariage of Sir Walter Raleigh, Knight, aswell in his Voyage, as in, and sithence his Returne; And of the true motives and inducements which occasioned His Majestie to Proceed in doing Justice upon him, as hath bene done* (London, 1618).

—— *The Letters and the Life of Francis Bacon*, (ed. James Spedding) (London, 1868–74).

Bell, Rev. A.H., *Some Account of the Parish of Poyntington* (1928).

Bergeron, David M., *Royal Family, Royal Lovers: King James of England and Scotland* (Columbia, 1991).

Bracken, C.W., *A History of Plymouth* (Plymouth, 1931).

Brushfield, T.N., 'Raleghana' Part VII, *Transactions of the Devonshire Association* (1905).

Camden, William, *Diary (1603–1623)* Hypertext ed. Dana F. Sutton (University of California, Irvine, 2001).

Chamberlain, John, *The Chamberlain Letters*, (ed. Elizabeth McClure Thomson) (London, 1966).

Coote, Stephen, *A Play of Passion* (London, 1993).

Davies, Rosalind, ' "The Great Day of Mart": Returning to Texts at the Trial of Sir Walter Ralegh in 1603', *Renaissance Forum*, 4, 1 (1999).

Edwards, Edward, *The Life of Sir Walter Ralegh*, 2 vols (London, 1868).

Fraser, Antonia, *King James VI of Scotland, I of England* (London, 1994).

Gill, Crispin, *Plymouth: A New History* (Exeter, 1993).

—— *Plymouth River* (Exeter, 1997).

Hariot, Thomas, *A Briefe and True Report of the New Found Land of Virginia* (London, 1588).

Harlow, V.T., *Ralegh's Last Voyage* (London, 1932).

Hume, Martin A.S., *Sir Walter Ralegh* (London, 1897).

Hutchins, John, *History of Dorset*, 3rd edn (London, 1861–70).

Irwin, Margaret, *That Great Lucifer* (London, 1960).

Kelsey, Harry, *Sir Francis Drake: The Queen's Pirate* (Yale, 1998).

Keymis, Laurence, *A Relation of the Second Voyage to Guiana* (London, 1596).

Lacey, Robert, *Sir Walter Ralegh* (London, 1973).

Latham, Agnes M.C., *Writers and their Work: Sir Walter Ralegh* (London, 1971).

—— 'Sir Walter Ralegh's Will', *Review of English Studies*, New Series, XXII, 86 (May 1971).

Latham, Agnes and Joyce Youings (eds), *The Letters of Sir Walter Ralegh* (Exeter, 1999).

Lloyd, Rachel, *Dorset Elizabethans* (London, 1967).

Lloyd-Williams, Norman, *Sir Walter Raleigh* (London, 1962).

M., R., *Newes of Sr Walter Rauleigh . . . sent from a gentleman of his fleet (R.M.) . . . November 17, 1617* (London, 1618).

March, Rosemary, *Sherborne Castle* (Sherborne, 1977).

Nicholl, Charles, *The Reckoning* (London, 1992).

—— *The Creature in the Map* (London, 1995).

Nye, Robert, *The Voyage of the Destiny* [novel] (London, 1982).

Ralegh, Sir Walter, *The Discoverie of the Large, Rich and Bewtiful Empyre of Guiana, with a Relation of the Great and Golden Citie of Manoa (which the Spaniards call El Dorado) . . .* (London, 1596).

—— *The History of the World* (London, 1614).

—— 'Journal of his Second Voyage to Guiana' (reprinted in Schomburgk).

—— *Everyman's Poetry: Sir Walter Ralegh* (ed. Martin Dodsworth) (London, 1999).

—— *The Works of Sir Walter Ralegh, Kt., now first collected: to which are prefixed the lives of the author* (ed. William Oldys and Thomas Birch), 8 vols (Oxford, 1829).

—— *Judicious and Select Essays and Observations . . . With his Appologie for his voyage to Guiana* (London, 1650).

Rowse, A.L., *Ralegh and the Throckmortons* (London, 1962).

Rye, William Brenchley (ed.), *England as seen by foreigners in the days of Elizabeth and James I* (London, 1865).

Schomburgk, Sir Robert H. (ed.), *The Discovery of the Large, Rich and Beautiful Empire of Guiana* (London, 1848).

Sheppard, Lilian, *Raleigh's Birthplace: The Story of East Budleigh* (East Budleigh, 1983).

Sinclair, Andrew, *Sir Walter Raleigh and the Age of Discovery* (London, 1984).

Smith, Ann, *Sherborne Castle* (Sherborne, 1999).

Stebbing, William, *Sir Walter Ralegh* (Oxford, 1899).

Strong, Roy, *Henry Prince of Wales and England's Lost Renaissance* (London, 1986).

(Stucley, John) *Affeton Castle: A Lost Devon Village* (1967).

Stucley, Sir Lewis, *Sir Lewise Stukelyes Appollogie* (printed as Appendix A to T.N. Brushfield, 'Raleghana' Part VII, *Transactions of the Devonshire Association* [1905]).

—— [Dr Lionel Sharpe], *The humble petition and information of Sir Lewis Stucley, Knight Vice-admirall of Devon, touching his own behaviour in the charge committed unto him, for the bringing up of Sir Walter Raleigh, and the scandalous aspersions cast upon him for the same* (London, 1618).

Sugden, John, *Sir Francis Drake* (London, 1990).

Trevelyan, Raleigh, *Sir Walter Raleigh* (London, 2002).

Winton, John, *Sir Walter Ralegh* (London, 1975).

Yonge, Walter, *Diary of . . . 1604–1628* (London, 1848).

Devon & Cornwall Notes & Queries
Transactions of the Devonshire Association

INDEX

Walter Ralegh and Lewis Stucley have been abbreviated to WR and LS in subheadings

Abbot, George 163
Acuña, Diego Palomeque de *see* Palomeque de Acuña
Acuña, Diego Sarmiento de *see* Sarmiento de Acuña
Alley, Peter 16, 20, 21, 27
Andrews, Peter 32
Anjou, Duke of 11
Anne, Queen 6, 7, 143, 146–7, 150, 151
Appollogie (Stucley) 153–5
Apsley, Sir Allen 137, 166, 168, 175, 183, 192, 202
Arundel, Lord 207, 210–11, 212
Arundell, Sir John 70

Bacon, Sir Francis 7, 10, 13, 57, 62, 146, 163
Baily, Captain 19, 104
Baines, Richard 68
Becher, William 180
Beeston, Sir Hugh 206
Belle, Antoine 124
Berrio, Antonio de 103
Berry, Leonard 6
Boyle, Sir Richard 4
Bull, Eleanor 68
Burghley, Lord Treasure 6
Bye plot 5

Caesar, Sir Julius 31, 163
Carapana (Indian chief) 48
Carew, Lady 176
Carew, Lord George 12, 40–1, 159, 176

Carey, Sir George 6
Carr, Robert, Earl of Somerset 7, 8, 76, 78
Cayenne 20–1
Cecil, Sir Robert 6, 8, 54, 68, 69, 78
Chapman, George 67
Charles, Prince 7, 50
Cholmeley, Richard 68
Chudleigh, John 173–4
Clarke (gunner's mate, *Destiny*) 173
Clifton Maybank 64–5
Coke, Sir Edward 163, 189
Coldwell, Dr 75
Cornelius, John 71–2
Cosmor, Captain 28, 46, 47
Cottrell, Edward 116, 130, 132, 136, 155
Court of High Commission 1594 (Cecil's) 69–70
Crab (servant) 18
Crowe, William 75
Cuthbert (LS's page) 52, 88

De la Chesnée, Davide de Noyon meets WR 123; introduces Le Clerc to WR 128, 129; curiosity about escape plots 130; Privy Council 164, 179, 180; WR's account 169–70, 175, 176; death 215
De la Forest (François de Vertou) 170, 178
Dee, John 8, 68
Des Maretz, Count 12, 124, 195

Destiny
    ordered 9–10; launched 11; Des
    Maretz 12; Thames 13; Plymouth
    15, 45; Guiana 17–18; Cayenne
    20, 21; mutiny 33, 41–2, 210;
    finances 136, 188; Guayacunda
    163
Digby, Sir John 76, 80–2
Doncaster, Lord 207
Doubleday, Edmond 164
Drake, Barnard 59, 60
Drake, Dorothye 60
Drake, Sir Frances 4, 11, 43, 54,
    59–60
Drake, John 60
Drake, Thomas 57
Duke, Richard 58
Durham House 8

East Budleigh 57–8
Eliot, John 216
Elizabeth, Queen 11, 35, 58, 59, 75
Errinetta, Captain 47
Essex, Earl of 68, 211–12

Faige, Charles 12, 13, 14, 124, 172,
    173, 184
Fanshaw, Mr 200
Ferne, Sir John 195, 211
fleet, WR's 12–13
Forman, Simon 68
Fowler, John 18
Francis (cook) 18
Fuller, Thomas 58

Gawdy, Justice 194
Gilbert, Adrian 58, 65, 74, 82
Gilbert, Humphrey 58
Gilbert, John (WR's half-brother) 58
Gilbert, Sir John (WR's nephew) 54,
    82
Giles, Edward 29
Gomera 20
Gondomar, Count de *see* Sarmiento
    de Acuña
Gorges, Sir Arthur 147
Grados, Geronimo de 47
Grenville, Sir Barnard 161
Grenville, Mary 160
Grenville, Sir Richard 51, 52, 54

Guattaral *see* Ralegh, Sir Walter
Guayacunda, Cristóbal 38–40, 49,
    56, 84, 106, 163, 164
Guiana 5–6, 10–11, 101–3, 106–14
Guyn, Dr 167

Hammond, Christopher 18, 187
Hampden, John 217
Hancock, Edward 49
Harcourt, Robert 17, 42
Harding, Thomas 15, 45
Harington, Sir John 82
Hariot, Thomas 8, 52, 67, 68, 78,
    145
Harris, Sir Christopher 43, 54, 55,
    56, 85
Harris, Lady Frances 54, 56
Harry the Indian 18, 20
Hart, Captain 116, 132, 134, 135,
    136, 155
Hastings, Edward 18, 20
Hawkins, Sir John 4, 54
Hayes Barton 58, 59
Henri, Duc de Montmorency 12
Henry, Prince 76, 147, 149, 150
Herbert, William 23, 116, 135, 136,
    140, 155, 168, 171–2, 188
Hervey, Sir George 144
The History of the World (Ralegh)
    147–50
Horsey, Mr 63
Horsey, Lady Edith 65
Horsey, Elizabeth 65
Horsey, George 65
Horsey, Sir John 64, 65
Horsey, Sir Ralph 65, 66, 70
Howard, Lord Admiral Charles 156
Howard, Lord Thomas 6, 70
Hues, Robert 67, 146

Ironside, Roger 66, 69, 70, 71

James I, King
    reprieves WR 5; petitioned by WR
    6; Spanish interests 7, 11, 50, 162;
    to Scotland 13; and Sarmiento de
    Acuña 18, 40; proclamation 9 June
    1618: 34; Prince Charles's marriage
    prospects 50; imprisons WR and
    Keymis 52; and LS 53, 152;

James I, King – *cont.*
  Sherborne 78, 80; Salisbury 93, 95;
  letter to Louis XIII: 180–1; visits
  Tower of London 183; Privy
  Council 190–1
Janson, Captain 20
Jones, Samuel 29–30, 43, 109–10
Jonson, Ben 8
Josef 39

Keymis, Laurence
  Guiana 1596: 6, 102, 103;
  Durham House 8; *Convertine* 14;
  Cape Cecyl 17; Baily's desertion
  19; Orinoco expedition 25, 106–7,
  110, 112, 171, 195; suicide 26,
  210; San Thomé 28, 32, 172, 195;
  WR's household 47–8; imprisoned
  52, 145; Sherborne 76, 78, 80
King, Samuel
  Plymouth 3, 39, 49; Guiana 46,
  47, 107; WR's escape plots 55–6,
  88, 95, 116, 125–6, 130; and
  Manoury 63–4, 208; Poyntington
  84; WR's escape attempt 132, 134,
  136; *Destiny*'s finances 188
King's Bench bar 199–202
Kyd, Thomas 68

Large Appologie for the ill success of his
enterprise to Guiana (Ralegh)
  99–109
Laud, Archbishop 7
Le Clerc
  and De la Chesnée 123; and WR
  128–30, 175, 185; and Manoury
  170, 178, 179; and Lady Carew
  176; Privy Council 180; declaration
  181
Leake, Mr 48
Leigh, Charles 17
Louis XIII 14

Madre de Dios 54
Manoury, Guillaume 117, 160, 181–2
  Radford 56; observes WR 62; and
  King 63–4, 208; Poyntington 84;
  and WR 86, 88–92, 94–5, 97–8,
  109, 115, 118, 121, 193; and LS
  117, 120, 121, 179, 182; and De

  la Forest 170, 178; Privy Council
  179
Marlowe, Christopher 67, 68
Masham, Thomas 102
Mearing, Robert 122, 163–4
Meere, John 79–80, 187
Mollineux, Mr 48
Molyneaux, Emery 68
Montague, Sir Henry 200–1
Montague, James 186
Moore, Richard 18

Naunton, Sir Robert 53, 96, 163, 177
Nevis 33
Newball (surgeon) 18
Newes of Sr Walter Rauleigh... (RM)
  21–2
Norris, Sir John 101
North, Roger 34, 172–3
Northampton, Lord 207
Northumberland, Earl of 145, 166

Orinoco region, Spanish presence in
  126
Osmund, Bishop 75, 86
Overbury, Sir Thomas 7, 76

Palomeque de Acuña, Diego 19, 28
Parham, Sir Edward 77, 78, 84, 209
Parham, Elizabeth 77
Parham, John 77
Parker, Charles 27, 28, 47, 107, 210
Parker, William 44
Pedro the Creole 38–9
Pennington, Captain 173, 196
Percy, Henry 67
Persons, Robert 67
Petition (LS's, written by Sharpe)
  157–60
Pett, Phineas 9, 11, 188
Peyton, Sir John 48
Philip III (the Pious) 19, 162, 189
Pigot, John 18, 20, 30
Plymouth 4, 14–15, 38
Pocahontas 52
Pope's donation 127
Poyntington Manor 77
Privy Council 162–5, 171–4,
  178–80, 189, 191–6
Pym, John 217

Radford 54, 55–6

Ralegh, Carew (WR's brother) 58, 66

Ralegh, Carew (WR's son) 10, 11, 35, 37, 49, 56, 88, 131, 145, 218

Ralegh, Damerei 37

Ralegh, Lady Elizabeth (Bess; née Throckmorton)
Destiny launched 11; Guiana expedition letters 16–33; invests in Guiana expedition 30–1, 188; marriage 35–7; to Plymouth 35; and King 43; WR's escape plots 55, 88, 131; Radford 56; Sherborne 65, 72, 76, 78, 146; house arrest 137, 189; Tower of London 143; WR in Tower 177–8; WR orders affairs before death 187; last visit to WR 204; life after WR's death 215, 217

Ralegh, George 25, 107, 110, 172, 173, 211

Ralegh, Katherine 58

Ralegh, Sir Walter
Guiana expedition 1–15, 16–33, 43–5; Tower of London 5, 8, 48, 52, 136–7, 139, 143–50, 167–70, 183–98; Winchester trial 5; fleet 12–13; injuries 30, 31; and Queen Elizabeth 35, 58, 75; marriage 35–7; Plymouth 40–9; appearance 46, 193–4, 205; suicide attempt 48; arrested 53–5, 136, 196; character 53; escape plots 55, 124, 125–6, 130, 196; Radford 55–6; birth 58; childhood 58; Sherborne 65–6, 74–6, 77–8, 82; School of Atheism 67; and Cornelius 71–2; and Manoury 86, 88–92, 94–5, 97–8, 109, 115, 118, 121, 193; feigns illness 87–93, 196; petitions to King James 96–7, 99–109; writings 99–109, 139, 147–50, 219; attempts to bribe LS 118–20; escape attempt 131–5; strokes 143, 146; and Mearing 163–4; and Wilson 167–70, 183–6; accuses LS of slander 168; orders affairs before death 187; Privy Council 191–6; sentenced to death 196–7,

199–202; execution of 202–14; forgives LS 208–9; corpse 217–18; image of 218–19; *see also* Ralegh, Lady Elizabeth

Ralegh, Walter (senior, WR's father) 58

Ralegh, Wat
Destiny launched 11; news of 18; mother's concern for 23; death 24, 25, 28, 47; burial 46; infant 72; Tower of London 143; Guiana 173, 210

Regapo, Leonard 17

Robin (WR's page) 39, 49, 88, 132, 136, 165, 166, 174

Rogers, Mathew 30

Rolfe, John 52

Roydon, Matthew 67

Salisbury 86, 87

Sampson (WR's technician) 144

San Thomé 25, 28, 32, 39, 42, 45, 47, 103, 111

Sarmiento de Acuña, Diego (Count de Gondomar) 11, 12, 40, 50, 53, 56, 81, 162

School of Atheism 67–9

Scory, Sylvanus 9

Sebastião, King Dom 51

Sharpe, Lionel 157–8, 159

Sheffield, Lord 206

Shelbury, John 78

Sherborne 65–6, 74–6, 77–8, 146

Simon, Pedro 39

Spain 7, 50, 126

St Christophers 23

St John, Sir William 116, 117, 136, 140, 155, 168

St Leger, Sir Warham 33, 110, 196

Steed, William 18

Stucley, John 52

Stucley, Sir Lewis
commanded to arrest WR 15, 40, 45; arrests WR 51–3, 60–1, 136, 196; Radford 56; WR feigns illness 63, 87, 88, 89–91, 92–3, 117; resumed journey to London 115; Andover 116; and Manoury 117, 120, 121, 179, 182; bribed by WR 118–20; London 125, 130; WR's

Stucley, Sir Lewis – *cont.*
escape attempt 132, 134, 135;
visits WR in Tower 140; decline
152–61; death 161; *Destiny's*
tobacco cargo 187; forgiven by WR
208–9
Stucley, Lewis (grandfather) 51
Stucley, Thomas 'Lusty' 51, 101

Talbot, John 18, 144, 187
Taylor, James 60
Thomas (son of Rolfe and
Pocahontas) 52
Thornhurst, Captain 26, 32
Throckmorton, Arthur 36, 85
Throckmorton, Elizabeth *see* Ralegh,
Lady Elizabeth
Thynne, Charles 204–5
Tilley, George 79
Tite, Lewis 9
Tounson, Robert 203–4, 205, 206,
213
travel 84–5
Trenchard, Sir George 66, 70–1

Turner, James 194
Turner, Peter 146

Vertou, François de *see* De la Forest
Villiers, George 7–8, 81, 116, 140

Waad, Sir William 145, 146
Warner, Walter 67, 145
'Walter' *see* Ralegh, Sir Walter
Weekes, Master 202
Whiddon, Jacob 5
Whitney, Captain 14, 27, 28, 47,
104, 106, 172
Whittle, Parson 66
Wilson, Edward 174, 177–8
Wilson, Sir Thomas 165–70, 174–7,
183–7, 189
Winwood, Sir Ralph 6, 8, 10, 23, 24,
195
Woolaston, Captain 27, 28, 47, 104,
106
Worcester, Earl of 163

Yelverton, Sir Henry 199–200